RAMPAGE

RAMPAGE

CANADIAN MASS MURDER AND SPREE KILLING

Lee Mellor

DUNDURN
TORONTO

Project Editor: Shannon Whibbs
Editor: Jenny Govier
Design: Courtney Horner
Printer: Webcom

Library and Archives Canada Cataloguing in Publication

Mellor, Lee, 1982-
   Rampage : Canadian mass murder and spree killing / by Lee Mellor.

Includes bibliographical references and index.
Issued also in electronic format.
ISBN 978-1-4597-0721-4

   1. Mass murder--Canada--History. 2. Mass murderers--Canada--Biography. I. Title.

HV6805.M447 2013   364.152'340922   C2012-904611-6

1   2   3   4   5   17   16   15   14   13

We acknowledge the support of the **Canada Council for the Arts** and the **Ontario Arts Council** for our publishing program. We also acknowledge the financial support of the **Government of Canada** through the **Canada Book Fund** and **Livres Canada Books**, and the **Government of Ontario** through the **Ontario Book Publishing Tax Credit** and the **Ontario Media Development Corporation**.

Care has been taken to trace the ownership of copyright material used in this book. The author and the publisher welcome any information enabling them to rectify any references or credits in subsequent editions.

J. Kirk Howard, President

Printed and bound in Canada.

Visit us at
Dundurn.com
Definingcanada.ca
@dundurnpress
Facebook.com/dundurnpress

Dundurn	Gazelle Book Services Limited	Dundurn
3 Church Street, Suite 500	White Cross Mills	2250 Military Road
Toronto, Ontario, Canada	High Town, Lancaster, England	Tonawanda, NY
M5E 1M2	LA1 4XS	U.S.A. 14150

This one is for the Brambergers:
Deborah, Peter, Raymond, and Liesa, who have always been there for me

CONTENTS

FOREWORD

Robert J. Hoshowsky

Memory is a peculiar thing. While most of us cannot remember specific details about uneventful activities like our Monday-to-Friday drive to work or school or what we ate for lunch from one day to another, the opposite holds true in times of tragedy. Unable to recall the trivialities of everyday life, we know precisely where we were the moment our nightmares became reality. When a loved one dies, we readily remember the time of day, sights and smells, and who we were with when we received the news. Like new earth created in time when leaves fall and plants decay, these memories mercifully remain buried, until something happens to reanimate them in monstrous detail.

When I heard from fellow true crime author Lee Mellor about his latest project — a book about spree killers and mass murderers — I immediately thought of an old friend who had suffered loss on such a scale as to be unimaginable: a murder-suicide that saw five members of his family dead in just minutes. In the initial confusion and shock, the awful details did not make themselves known right away, but unfolded over several horrifying hours.

Back in late March of 1985, I was at the Glendon Campus of York University in Toronto. Unlike the formidable Keele Street campus, the Glendon Campus in the city's north end has an almost village-like feel to it, a mixture of noncommittal sixties-style beige structures alongside gorgeous historic buildings crafted from brick and stone, surrounded by old trees and footpaths. At the gym sign-in desk, I met someone I hadn't seen since grade school. We spoke for a few minutes, while in the background breaking news came over the radio about a shooting in the city's west end. I didn't pay a great deal more attention until after my workout, when I passed the desk and heard another news announcement, this time stating that more than one person had been shot and killed on Quebec Avenue. *I know someone who lives on Quebec Avenue*, I thought. *Could it be Marko?* The thought bothered me as I walked back to my parents' home, where my mother immediately said, "Did you hear about the murders in the west end? Doesn't your friend Marko live on Quebec Avenue?" I started to feel something was terribly, irreparably wrong.

She was referring to Marko Bojcun, the editor of an English-language Ukrainian newspaper called *New Perspectives*. Just twenty at the time, I had been contributing to the paper for several years, writing articles and taking photos mainly of community and political events. Marko was not only a mentor to me when I started submitting pen-and-ink drawings to the publication while in my teens, but a gentle, highly intelligent, kind-hearted, and patient man who tolerated my youthful enthusiasm and utter lack of experience with sound advice and a ready smile. I immediately called the west-end apartment he shared with his wife. A gruff-sounding man answered the phone during the first ring. I asked to speak with Marko. The man on the other end identified himself as a Toronto Police detective, and asked who I was. "A friend," I responded, feeling as though hands were around my throat, choking me. In the background, I heard male voices muttering, "Oh, Jesus," and, "Goddamn it!" After a moment, I croaked, "Can I speak to Marko?" My request was followed by a very long pause, after which the detective softly replied, "No … not now," and hung up. It was at that moment I knew something tragic had happened, and ran to the living room to turn on the television.

We watched as station after station put together details from neighbours and police about what happened: a man who had come to Canada from the United States had shot and killed four relatives before turning the weapon on himself. That man was Marko's brother-in-law, and the family members were the killer's parents, an uncle, and his sister — Marko's wife, Marta.

Minute by minute, other facts emerged. Marko's brother-in-law was Wolodymyr Danylewycz, a thirty-three-year-old from Cincinnati, Ohio.

A disturbed soul, he came to Toronto for a visit with other family members, bringing along with him a hidden handgun. On that sunny Sunday, March 24, the family was gathered in the triplex apartment, when Danylewycz asked Marko to get ice cream from the local store. Soon after he left, a loud discussion erupted, and shots were fired around 3:00 p.m. Neighbours called police. Returning to the apartment, Marko found the door unlocked but chained, and he was able to see the carnage inside. Police cars arrived and closed off intersections. Members of the Toronto Emergency Task Force lobbed tear gas into the apartment. Faces covered by gas masks, they stormed inside to discover five bodies in different rooms, all dead. The final gunshot had come from the bathroom, when Danylewycz put the barrel of his gun in his mouth and pulled the trigger.

Investigations by Toronto Police and American authorities soon revealed that Danylewycz was mentally ill and had received psychiatric treatment in Cincinnati. Described as clean-cut and a loner, Danylewycz had unexpectedly quit his job — working as an Easter Seals driver for handicapped persons — just days before coming to Toronto. Police soon found another handgun and notes in which the killer described how he would carry out the murders.

Several days after the murders, I attended the visitation at a funeral home in the city's west end. All five oak caskets were closed, name cards atop each, and arranged in a semi-circle. When I shook Marko's hand, I felt grief for another human being I had never felt before or have since. In time, Marko moved on, becoming a highly respected scholar and author.

There are few things more frightening than the thought of being in a comfortable, seemingly safe place — our living room or backyard, or a restaurant, movie theatre, church, or school — and having that serenity destroyed in moments by a madman armed with guns, knives, bombs, or other weapons. Tragically, mass murders and spree killings are becoming more common worldwide, and although police are able to piece together why someone chose to kill masses of innocent people, we are — despite the work of investigators, psychiatrists, and other experts — no closer to *preventing* these massacres from occurring. History is full of accounts of mass murderers, targeting groups based on race, gender, familial relationship, or any other reasons they justify in their delusional minds. As one fades from memory, he is replaced by another. Yesterday's Charles

Whitman — who stole fourteen lives while shooting from the tower at the University of Texas at Austin in August of 1966 — will be replaced by Norwegian mass murderer Anders Behring Breivik, who massacred seventy-seven in July of 2011, and James Holmes, who murdered twelve and wounded fifty-eight others during a premiere of the Batman movie *The Dark Knight Rises* in Colorado a year later.

Along with Whitman, Breivik, and Holmes, there have been many others who, feeling marginalized and fuelled by loathing, chose to kill. In December of 1989, twenty-five-year-old Marc Lépine slaughtered fourteen young women at Montreal's École Polytechnique. Rather than address his own inadequacies as a man, Lépine blamed "feminists" for taking over non-traditional jobs. In a disturbing twist, a friend of mine, a female student at the École Polytechnique, had mercifully left twenty minutes before Lépine's rampage.

As someone who has devoted a considerable amount of his life to writing about crime, I find nothing more terrifying than mass murderers and spree killers. Serial killers tend to target victims based on any number of factors, including gender, appearance, and race. Ted Bundy preferred brunette females, and John Wayne Gacy targeted young men. Mass murderers and spree killers think nothing of killing friends, family, and anyone else unfortunate enough to get in the way.

In *Rampage: Canadian Mass Murder and Spree Killing*, Lee Mellor has done an admirable job of bringing dozens of cases to light. Some, like the École Polytechnique massacre, are well known, while others have remained hidden — until now. Detailing not only the crimes committed, Mellor explores the twisted mindsets and motives behind these killings, and has created a work that will undoubtedly lead to a greater understanding of why these massacres occur, and what can be done to prevent tragedies in the future.

PREFACE

In my first work, *Cold North Killers*, I documented and analyzed the history of serial murder in Canada. *Rampage: Canadian Mass Murder and Spree Killing* continues in the footsteps of its predecessor, shifting focus to multiple murderers who are slightly more hot-blooded in nature. Unlike serial slayers, mass murderers and spree killers do not experience the cooling-off period that would allow them to retreat back into anonymity. Rather, like bombs, they explode upon society, either in a single act of abrupt devastation or a rapid chain of smaller eruptions. This is not to say that their crimes are spontaneous; in many cases, they have spent months or years planning and working themselves up psychologically to the big event. As we will see in the cases of **Thomas Easby** (Chapter 3) and **Albert Guay** (Chapter 12), when a mass murderer successfully eludes capture, he typically does not go on to kill again. However, the case of **Alexander Keith Jr.** (Chapter 3) indicates that there are exceptions to this rule (see also the serial killers Dennis Rader, Anatoly Onoprienko, and Nathaniel Code).

Contrary to the methods of serial killers, most rampage murderers do not take precautions to ensure their own freedom and survival. In fact, to borrow from T.S. Eliot's "The Hollow Men," many have opted to end their miserable lives with a bang rather than a whimper. Like **Denis Lortie** (Chapter 11) or **Marc Lépine** (Chapter 1), they may feel they are making a profound final "statement" directed at a world that has denied them their rightful place. They conclude that society has driven them to suicide, and rather than meekly ending their own lives, decide to take as many others with them as possible. After all, in their paradigm we are responsible for the misery of their existence. This is truer in some cases than others. The unfortunate tragedy of **Pierre Lebrun** (Chapter 10) reveals that bullying and cliquism may contribute significantly to a mass murderer's psychological destabilization. Severe mental illness, in which the subject experiences a break from reality, is also more common in rampage killers than in serial offenders, as the cases of **Victor Hoffman** (Chapter 13) and **Swift Runner** (Chapter 2) illustrate.

As Fox and Levin have astutely observed in *Extreme Killing: Understanding Serial and Mass Murder*, "In striking contrast to the expanding scholarly interest in serial homicide … the slaughter of several victims during a single act or a short-lived crime spree — have received relatively little consideration."[1] The authors go on to provide a series of plausible explanations for this: the lack of a mysterious identity for police to uncover, reactions of horror as opposed to apprehension about becoming the next victim, and the typical absence of sensationalistic acts of sex or sadism (though strangely, the Canadian rampage murders committed by **Swift Runner, Dale Merle Nelson, David Shearing, Jonathan Yeo,** and **Robert Poulin** are equally or more depraved than many of the cases I examined in *Cold North Killers*). I have chosen to write this book partially because I concur with Fox and Levin that rampage murderers have been underemphasized compared to serial multicide. For this reason, I have included significantly more personal analysis and opinion in *Rampage* than I did in *Cold North Killers*. I believe the field could benefit from a greater plurality of interpretations. In Part C, I have proposed what is, to my knowledge, the first in-depth typology of spree killers. As my formal academic background is currently in history rather than criminology or psychology, I anticipate this will ruffle some feathers. That said, I have gone to great lengths to educate myself in these areas, and have studied much of the current literature relevant to this topic.

As I did in my earlier work, I would like to reiterate that the primary intent of this book is to serve as a didactic encyclopedia. Again, I have purposefully avoided glorifying the killers or canonizing their victims. Nor have I bowdlerized the gruesome details of these murders. To understate the magnitude of what happened would be dishonest, as well as potentially dangerous, since some of the offenders are coming up for parole. It would also be unfair to those who suffered profound agony and indignity.

Let the lesson not be "fear," but "vigilance."

ACKNOWLEDGEMENTS

I would like to begin by thanking Michael Carroll at Dundurn for proposing this book and offering to publish it: mind-reader! Cheers also to my agent, Robert Lecker, for facilitating the contract, and for his continued friendship and support.

Of all those who contributed their time and efforts to *Rampage*, one name deserves special mention. Christina FitzGerald spent countless hours scouring online newspaper and library archives to ensure I had as much information to work with as possible. Without her efforts, this book would be significantly less detailed and thorough. Thank you for your hard work and dedication.

My utmost gratitude also goes out to the author Robert Hoshowsky *(The Last to Die; Unsolved: True Canadian Cold Cases)* for sharing your account of the Bojcun/Danylewycz murders in the Foreword. After twenty-seven years, revisiting this tragedy must have been a harrowing experience. I thank you for adding a much-needed personal perspective and illuminating Marko Bojcun's incredible resilience.

Once again, I am highly indebted to Kay Feely, Andre Kirchhoff, and Elizabeth Roth for their wonderful illustrations. If my ship ever comes in, I'll take you all on a cruise. In the meantime, your generosity and talent are deeply appreciated.

I would like to thank my colleagues at the Multidisciplinary Collaborative on Sexual Crime and Violence for accepting me into your fold. I hope that *Rampage* does something to further our collective understanding of the underexplored phenomena of mass and spree killings. For those who attended the San Antonio conference, forgive my resurrection of the spree murderer. I just don't think they have been given a fair shake.

Finally, to my lioness, Jenn: for your love, support, and patience during this arduous process. Here's to all of the ghoulish conversations yet to come!

PART A

DEFINING MASS MURDER AND SPREE KILLING

If you have purchased this book expecting to find names like Paul Bernardo, Karla Homolka, or Robert Pickton, then you are likely one of the many people who confuses a mass or spree murderer with a serial killer. Don't lament — the media hasn't made it easy for you. Before the term *serial killer* entered public consciousness with the release of Thomas Harris's *The Silence of the Lambs*, serial murders were routinely referred to as mass murders. To this day, the twenty-seven serial slayings perpetrated by Dean Corll are anachronistically known as "The Houston Mass Murders." In the 1994 cult film *Natural Born Killers*, there is a misleading scene in which Wayne Gale (Robert Downey Jr.) is attempting to convince the psychopathic Mickey Knox (Woody Harrelson) to be interviewed for his sensationalist television program *American Maniacs*.

Wayne: I have a television show. And every couple of weeks we do — it's our thing about "Current America" — we do a profile on a different *serial killer*.
Mickey: Technically, *mass murderer*.
Wayne: Well, whatever you want.[2]

Technically, neither Wayne nor Mickey was correct in their classification of the crimes portrayed in the film: the Knoxes were quintessential spree killers. Over the eighties and nineties, there were numerous paperback encyclopedias of "mass murderers" published consisting mainly of serial and spree slayers. Even as recently as 2011, the authors Kerr and Castleden entitled their book the blatantly oxymoronic *Spree Killers: Ruthless Perpetrators of Mass Murder*.

Given the frequent contradictions and misrepresentations of these terms, Chapter 1 is devoted to outlining the differences in multicide (a.k.a. multiple murder). Chapter 2 examines four cases from the great white north that illustrate the difficulty in attempting to sort every multiple murderer according to these classifications. After I've discussed how to discriminate between the various types of killers, Chapter 3 picks up where this book would have begun if it hadn't been for the semantic confusion: chronicling the first four mass murderers in Canadian history.

If indeed you were looking for Bernardo, Homolka, and Pickton, please do not despair. Many of the cases in this book are as lurid and compelling as those of Canada's most reviled serial killers. You just don't know it yet.

CHAPTER 1

TWO KINDS OF RAMPAGE MURDERERS

Table 1: Multiple Homicide Classification by Style and Type[3]

	Mass Murder	Spree Killing	Serial Murder[4]
Number of Victims	4+	2+	3+
Number of Events	1	1	3+
Number of Locations	1	2+	3+
Cooling-Off Period	N/A	No	Yes

Rampage murder is a term commonly used to encompass the first two categories in Table 1: mass murder and spree killing. The FBI's *Crime Classification Manual* originally defined mass murder as, "Any single event, single location homicide involving four or more victims," though it drew a distinction between classical mass murder and family mass murder. According to the text, classical mass murder

> [I]nvolves one person operating in one location at one period of time. The time period could be minutes or hours or even days. The prototype of a classic mass murderer is a mentally discolored individual whose problems have increased to the point that he acts out toward a group of people who are unrelated to him, unleashing

his hostility through shootings or stabbings.[5]

A family mass murder, on the other hand, occurs "if four or more family members are killed ... without [the offender committing] suicide."[6] These first attempts at defining the phenomenon suffered from being too narrow; for example, the specification that mass murder "involves one person" excludes textbook cases such as the April 20, 1999, Columbine High School shootings perpetrated by Eric Harris and Dylan Klebold, and those by their lesser-known predecessors in Jonesboro, Arkansas. The stipulation that an offender committing suicide alters a family mass murder into a simple murder-suicide has also recently been overhauled. In their *Mass Murder in the United States*, Holmes and Holmes fold multiple murders occurring during a single incident within a domestic situation into a sub-category of mass killer known as The Family Annihilator. They also remove the suicide clause altogether and reduce the tally of victims necessitating a mass murder from four to three. Regarding numbers, I believe the most pragmatic parameters are those proposed by Dr. Katherine Ramsland in her *Inside the Minds of Mass Murderers: Why They Kill*:

> For the purpose of this study, I tend to focus primarily on those who have killed at least four victims, but I sometimes make exceptions when it is clear that the killer's intent had been to annihilate far more....[7]

In this book, I've made similar exceptions for **Denis Lortie** (three killed/thirteen injured) and **Joel Egger** (three killed in Canada, probably more overseas). I also follow Holmes and Holmes's lead in doing away with a separate family mass murderer, including it as a permutation of a general mass murderer type. Whether the murderer committed suicide or not has no bearing on my classification, as I see the inclusion of this specification as completely arbitrary.

The definition of spree killing has proved so contentious that in recent years the FBI has deemed it merely a subtype of serial murder. Fox and Levin were the first to propose eliminating the category altogether, claiming that focusing "on motivation rather than timing eliminates the need for a spree killer designation — a category sometimes used to identify cases of multiple homicide that do not fit neatly into either the serial or mass murder types."[8] John Douglas, one of the pioneers of the FBI's Behavioural Sciences Unit, defined a spree murderer as "someone who murders at two or more separate locations with no emotional cooling-off period between the homicides. Therefore, the killings tend to take place in a shorter period of time [than most serial killers]...."[9] In this book, I make a case for the usefulness of designating spree murder as a separate phenomenon from serial murder, and propose a clearer definition and criminological understanding in Part C. The reader should also note that the FBI's criteria for serial murder has recently changed to two or more victims in two or more separate events, with location no longer considered a factor.

Unlike in my first book, *Cold North Killers: Canadian Serial Murder*, I have made no attempt to create an exhaustive work. However, I have assembled a basic chronology of Canadian rampage murders in Table 2.

Table 2: A History of Canadian Rampage Murderers, 1828–2012
Italics denote cases included in this book.

Name	Date and Duration of Rampage	Type	Killed
Thomas Easby	*December 1828*	*Mass Murder — Family Annihilator*	*Five*
Henry Sovereign	*January 23, 1832*	*Mass Murder — Family Annihilator*	*Eight*
Patrick Slavin	*October 24, 1857*	*Mass Murder — Family Annihilator*	*Six*
Mathilde Laventure	July 20/21, 1862	Mass Murder — Family Annihilator	Seven
Alexander Keith Jr.	*December 11, 1875*	*Mass Murder — Set and Run*	*Eighty-one*
Swift Runner	*Winter of 1878/79*	*Difficult to classify*	*Eight*
Black Donnelly Massacre	February 4, 1880	Mass Murder — Family Annihilator	Five
John Mychaluk	April 1916	Mass Murder — Family Annihilator	Five
Grand Prairie Massacre	June 1918	Mass Murder — Unknown	Six

Vernon Booher	July 8, 1928	Mass Murder — Family Annihilator	Four
Andrew Day	December 16, 1929	Mass Murder — Family Annihilator	Eight
Thomas Hreczkosy	January 29, 1932	Mass Murder — Family Annihilator	Seven
Rosaire Bilodeau	*October 25, 1934*	*Difficult to classify*	*Six*
Kalmakoff, Posnikoff, and Wolken	October 5–7, 1935	Spree Killer — Utilitarian	Four
Albert Guay	*September 9, 1949*	*Mass Murder — Set and Run*	*Twenty-three*
John Petlock	August 29, 1955	Mass Murder — Family Annihilator	Five
John Etter Clark	June 3, 1956	Mass Murder — Family Annihilator	Seven
Robert Cook	*June 25, 1959*	*Mass Murder — Family Annihilator*	*Seven*
Abel Vosburgh	December 29, 1960	Mass Murder — Family Annihilator	Twelve
Leonard Hogue	*April 19 or 20, 1965*	*Mass Murder — Family Annihilator*	*Seven*
Victor Hoffman	*August 15, 1967*	*Mass Murder — Psychotic*	*Nine*
Frederick McCallum	January 30, 1969	Mass Murder — Psychotic	Seven
Louis Chiasson	*December 2, 1969*	*Mass Homicide — Set and Run*	*Forty*
Dale Merle Nelson	*September 4–5, 1970*	*Spree Killer — Signature*	*Eight*
O'Brien, Boutin, and Eccles	September 1, 1972	Mass Homicide — Set and Run	Thirty-seven
Gargantua Nightclub Fire	January 21, 1975	Mass Murder — Gangland	Thirteen
Robert Poulin	*October 27, 1975*	*Difficult to classify*	*Two*
Lorne Acquin	July 22, 1977	Mass Murder — Family Annihilator	Nine
Gregory McMaster	*July 27–August 2, 1978*	*Spree Killer — Utilitarian*	*Four*
Rene Paul	January 4, 1981	Mass Murder — Family Annihilator	Five
David Shearing	*August 1982*	*Difficult to classify*	*Seven*

Bruce Blackman	January 18, 1983	Mass Murder — Psychotic	Six
Denis Lortie	*May 8, 1984*	*Mass Murder — Disgruntled Citizen*	*Three*
Wolodymyr Danylewycz	*March 24, 1985*	*Mass Murder — Family Annihilator*	*Four*
Air India Bombings	June 23, 1985	Mass Murder — Set and Run	329
Marc Lépine	*December 6, 1989*	*Mass Murder — Disgruntled Citizen*	*Fourteen*
Peter John Peters	*January 20–25, 1990*	*Spree Killer — Utilitarian*	*Two*
Mark Wells	June 15, 1990	Spree Killer — Signature	Four
Gavin Mandin	August 6, 1991	Mass Murder — Family Annihilator	Four
Jonathan Yeo	*August 9–14, 1991*	*Spree Killer — Signature*	*Two*
Roger Warren	September 18, 1992	Mass Murder — Set and Run	Nine
Valery Fabrikant	*August 24, 1992*	*Mass Murder — Disgruntled Citizen*	*Four*
Order of the Solar Temple	*October 4–5, 1994*	*Mass Murder — Ideological/Disciple*	*3+*
James Huang	January 5, 1996	Mass Murder — Family Annihilator	Four
Mark Chahal	April 6, 1996	Mass Murder — Family Annihilator	Nine
Marcello Palma	*May 21–22, 1996*	*Spree Killer — Exterminator*	*Three*
Abbotsford Cocaine Murders	September 12, 1996	Mass Murder — Gangland	Five
Ludvic Kirec	April 13, 1997	Mass Murder — Family Annihilator	Five
John Gorton	September 19, 1997	Mass Murder — Family Annihilator	Five
Pierre Lebrun	*April 6, 1999*	*Mass Murder — Disgruntled Employee*	*Four*
Bill Luft	November 10, 2000	Mass Murder — Family Annihilator	Five
John Bauer	September 20, 2001	Mass Murder — Family Annihilator	Six

Magloire Poissant	December 29, 2001	Mass Murder — Family Annihilator	Four
Jay Handel	March 11, 2002	Mass Murder — Family Annihilator	Six
Peter Kiss	June 14, 2002	Mass Murder — Family Annihilator	Four
James Roszko	*March 3, 2005*	*Mass Murderer — Disgruntled Citizen*	*Four*
Frank Mailey	April 2, 2006	Mass Murder — Family Annihilator	Four
Bandidos Massacre	April 8, 2006	Mass Murder — Gangland	Eight
Stephen Marshall	*April 16, 2006*	*Spree Killer — Exterminator*	*Two*
Glen Race	Early March 2007	Spree Killer — ?	Three
Jesse Imeson	*July 18–31, 2007*	*Spree Killer — Utilitarian*	*Three*
Peter Hyun Joon Lee	September 4, 2007	Mass Murderer — Family Annihilator	Four
Dennis Karbovanec	October 19, 2007	Mass Murderer — Gangland	Six
Joshua Lall	May 27, 2008	Mass Murderer — Psychotic	Four
Mohammed, Tooba, and Hamed Shafia	June 30, 2009	Mass Murderer — Family Annihilator	Four
Winnipeg Spree Killer	October 23, 2010	Spree Killer — ?	Two

The first two slayers we look at represent the most infamous examples of Canadian mass murderers and spree killers. **Marc Lépine** stunned the world on December 6, 1989, when he callously executed fourteen female engineering students at Montreal's École Polytechnique, sparking debates over misogyny and national gun laws. Though spree killer **Peter John Peters** would not receive any level of international recognition or lasting notoriety, in January 1990 he held Ontario in the grip of terror for nearly a week. These men are similar in that they embarked on rampage-style murders just over a month apart. Yet in many aspects of their character, they are polar opposites. Lépine and Peters have been selected as introductory models, not just because of their infamy, but also because they reflect the fundamental difference between a mass murderer and a spree killer.

Andre Kirchhoff

Marc Lépine
The Polytechnique Gunman

"Ah, shit."

Victims: 14 killed/14 wounded/committed suicide
Duration of rampage: December 6, 1989 (mass murder)
Location: Montreal, Quebec
Weapons: Sturm Ruger Mini-14 .223-calibre semi-automatic rifle

RAINING ICE

December 6, 1989, was a surprisingly mild day for a Montreal winter, the freezing rain spattering against the yellow brick exterior of École Polytechnique like tears of ice. Twenty-five-year-old Marc Lépine sat awkwardly on a bench in the office of the registrar, dark eyes peering from beneath the brim of his "Tracteur Montreal" baseball cap. Hours before, the barber had scraped a razor over his acne-marred skin, his brown tousled hair tumbling to the floor: shorn, like his dreams. Beneath his grey windbreaker and blue-striped sweater, he could feel the sheath of the hunting knife pressing against his body. Nervous, he patted the bulky green garbage bag concealing his .223-calibre semi-automatic rifle. Two months earlier he had purchased the Sturm Ruger Mini-14 at Checkmate Sports on St. Hubert, ostensibly for hunting small game. These hypothetical ducks and rabbits would have stood no chance — police SWAT teams routinely employ the same firearm. Though the scrawny young man did his best to avoid attention, he had seated himself by the office door, making it difficult for students to enter. After forty minutes, a female office employee politely inquired if he needed assistance. Without uttering a word, Lépine rose and relocated to somewhere less conspicuous.

It was close to 5:00 p.m., and through the windows the light was quickly fading. Many of the faculty and students were leaving the building to begin their Christmas holidays. This was the moment he had been waiting for: empty hallways meant less chance of somebody being alerted to the impending massacre.

He made his way to the second floor, where an engineering class was being held. The green bag fluttered to the tiles as he unveiled the Sturm Ruger and proceeded calmly through the doorless entrance into C-230. At first, neither of the two professors or sixty-nine students packing the room noticed anything amiss. Lépine smiled as if to acknowledge his tardiness. One of the students was giving a presentation on heat transference. Lépine surveyed the crowd, noting where the female pupils were seated, and moved toward the presenter.

"Everyone stop everything!" he barked. One of the professors cast him a stern glance. He did not recognize this "student." Continuing in French, Lépine ordered the women to move to the left side of the room and the men to the right. Instead of compliance, his demands were met with laughter. Lépine felt the anger welling up inside him. Even now, in what should have been his moment of supreme control, they mocked him. In reality, most of the students had simply assumed it was an end-of-term practical joke. Furious, Lépine hoisted the Sturm Ruger and fired two shots into the ceiling. The room fell silent. Laughter became the first casualty in his personal war.

"I want the women!" Lépine roared. "You're all a bunch of feminists, and I hate feminists!" Terrified, the two sexes separated accordingly.

"Okay, the guys leave," he motioned toward the exit. "The girls stay there." As the sixty male students and two professors reluctantly vacated, Lépine approached the nine remaining female students and ushered them into a corner.

"Do you know why you are there?" he asked. "I am fighting feminism." When student Nathalie Provost attempted to explain that they were not necessarily feminists, Lépine proved his intellectual superiority by spraying the women with ammunition from left to right, until they lay in a crumpled mess of blood and limbs. He had fired approximately thirty bullets.

Outside the classroom, the exiled males listened in disbelief as gunshots and screams rang out in grim cacophony. As several hurried down the hallway to warn the rest of the school, Lépine exited C-230 and pointed the gun at the remaining men until they cleared a path. Keeping his back to the wall, he continued down the main corridor, firing into the photocopying centre and injuring three more victims: two women and one man. Turning, he strode into the doorway of C-228 and aimed at another female student. Fate intervened, and the Sturm Ruger malfunctioned. Frustrated, Lépine took cover in the emergency stairway near room C-229 and checked the weapon. As his fingers worked feverishly at a solution, an unsuspecting student descended the steps and brushed past him.

"Ah, shit, I'm out of bullets," Lépine said aloud. The student remained oblivious, continuing down the hallway to the photocopiers. When he saw the bodies, he realized what was happening and raced for the escalators.

Meanwhile, several of the male engineering students had returned to room C-230 to find their classmates lying beneath a mural of blood. Some of the women were moaning in agony; some wept — others stayed horribly silent. As ambulances raced through the sleet, Lépine reloaded and made his way back to C-228. By now the door had been locked. Frustrated, he fired three shots into it, then proceeded to the foyer, past three wounded victims. Entering the foyer, he spied a female student stepping off the escalator, and shot her. She was injured but managed to escape via the emergency staircase, and took refuge on the fifth floor. Calmly changing his magazine, Lépine strode over to a person hiding behind a counter and fired twice, missing on both occasions. He moved across the cafeteria terrace to room B-218 — the financial services office — where a woman hastily locked the door. Lépine sighted her through the door window and shot her fatally through the glass. He had quit many things in his life, but in murdering women, he was surprisingly resolute.

LIKE FATHER, LIKE SON

Canada's most notorious mass murderer had not always been named Marc Lépine. On October 26, 1964, Gamil Rodrigue Liess Gharbi was born to a French-Canadian mother, Monique, at Montreal's Sainte-Justine Hospital. His Algerian father, Rachid, was notably absent, favouring a Caribbean business trip over his family obligations. Nevertheless, Rachid had left specific instructions that the boy was to be named Gamil, which meant *handsome* in Arabic. During her stay at Sainte-Justine, Monique learned from an admissions clerk that another "Monique Gharbi" had given birth at the hospital only a week earlier. Interestingly, this woman's partner had also been called Rachid Gharbi. As the surname was rare in Montreal at the time, Monique deduced that her husband was carrying on an affair.

Shortly after returning to their home on Ridgewood Avenue, she checked his income tax returns, and found confirmation in the form of child support payments to two local children.[10] Confronted by Monique, Rachid confessed to the affair, but assured her that it had ended. She knew better than to believe him — while he had been away on business, a delivery truck had arrived from Eaton's department store. Though Monique had ordered one of the items, the deliveryman insisted that he also had an expensive baby carriage for her. When she denied making the purchase, he checked his records and realized that it was intended for another Monique Gharbi who resided only blocks away. Given Rachid's history, the revelation of his infidelity was hardly surprising.

Monique Lépine had first met the silver-tongued aircraft mechanic in 1961, when a female workmate invited her out for drinks with "two charming young men." With his flashy clothes, confidence, and fluency in four languages, Rachid Gharbi swept the twenty-two-year-old nurse off her feet. He was unlike the hockey-obsessed suitors Monique had encountered before, and the two soon began a relationship. From the get-go, Rachid pressured her to have sex, but Monique, who was raised in a devout Catholic family, resisted his advances. After three months, she conceded when he threatened to break up. Sadly, the birth control pill was not easily available or acceptable in Quebec at the time, and Rachid stubbornly refused to wear a condom. The result was that Monique underwent three illegal abortions between May 1961 and October 1963, sparing her family the shame of bastard children. Though Rachid grudgingly footed each of the $300 fees, he made no bones about his unhappiness with the situation. As a non-practising Muslim, his concern was not with the termination of the pregnancies, but the financial cost of the operations.

When Rachid proposed marriage to Monique on October 13, 1963, she accepted because she feared becoming an old maid. In retrospect, she realized it was a foolish decision. Rachid was a volatile and controlling man, often calling her several times a day to check on her, despite his own infidelities. He would fly into a rage at the slightest provocation, and Monique, who had been taught by nuns to placate her husband, unfailingly submitted to his will. Things only worsened after their marriage, as the abuse extended from the emotional realm to the physical. Though he forbade her to work outside the home, Rachid expected Monique to serve as his personal typist, slapping her whenever she made a mistake and forcing her to re-type the entire page. So relentless was her work that she was often unable to comfort her crying infant. When Gamil realized his screams would go unanswered, he sunk into a telling silence. In a vain attempt to become closer to her absentee husband, Monique uprooted to Puerto Rico with him when Gamil was just over a year old. Contrary to her expectations, she saw even less of Rachid, and he remained as selfish as ever. On one occasion he insisted that Monique go to the cinema with him, even though there was no babysitter available. The two went out for a night on the town, leaving the eighteen-month-old Gamil slumbering in his crib. When they returned, they found him sobbing in the middle of the bedroom floor. The abandoned child had climbed out of his crib, shattering a nearby lamp in the process.

In 1966, Monique discovered she was pregnant again, and decided to move back to Montreal to have their second child. On April 7, 1967, she gave birth to a healthy daughter, Nadia, in the same room at Sainte-Justine Hospital where Gamil had been born. Instead of adoring his baby sister, Gamil was fiercely jealous. The newborn hadn't been home for a day when Monique discovered Gamil violently rocking her cradle as if he were trying to tip Nadia onto the floor. Monique would later describe him as "a very possessive child" who "always wanted to be close to me, to the point of getting angry when I was absent, even for a short time and sulking when I looked after his little sister." There were other problems too. By now Rachid's violent temper had turned against his children; Gamil was already being spanked much more frequently and severely than was merited. One morning in 1970, the six-year-old had risen early, and inadvertently woke his father by singing. Enraged, Rachid burst into the room and struck Gamil across the face, bruising him badly. As the child sat weeping, Monique went to comfort him, but her husband intervened, ordering her not to "pamper" him. It was the last straw. The couple officially separated in July 1971, and she gained custody of the children. Their divorce would not be finalized for another five years. Angered by the split, Rachid took all of the photographs of the children with him, refusing to pay alimony or his $75-per-month child support. It wasn't long before bailiffs descended upon their Prieur Street home, repossessing all of the furniture save for the beds, a table, and chairs. Monique learned that Rachid had secretly taken out a second mortgage on the property but had ceased making payments. Within days, what little they had left was lost, and Monique and her children had no choice but to move in temporarily with a kindly neighbour.

Rachid was permitted to see his children once a week, albeit under the supervision of a social worker. Gamil never looked forward to the visits. On one occasion, Monique was driving them to meet Rachid at an ice cream parlour when she informed her son that he was going to see his daddy. Without warning, the six-year-old seized the steering wheel and attempted to veer the vehicle off road. Fortune prevailed and nobody was hurt, but it would be the last occasion Gamil would ever spend in Rachid's company. In fact, he never spoke of his father again unless he was forced to. Not long after, Monique discovered Gamil cowering behind a cupboard because he was afraid that a workman at their new apartment would hit him.

Desperate, Monique applied for social assistance, but was unable to get by without Rachid's financial support. With few options, she returned to nursing full time at Royal Victoria Hospital, hiring a Francophone family in Pointe-aux-Trembles to care for her children. Overworked and taking professional development courses three nights a week, in 1972 Monique decided to leave Gamil and Nadia with their caregivers throughout the week. They would stay with her on weekends at her Sherbrooke Avenue apartment, where they would play board games and enjoy home-cooked chicken dinners. In January 1974, their caregivers moved away, and Monique passed them off to a retired nurse in Saint-Michel. The children did not adjust well to the disruption. Their school marks plummeted, and Nadia began bedwetting. After several months, Monique found another family for the children to live with during the week: two ex-teachers who owned a farm in the Eastern Townships village of Bethanie. To Monique, Gamil and Nadia seemed happier there, and they attended the same school as the couple's daughters. Little did she know that her children were feeling increasingly abandoned by their mother, creating emotional instabilities that would ultimately lead them both to early graves. One of Marc's caretakers would later tell Monique:

> We had to watch your son closely. Once, when we were camping, my husband asked him to get a propane tank from the car. When he came back with it, for no apparent reason, he threw it into the campfire, where it exploded. Luckily no one was hurt. Another time, after all the equipment was packed up on top of the car, he undid the straps that held it in place. Again, it was just by chance that we noticed before we got on the road.[11]

SIBLING RIVALRY

When Monique's expensive divorce was finalized in 1976, her financial situation improved, and Gamil and Nadia begged to move back in with her. Having worked her way to the position of director of nursing care at the Montreal Convalescent Hospital, Monique agreed. She rented a three-bedroom apartment for them on rue Van Horne, and left twelve-year-old Gamil to care for his sister while she worked. The following year, she purchased a bungalow in suburban Pierrefonds. Here, the first signs of Gamil's disturbance came to light. In one eerily prescient incident, he had been fighting with his sister during the day and had become extremely upset. As the sky darkened over the sleepy subdivision, he grabbed a shovel and began digging a hole in the backyard. By the time he was finished, an empty grave lay gaping in the moonlight. Acting as if on autopilot, Gamil fashioned a makeshift tombstone upon which he wrote NADIA, and attached a photograph of his little sister to it. With his work complete, he stepped back and stood staring blankly at his creation. Monique accused him of bad taste and told him to get rid of it. Gamil complied without protest, disassembling the monument in the same methodical manner with which he had erected it. Months later, Monique's beloved cat disappeared. When she asked her children if they had seen it, Nadia confided that she had watched her brother bind a rope around its neck. Confronted by his mother, Gamil denied any responsibility. Monique never saw her pet again.

Despite these seemingly isolated incidents, young Gamil was a great help around their new home — shovelling snow, mowing the lawn, and fixing things for his mother. Regardless of what Gamil may have thought about Monique, one thing is abundantly clear: he despised his father. In his first day of classes at Pierrefonds High School, a teacher requested that each student stand when he read their name for roll call. When the words "Gamil Gharbi" stumbled from his lips, nobody rose. He repeated them. After a long pause, the boy slowly rose to his feet at the back of the class, glaring at the rest of the students: "Present." At age thirteen, sick of being called "Arab" and having to explain about his loathed Algerian father, Gamil Gharbi officially changed his name to Marc Lépine.

During his stint at Pierrefonds High, Marc befriended Jean Belanger. They had first met on a school bus in September 1977, when Jean had noticed Marc sitting alone and decided to talk to him. The two became best pals, shooting at pigeons with air rifles from the Bordeaux Bridge. The only negative experience Jean recalls was the time he asked Marc where his father was. Angered, Marc told him that he had probably moved back to Algeria and to mind his own business. Jean got the message and never broached the subject again. It was obvious that his friend was struggling with some major issues. Marc was painfully shy, so much so that he struggled to say hello to Jean's parents, despite the fact that they repeatedly demonstrated their fondness for him. More confident than his friend, Jean began dating Gina Cousineau. There was many a time when Marc stood awkwardly by, not knowing what to do, as the two lovers made out. When he finally tried his luck with a neighbourhood girl one summer afternoon, Nadia spotted them kissing in the backyard and laughed mockingly. Furious, Marc pushed the confused girl away, choosing solitude over his sister's jibes.

Jean disliked Nadia and the way she treated his friend. She was constantly calling Marc names in front of other people, accusing him of "having no balls," and insinuating that he was homosexual. Whereas Jean and Marc devoted themselves to constructive intellectual pursuits like building electronic gadgets in the basement, Nadia fell in with a bad crowd, and began drinking and taking drugs.

What remaining close relationships Marc had established perished in the summer of 1982, when his mother sold the family home in Pierrefonds and moved with her two children to a rented two-storey row house in the suburb of Saint-Laurent. Life at 2675 Marlborough Court had the advantage of being closer to St. Jude's Hospital in Laval, where both Monique and Marc were employed; the former as a nursing director and the latter washing dishes in the hospital kitchen. By September, Marc had finished his summer job and was entering his first semester of a two-year CEGEP program in Pure Sciences at Saint-Laurent Junior College. At the same time, he was beginning to show signs of mental disturbance. Just after his seventeenth birthday he was debating a "controversial topic" with his mother when suddenly he seized her arm and gouged his fingers into her skin. When she threatened to kick him out of the home, Marc snapped out of his trance and let go, retreating in shame to his bedroom. Often he had professed to friends that he wished he had been able to save Monique from Rachid's abuse — now, for an instant, he had taken his father's place.

It was merely the beginning. After excelling academically in high school, Marc failed two classes in his first term at CEGEP, spending most of his time locked in his cluttered room playing on his computer or reading. He applied for the army that same year but was rejected for displaying anti-social behavioural traits. In order to best understand Marc Lépine's state of mind in 1982, we need only look at one of the first lines in his 1989 suicide note: "It has been seven years that life does not bring me any joy." If we are to trust the judgment of the gunman himself, this period marked the beginning of a radical negative shift in his emotional well-being.

SEVEN YEARS OF SORROW

Without the benefit of hindsight, in 1983 Marc Lépine seemed angelic compared to his sister, Nadia, whose habitual disobedience had landed her in a boarding school for troubled teens. Lépine was not sorry to see her go. For years she had constantly taunted him in front of his friends, exacting a devastating toll on his fragile self-esteem. Though Lépine had fared poorly in his fall 1982 term at CEGEP, by winter 1983 he had revitalized his academic performance, earning grades which ranged from the seventies to the nineties. His boyhood dream of entering the engineering program at École Polytechnique was now close to becoming a reality.

In the meantime, he continued to work part-time as a custodian at St. Jude's Hospital, and was also responsible for serving meals to patients. Here his social shortcomings became increasingly evident. Considered weird and loud by his workmates, Lépine was judged to be seeking attention. Though he made friends, he argued with them constantly, a trait which some found annoying. Nicknamed "James Bond" for his high IQ and puzzle-solving abilities, sadly Lépine lacked 007's confidence and easy charm with the ladies. He would routinely take meals and breaks with female co-workers, but was stifled in his efforts to court them by his crippling shyness. Plagued by terrible acne, instead of opening up to women, he continually guided conversations back to areas of his expertise, where he felt self-assured. Like the computers he so revered, Lépine was intelligent but unable to effectively process emotions. He also struggled with authority, slacking on his hospital duties and treating his bosses with disdain. Chronically distracted, he was prone to making simple errors in day-to-day tasks, which he would unfailingly acknowledge with his token "Ah, shit."

When autumn of 1983 came, Lépine suddenly changed academic direction, dropping out in the middle of his two-year Pure Sciences program in favour of a three-year vocational trade program in Electronics Technology. He continued to achieve good grades, including an 82 in Industrial Electronics and an 87 in Control Systems. However, in both the school and the workplace, he was regarded as high-strung — a bundle of nerves who was "always in a hurry." Lépine would often slam meal carts, spilling soup, which his co-workers interpreted as aggression, though it is possible that his attention and coordination were distracted by his overwhelming anxiety. During this period, Nadia and Isabelle Lahaie, her roommate at boarding school, often visited the apartment at 2675 Marlborough. Isabelle remembers Marc as a "good guy" but "closed" with a "strange look — his eyes were lit up, he had the same smile all the time … You could see he was unhappy."[12] A troubled teen herself, Nadia seemed indifferent to her brother's problems, even advising Isabelle that the best ways to "get him mad" were to "call him Gamil, and tell him he is ugly and stupid." Unsurprisingly, when Nadia returned to living at 2675 Marlborough in 1986, Lépine's behaviour took a turn for the worse. With only nine courses left before graduating CEGEP in Electronics Technology, on January 31, 1986, the twenty-one-year-old simply stopped attending classes. He applied for the engineering program at École Polytechnique and was predictably rejected. Next he enrolled in summer courses, but dropped out. When July came, Lépine relocated to apartment 401 at 4185 St. Martin Boulevard in suburban Laval, away from his sister's acerbic tongue.

Lépine's habitual clumsiness resulted in him being transferred to the cafeteria at St. Jude's, but the constant steam from the kitchen only worsened his repulsive acne. Fellow employees mocked him and refused to let him serve their meals. Lépine grew a patchy beard in an attempt to disguise his complexion, but if anything, it only accentuated his imperfections. Eventually, he was relegated to the back of the kitchen where nobody could see him — a modern Quasimodo, whose deafening "bells" were grease and steam.

That summer, Lépine befriended nineteen-year-old Dominique Leclair, the daughter of the man who ran the hospital. "I was kind to him because he was so hyperactive and nervous," Dominique recalled. "Nobody would talk to him at lunch or break time.... Everyone else tried to avoid him because he was a bit strange because of his shyness.... He was always rushing things. He would never be calm."[13] Regarding his co-workers, she readily admitted, "They were mean." If Lépine ever had any romantic interest in Dominique, she did not pick up on it. Even when they dined together, he kept his eyes on his food, stirring it continuously.

"I've asked a lot of girls out, but they have all refused," he once confessed to her. "I know so many girls, but they won't go out with me. I'm not good looking...." The two finally went their separate ways in September 1987, when Dominique returned to school. Lépine was fired from his job at the hospital and attended a CEGEP in Montmorency.* Although he received a $2,400 severance package, he was infuriated. One witness remembers him threatening to go on a killing rampage that would culminate with his own death. In a chilling coincidence, the last victim of the Polytechnique massacre would turn out to be Dominique's cousin Maryse. He had repaid her kindness with a lifetime of agony.

---

* Some sources say that Marc was fired in 1984. Perhaps owing to his mother's position at the hospital, he was granted a second chance before blowing it again in 1987.

"AH, SHIT"

The cafeteria at École Polytechnique was adorned with red and white balloons to mark the holiday season. At 5:18 p.m., approximately one hundred people were gathered around the tables, chatting, eating, and sipping complimentary wine to celebrate the end of term. Stepping off the escalator, Marc Lépine entered the cafeteria and opened fire, striking a female student by the kitchen. Terrified onlookers began to flee the cafeteria in droves. When his victim fell dead, Lépine stalked across the large room, firing and wounding another. He reached a storage area known as the Polyparty, where he encountered two more female students and unloaded the Ruger, killing them. He spotted a male and female student attempting to conceal themselves beneath a table, and ordered them to "get out from there." For unknown reasons, he allowed them to escape unharmed.

Exiting the cafeteria, Lépine roamed around aimlessly for a number of minutes before stomping up a non-functional escalator to the third floor. There he encountered a group of students in the hallway and opened fire, wounding three: two men and one woman. Continuing down a short corridor, he turned left and entered room B-311, where three students stood on a raised platform. Clad in a brand-new red sweater, Maryse Leclair had her back to him and was scribbling on the blackboard.

"Get out, get out," he snarled, firing and hitting Maryse. Pivoting, he began spraying bullets at the students seated in the front row. Two women made a dash for the front doorway, but the Ruger roared, fatally wounding them. Those who chose to escape through the back exit were more successful. Lépine stalked down the aisle, firing at students hidden among the desks. One of the four he hit would eventually succumb to her injuries. Pacing up and down the aisle as if engaged in a tedious argument with himself, Lépine then clambered on top of a desk and exchanged his empty magazine for a full one. His mind clearly disintegrating, he fired wildly: nowhere; everywhere. In the silence that followed, he heard Maryse Leclair murmuring for help from the platform. Climbing onto the dais, he drew his six-inch hunting knife and plunged it three times into her chest. Then, placing the dripping blade, two boxes of ammo, and his cap onto the instructor's desk; he sat on the platform and wrapped his windbreaker around the barrel of the Ruger.

"Ah, shit," he muttered. Seconds later, he blasted the remaining bullet in the magazine through his own skull, bringing the Polytechnique massacre to its conclusion.

CONTROL DATA

A month and a half after losing his job at the hospital, Marc Lépine turned twenty-three. Living off unemployment insurance, he managed to obtain good grades during his fifteen weeks at CEGEP Montmorency, including an 84 in Mass Communications, 81 in Advanced Algebra, and 75 in Ethics of Politics. After purchasing a computer with his savings from the hospital, he spent most of the winter cooped up in his apartment playing on it. On February 29, 1988, he applied to study Computer Programming at Control Data, a private post-secondary school in downtown Montreal. Earning a 90 grade on his admissions exam, he began attending classes on March 11. The fifteen-month program cost $9,000, two-thirds of which he took care of with a student loan, covering the rest with monthly payments of $200. While his work at other institutions had ranged from "good but unremarkable" to "terrible," at Control Data he truly shone. The school's director, Jean Cloutier, recalls "an isolated hard worker. Very much above average.... His marks throughout were probably in the top fifteen percent."[14]

Outwardly, things seemed to be looking up for Lépine. Having reconnected with his old buddy Érik Cossette from Pierrefonds High School, in June the two moved into a second floor apartment at 2175 Bordeaux. Érik, shorter and fairer than Lépine, was studying theatre at the University of Quebec at Montreal, while Marc entered a chemistry course at CEGEP du Vieux Montreal. Strangely, during Lépine's last meeting with his former building superintendent Luc Ripoel, he made no mention of his academic pursuits, only of leaving to join the armed forces.

Lépine's new apartment was a striking departure from his previous residences. Located in Montreal's downtown east side, the red brick duplex lay within walking distance of some of Canada's most exciting nightlife. He decided to forego this opportunity to have fun, continuing to live as a hermit. Nadia's ex-boyfriend Jacques recalled his futile attempts to help Lépine break out of his shell:

One evening, to help him out, I took him to a bar on St. Denis Street and bought him a rum and Coke. That was his favourite drink, although he wasn't really much of a drinker. I hoped it would help him relax a bit because he was so nervous he was starting to sweat. He had no idea how to talk to the girls I introduced him to and ended up going home early. When Nadia and I went out with friends, we would often ask him to join us, but he usually said no.[15]

At 2175 Bordeaux, Lépine ended up with the smaller of the two rooms, spending the last two and a half years of his life sleeping on a sofa bed in an eight-by-ten-foot box. The only window in the room overlooked a network of telephone wires obscuring the alley below. Monique, who had moved into a condominium three blocks away, had helped her son paint the walls turquoise. As a finishing touch, he added two prints, one depicting an epic battle scene.

The following month, Lépine arrived at his Class of '82 Pierrefonds High School reunion, looking uncharacteristically suave in a black button-up shirt and dress pants. One of his few friends, Jean Belanger, was absent from the gathering, having accidentally crushed his leg with a garage door. Jean's ex-girlfriend Gina Cousineau, however, was happy to see him. "He looked like he always looked, that big smile," Gina recalled in an interview with the *Ottawa Sun*. "He always had that smile on his face, even if things weren't going so well." Lépine spent most of the evening drinking Coca-Cola and clinging to Gina and her fiancé. Though he was halfway through his studies at Control Data, he did not speak of it, saying only that he was attending university in the fall. When Gina inquired about his love life, Lépine said something about a girlfriend who had recently dumped him. He also claimed to have been fired from the hospital by a woman during his three-month probationary period because of one simple error. His replacement was another female employee, a point upon which he seemed particularly angry. The day after the reunion, Lépine called his injured friend Jean and informed him that he was considering a career in the military.

Chemistry at CEGEP du Vieux Montreal commenced in February 1989. From 1:00 p.m. to 6:00 p.m., Lépine attended Control Data, devoting two nights a week to his new course. He became lab partners with Sylvie Drouin: a shy twenty-eight-year-old Laval University arts graduate. Like him, she was taking the class as a prerequisite for applying to engineering school. Initially, Sylvie found Lépine attractive, but was quickly turned off by the "fascist" side of his personality. During the first few weeks he criticized her constantly, called her "Fräulein," and ordered her to wash and fetch things for him. When Sylvie threatened to change lab partners if he didn't stop, Lépine responded with a silent scowl. For the rest of the term, he was notably more considerate. Paradoxically, the little führer was constantly bungling experiments, dismissing his absent-minded failings with his signature "Ah, shit." "He was good at the theory, but at practical things he was no good," Sylvie would later explain. "He was so nervous, he would make mistakes. His mind would wander. He would put too many drops in the solution, that kind of thing."[16] Despite his disorganized headspace, Lépine's raw intelligence managed to earn him an A+ in the course.

Sylvie Drouin's relationship with Lépine was remarkable in that she was one of the few women he allowed into his personal life. When she learned that he was a wizard with computers, Sylvie asked if he would mind helping her with homework for a night course she was taking on the subject. Lépine was eager to assist, and on her first visit to 2175 Bordeaux, she thoroughly enjoyed watching him demonstrate 3-D modelling techniques and colouring on his computer. Unfortunately, it soon became apparent that his intentions were not to teach her, but to wow her with his outstanding computer prowess. "He needed to feel important to other people," Sylvie perceived. "He didn't teach me. He just wanted to solve the problems himself and hand them to me." In her opinion, the controlling and patronizing approach Lépine took to teaching and teamwork would have adversely affected his love life:

> I think in his mind, the girl has to worship everything he does, that everything he does is right. Like in those first few labs.... If you follow him and his ways, things are fine. If you don't, there is nothing. He gets very cold

and withdrawn.... I like the different kind, not whackos,
but different. But to be with a guy like that, you would
have to give your whole life to him, just follow him.[17]

Lépine's patriarchal views were not confined to his private life.
Laboratory assistant Andre Tremblay recalls the twenty-two-year-old
bringing a tabloid newspaper into class featuring a story about a female
police officer who had rescued an elderly man from a house fire. Lépine
had launched into an irrational polemic about how women were not physically fit to work in law enforcement, mentioning that there were only six
employed on the Montreal police force. Incredulous, Andre asked where
he had obtained such information, to which Lépine replied, "To date,
I have only found the names of six of them in newspaper stories...."[18]
For a man of supposedly high intelligence, Lépine had seemingly missed
two salient points: 1) the article intrinsically disproved his notions about
female police competence; and 2) counting names featured in newspapers was hardly a logical way to collect statistics regarding gender rep-
resentation in the Montreal police. If he were counting the male officers
chronicled in the media, for instance, he would undoubtedly arrive at a
smaller number than those employed by the force. At this juncture, one
can only wonder: was the cheese beginning to slide off Lépine's cracker?

With only two months left in his education at Control Data, on
March 31 Lépine followed the same academic pattern he had his whole
life: he quit. Jean Cloutier remembers his astonishment: "With his background in electronics, plus his high standings in programming, he was
well on his way to becoming a computer genius."[19] Two weeks later,
Lépine stopped by Control Data to return some books, dismissing questions about his sudden lack of attendance with a few vague sentences
about pursuing another career. Although he continued to attend chemistry class, pretending to Sylvie Dourin that he was still taking courses at
Control Data, she began to perceive him becoming withdrawn. Andre
Tremblay noticed that Lépine's eyes were red, as if he hadn't been sleeping well. In an attempt to coax him out of his shell, Sylvie invited Lépine
to a Thursday-night party at a downtown bar, but he refused, saying,
"No, I don't drink and I never go in that kind of place." He once asked if
she would like to hang out after their weekly computer lessons, but all he

wanted to do was watch violent movies on videotape — not exactly her cup of tea. The last time Sylvie ever saw him in person was a week and a half after their chemistry class had ended:

> I had come away from there with a very strange feeling like I would never see him again, that I didn't want to see him again and I didn't. I told him I might call in the summer but I never did.... [He was] very strange, in a very hurried state, like someone with something very important on his mind. It was as though he had something to do that no one else could know about....[20]

Ultimately, Sylvie was accepted into the University of Quebec's engineering program in the nearby city of Trois-Rivières. For his part, Lépine claimed he would be attending École Polytechnique for engineering in the autumn.

Of all the people who knew Marc Lépine in the year leading up to the massacre, Érik Cossette probably had the closest view, once describing his roommate as "emotionally repressed." He recalls witnessing Lépine flying into a rage after dropping a chicken on the floor. On another occasion, Lépine burnt some meat and punched a hole in the wall. Aside from these incidences, Cossette maintains that there was nothing particularly nefarious about his friend's behaviour. The sexist remarks he made were "no more disturbing than what one hears from many men," and Cossette chalked his fondness for gun magazines down to "an interest like any other."[21] In fact, according to Cossette, Lépine had a number of good qualities: his insatiable intellectual curiosity for history, science, politics, and technology; his childlike fondness for cartoons; and his willingness to help out a friend. "Doing favours was his way of expressing his affection for people."

As the summer of 1989 came to a close, Érik left 2175 Bordeaux Street to backpack in South America, and was replaced by Lépine's younger cousin Michel Thiery. On August 29, Lépine procured a firearms acquisition certificate application from the Sûreté du Quebec. He bumped into Isabelle Lahaie while exiting the SQ's Montreal headquarters, and explained he was trying to obtain a gun for hunting. The application was filled out and in police hands, along with the customary $10 charge, by Labour Day, but due to the demand before hunting season, it wasn't until mid-October that permit number AA2092373 bearing the name "Marc Lépine" appeared in his mailbox. Soon after, the gangly young man began appearing at Checkmate Sports on St. Hubert, inquiring about firearms. On the afternoon of November 21, Lépine finally purchased a semi-automatic Sturm Ruger Mini-14 with a banana clip capable of holding thirty bullets. Including the carrying case and five boxes of Remington .223 bullets — one hundred in total — his bill came to $765.03.

"Ah, shit." Lépine blushed. He had purchased the cheapest ammo available and was still short on cash. Leaving a $100 deposit, he hurried to the bank and returned in thirty minutes with the balance.

Aside from his daytrips to the sporting goods store, Lépine lived the life of a recluse throughout the fall, routinely ordering grocery deliveries from the store across the street. Monique remembers that he brought her an early birthday present, and though he was uncomfortable with physical affection, told her, "You can kiss me." Neighbours recall his chilling laughter in the middle of the night, cascading down from his bedroom window into the alleyway below.

AUTOPSY

By the time the zipper was closed on Marc Lépine's body bag, fourteen innocent women lay dead, with another ten women and four men suffering injuries. The tragedy at École Polytechnique was followed by three official days of mourning in the province of Quebec. At Montreal's Notre-Dame Basilica, a joint funeral was held for the nine victims of Roman Catholic faith, along with an official recognition of the massacre. The bodies of the slain were displayed in pearl caskets in a chapel below the University of Montreal tower, where tens of thousands of grieving Canadians lined up in the winter cold to pay their respects. Across the country, public and private vigils were held for the deceased. The fallen were Geneviève Bergeron, Hélène Colgan, Nathalie Croteau, Barbara Daigneault, Anne-Marie Edward, Maud Haviernick, Barbara Marie Klueznick, Maryse Laganiere, Maryse Leclair, Anne-Marie Lemay, Sonia Pelletier, Michèle Richard, Annie

St-Arneault, and Annie Turcotte. The only people in attendance for Lépine's funeral at a Boucherville crematorium were his mother, his sister Nadia, her boyfriend, and a few members of Monique's church.

Marc Lépine had left three documents in his pocket: a suicide note (which we will examine in detail later) and two letters to his friends. In the latter two, he instructed them to give his fridge to his landlord to compensate for missed rent, and everything else he owned he left to his old school chum Jean Belanger. Interestingly, one source claims that on December 7, an unnamed friend of Marc's received a letter bequeathing him some personal belongings. We will refer to the mystery friend as "James." Lépine's cryptic letter suggested that the motive for the murders was hidden somewhere at 2175 Bordeaux. Donning a ski mask to hide his identity, James accessed the apartment using a key Lépine had entrusted to him, and passed through the narrow, linoleum-floored hallway into his late friend's bedroom. The turquoise lair was piled high with books on science and the Second World War, along with videocassettes of violent pay-TV movies and a plastic skull. As journalists hammered on the windows and doors, James began to explore, and spotted a sliver of paper lodged between the floorboards. "The author is the solution," it read. "If you have found this, it means you are already in the know." The note suggested looking on the shelf for a book by an author mentioned in the earlier letter. It turned out to be a biography of American pilot Chuck Yeager, who in 1947 became the first person to break the barrier of sound. Inside the pages, James discovered a second message: "If you have found this letter you are on the right track. It contains my last wishes. At the back of the room is a suitcase with a few things I would like to pass on." Given the context of this scavenger hunt, its contents were anticlimactic to say the least: hardware and computer games — hardly the secrets of Lépine's derangement.

Overwhelmed by the magnitude of what had happened, Monique Lépine sought refuge with friends in Switzerland immediately after the massacre. Upon returning in January 1990, she discovered two bulky black garbage bags in her closet. The first was stuffed with Marc's bedding, movies, and a Beta video player, while the second contained his outstanding report cards — a reminder of the potential he had once exhibited as a little boy. There was also a brief handwritten letter that read, "I am sorry, Mom. This is inevitable." Without her knowledge, in the days preceding the murders, Marc had entered her condo while she was out and deposited the garbage bags.

To this day, the echoes of the Polytechnique massacre continue to reverberate. Many survivors of the massacre developed post-traumatic stress disorder and were haunted by terrible nightmares. On August 20, 1990, former student Sarto Blais hanged himself in his apartment bathroom. Among the reasons the Gaspé native offered in his suicide note was, "[I] could not accept that as a man I had been there and hadn't done anything about it."[22] Though Blais had finished school and found work with a Montreal construction firm, his guilt combined with the memories of blood-drenched hallways was unbearable. Within a year of his suicide, Blais's parents killed themselves — the seventeenth and eighteenth lives annihilated by Marc Lépine's actions.

The impact on Lépine's own family was devastating. Twenty-two-year-old Nadia was looking forward to beginning a philosophy course at CEGEP du Vieux Montreal when the massacre occurred. Unable to cope, she became addicted to heroin and cocaine, eventually turning to prostitution to support her habits. On March 1, 1996, Nadia overdosed on cocaine and was taken to Notre-Dame Hospital, where doctors determined that she had severely damaged her cerebral cortex. After twelve hours of watching her daughter slip slowly into the abyss of death, Monique gave her approval to unplug her life support machines. The twenty-eight-year-old was buried next to her brother in a family plot at Notre-Dame-des-Neiges cemetery.

The unfathomable depth of Monique's suffering is detailed in her courageous book *Aftermath*, in which she writes not only of losing two children, but also of recurring nightmares that her son is coming to kill her. Even the chief investigator of the massacre, André Tessier — a man who had been exposed to countless acts of barbarism during his career — would be emotionally scarred by the events of December 6, 1989. For him, not only was the scope of the murders overwhelming, but the daughter of a friend had been among the victims.

In the end, Marc Lépine's crude efforts to fight feminism backfired, and December 6 is now a National Day of Remembrance and Action on Violence Against Women in Canada. Female enrollment in Canadian engineering programs rose from 13 to 19 percent between 1989 and 1999. The Polytechnique massacre was to be the last in his long litany of failures. One can almost hear his pitiful voice muttering a final "Ah, shit" through the gates of Notre-Dame-des-Neiges cemetery.

Lépine's crimes created a dialogue surrounding the issue of misogynist violence in Canada and raised important questions regarding national firearms laws, spawning the Coalition for Gun Control. Many Canadians wondered how somebody as emotionally disturbed as Marc Lépine could gain access to such a powerful weapon. When Justice Minister Douglas Lewis promised to examine the issue, but warned, "We can't legislate against insanity," it seemed that the motivation for the attacks was being misinterpreted. Lépine had no known history of psychosis and had been plotting the murders in one form or another for years. Police learned that he had been spotted at the school on no less than seven occasions between October 1 and the murders. Given these facts, should we really dismiss the massacre as simply the work of a madman? There is wisdom in the words and actions of Nathalie Provost, the brave young student who had tried to reason with Lépine. A survivor of four bullet wounds, she went on to defy his plans for her by becoming a mechanical engineer. Speaking with the *Globe and Mail* on the twentieth anniversary of the massacre, Provost expressed her reluctance to label her attempted murderer as a monster:

> That man was first a little baby, a child, a little boy who played ball, who tried to be loved by people around him; he was all kinds of things before he did what he did. I have four children and I try to love them with all my heart, but I know perfectly well that I don't always control them. The horror was in the act he committed, which is unpardonable, horrible, and abominable. But behind the act was a human being.[23]

In this spirit, let us now endeavour to understand Lépine's psyche.

A FRUSTRATED, FURIOUS FAILURE

The suicide note retrieved from Marc Lépine's pocket by police provides us with precious insight into the mind of a killer. As in many cases, what the murderer intends us to believe is of infinitely less value than the reality he attempts to cover up:

> Forgive the mistakes. <u>I only had 15 minutes to write this</u>. (See also Annex)
>
> **Please note that if I commit suicide today 89/12/06 it is not for economic reasons (for I have waited until I exhausted all my financial means, even refusing jobs) but for political reasons.** For I have decided to send the feminists who have ruined my life to their maker.
>
> It has been <u>seven years that life does not bring me any joy</u> and being totally blasé, I have decided to put an end to those viragos.
>
> *I had already tried as a youth to enlist in the [Armed] Forces as an officer cadet, which would have allowed me to enter the arsenal and precede Lortie in a rampage.* They refused me because of asociality.
>
> So I waited until this day to carry out all my projects. **In between, I continued my studies in a haphazard way for they never really interested me, knowing in <u>advance my fate</u>. Which did not prevent me from obtaining very good marks despite not handing in my theory assignments and studying little before exams.**
>
> Even though the Mad Killer epithet will be attributed to me by the media, **I consider myself a rational and erudite person** that <u>only the arrival of the Grim Reaper has forced to undertake extreme acts.</u>
>
> For why persevere in existing if it is only to please the government? Being a backwards-looking thinker by nature (except for science), I have always been enraged by feminists.
>
> They want to retain the advantages of being women (e.g., cheaper insurance, extended maternity leave

preceded by a preventive leave) while trying to grab those of the men.

Thus, it is self-evident that if the Olympic Games removed the Men/Women distinction, there would only be women in the graceful events. So the feminists are not fighting to remove that barrier.

They are so opportunistic that they [never] neglect to profit from the knowledge accumulated by men throughout the ages. They always try to misrepresent them every time they can.

Thus, the other day, people were honouring the Canadian men and women who fought at the frontlines during the world wars. How does this sit with the fact that women were not authorized to go to the frontline at the time??? Will we hear of Caesar's female legions and female galley slaves who of course took up 50 per cent of history's ranks, although they never existed? A real Casus Belli.

Sorry for this too brief letter.

Marc Lépine

Annex

[Nineteen women's names, including the six police officers he'd identified in the media] nearly died today. The lack of time (because I started too late) has allowed those radical feminists to survive.

Alea Jacta EST.[24]

Besides Lépine's obvious misogyny, several subtler themes are evident. In the first half of the letter, he is obsessed with convincing society that he is a martyr instead of a failure (see text in **bold**). Yet he betrays himself by admitting that he was unable to realize the full extent of his mission because he "started too late." Taking into account the brevity of the letter, there is also an abundance of references to the military, warfare, and Rome, including Latin terms (see text in *italics*). It is interesting to note that Lépine's historical references seem to focus solely on military aspects, reinforcing the idea that he was enamoured with violence. There are also fatalistic overtones (underlined), as if he viewed his actions and personal situation as being totally out of his control. Lépine wrote that he was "forced" to kill because the "world doesn't bring [him] any joy." Instead of taking the time to prepare the perfect suicide note during his alleged years of planning, he lamented that he "only had fifteen minutes to write this," as if he were lacking agency altogether.

Where the massacre certainly brought attention to the issue of misogyny in Canadian society, the origins of Marc Lépine's contempt have rarely been discussed beyond the simplistic "like father, like son" argument. Lépine's hatred of women resulted from a variety of individual experiences, which were shaped by a major personality disorder. Rachid Gharbi beat and dominated his wife, but to say that Lépine emulated his father would be to ignore the fact that he absolutely hated him. This early exposure to misogynist violence may account for elements of Lépine's psychology; however, by examining the role that his mother and sister took in his life, we gain a much broader perspective. During Marc's childhood, his mother spent very little time with him. Since he had already suffered psychologically as a result of his father's abuse, this increased his vulnerability to negative emotions. Rather than rationally understanding his mother's plight as an overworked single parent, Marc felt simply abandoned. To make matters worse, his sister, Nadia, mocked him mercilessly during his teens and early twenties. With the two primary female figures in his life projecting the notion that he was unworthy of a woman's love (Monique doing so unintentionally, Nadia maliciously), the acne-ridden, bookish Lépine was unable to envision a woman ever wanting a romantic relationship with him. These impressions laid the groundwork for his misogyny, which his narcissistic intellect forged into ideology. Ultimately, this ideology created political justifications that masked the insecurities underlying his hatred of women. I present this as an explanation, not a justification.

Underpinning Lépine's misogyny, obsession with violence, fatalism, and need to convince the world that he was a "somebody" was his extreme narcissistic vulnerability. We will explore the criteria for narcissistic personality disorder later, in the case of fellow Montreal school shooter **Valery Fabrikant** (Chapter 4). To quote Monique Lépine,

For him [Marc] … everything was, categorically, either black and white, good or bad, total belief or outright defiance. He could never be cheerful if he was down or believe he could succeed if anyone (his sister for example) thought he was a loser.… Because he couldn't love himself, he became convinced that no member of the opposite sex could ever love him.… He was narcissistic, anti-social, and extremely sensitive to rejection. Whenever he experienced setbacks, he took refuge in violent, extravagant daydreams that compensated for his feelings of incompetence.[25]

Andre Kirchhoff

Peter John Peters
Tattoo Man

"When the police find you, make sure you tell them that I was a real nice guy."

Victims: 2 killed/1 wounded
Duration of rampage: January 20 to 25, 1990 (spree killer)
Locations: London, Ontario; Toronto, Ontario
Weapons: Manual strangulation/plastic bag suffocation; iron bar

NO GOOD DEED GOES UNPUNISHED

Before dawn on Monday, January 22, 1990, Albert Philip rolled from the warmth of his bed and glanced out the window. In the dim glow of the streetlights, snowflakes were falling on Ellis Avenue, as if powdering a corpse for burial. Beneath the blankets, Albert's wife lay sleeping.

Careful not to wake her or their thirteen-year-old daughter, the age-ing man put on his coat, slipped out the front door, and drove to the downtown Toronto parking garage where he worked as an attendant. He was a kind and considerate man, known for providing food to the homeless. Albert clocked in for his shift and began readying himself for work, intending to rouse his wife shortly after with a routine wake-up call. Sadly, his life of peaceful order was about to be interrupted by the savage forces of chaos.

Albert's wife arose late at 7:30 a.m., surprised not to have been woken by her husband's gentle tone. When she telephoned the parking build-ing's office to check on him, she received no answer. Concerned, Mrs. Philip called another employee and asked him to investigate. Heading downstairs to the office, the co-worker came face to face with a bloodied Albert Philip — unconscious and barely breathing. Police and paramed-ics arriving on the scene doubted the sixty-three-year-old would survive his attack. Albert's skull had been fractured several times, propelling his false teeth under the radiator. He had also sustained numerous defence wounds to his hands. The murder weapon — a blood-stained metal bar — was discovered nearby, along with a knapsack full of clothing. Albert's wallet and vehicle were missing.

Reconstructing the timeline, investigators concluded that he had been viciously assaulted shortly after punching his card for work. The battered attendant was rushed immediately to the emergency room at St. Michael's Hospital to have surgery performed on his scalp. Meanwhile, a solemn policeman assured the Philip family that Albert's attacker would be found and punished. The promise would go unbroken.

THE WOLF AND THE WOODCUTTER

Until the 1991/92 torture-murders committed by Paul Bernardo and Karla Homolka, the community of St. Catharines, Ontario, had been considered largely untainted by violent crime. The events of January 22, 1990, were a shocking exception.

At 1:15 p.m. that day, twenty-eight-year-old Sandie Bellows parked outside a local credit union. As she exited the vehicle, she spotted a man with long blond hair seated in a mid-eighties estate car.

The two exchanged smiles, and the newlywed Sandie continued to the credit union to conduct her business. After returning to her car, she was putting the keys in the ignition when she felt a cold blade against her neck.

"Shut up!" the blond man barked, no longer smiling. "Get over!" He pushed Sandie over to the passenger side, and climbed into the driver's seat. Terrified, she repeatedly begged him to release her as he drove the car out of the parking lot and onto the road, heading west. Her abductor responded by threatening to stab her if she didn't shut up and pay attention. He informed her that he was on the run from the police, and that he and Sandie had to look like a married couple. If she complied, he promised to set her free once he was out of harm's way.

"When the police find you," his green eyes pierced the windshield, "make sure you tell them that I was a real nice guy." The man claimed his name was John, and that something that he hadn't meant to happen had gone "really, really wrong."

"I don't want to know anything," Sandie sobbed. John's behaviour was already disturbingly erratic; though he seemed to be trying to befriend her, he continued to remind her that if she screwed up he would kill her.

Just over an hour into their flight west, John veered the car into a wooded area near Paris, Ontario. Realizing that if he tried to kill her nobody would hear her screams, Sandie began to panic. Worse yet, her captor's mood had taken a turn.

"What are you doing?" Sandie protested. "You promised to let me go."

"I'm going to have some fun with you," he responded. "I'm going to rape you." John forced her into the back seat and beat her into submission. As John penetrated her, Sandie could only think that she would soon be murdered. Fortunately, a valiant woodcutter was coming to her rescue. While logging in the forest, retired Ontario provincial policeman Alan Pike spotted Sandie's car and drove his tractor over to investigate. Alarmed by Pike's approach, John warned Sandie to "get up and not do anything stupid." As her attacker climbed out the right rear door and began to pull his pants up, Sandie sprang from the back seat and ran toward the forest. Before she knew it, John had struck her forehead, knocking her to the ground. Al Pike threw the tractor into full throttle as the blond man kicked the helpless woman in the skull. John then began stabbing a blade repeatedly into Sandie's torso. Luckily, Alan Pike had an axe lying on the tractor floor. As John raised the blood-stained knife to deliver a fatal blow through Sandie's breast, he spotted Pike hurrying toward him. Leaping aside, John sprinted back to Sandie's car, and with a screech of tires began to pull away. Adrenaline surging, Pike followed and managed to shatter the right rear window with his axe. The relentless retiree attempted to climb into the departing vehicle, but was unsuccessful. Exhausted, he watched in frustration as it rounded the bend and disappeared from his sight.

As emergency respondents sped toward the scene, John managed to bog down the car on a snowy back road. He continued on foot until he reached a nearby farm house, where he robbed sixty-seven-year-old Jenny Whiting of her car at knife point. From there, he drove to downtown Paris and held up a Bank of Montreal for $2,000. Within half a day, the mysterious "John" had accumulated a list of charges that included rape, two counts of attempted murder, and armed robbery. Numerous police agencies were now hot on his trail. When investigators found Albert Philip's empty car in the St. Catharines parking lot where Sandie had been kidnapped, they realized that the same offender was at work. Mustering her strength, Sandie Bellows provided the police with a description of her attacker, including one particularly important detail: tattoos — he was covered in them. Specifically she remembered seeing the name "Johnnie" or "Joannie" inked into his forearm. By evening, Albert Philip was dead.

The following day, inside a police warehouse, a forensics team meticulously tore the stolen vehicles apart in search of evidence. On the inside door handle of Albert Philip's car they discovered a partial fingerprint, which was immediately flown by plane to the national police database in Ottawa. To the investigators' disappointment, it could not be processed by computer. As the moon hung over the Ontario snows, a sad truth settled into the hearts of the policemen: a good man lay dead, and a tattooed monster was still roaming the streets.

BREADCRUMBS

The morning of Wednesday, January 24 would finally shed light on the blond man's identity. After three days of fruitless searching, the friends and family of twenty-five-year-old Charlene Brittain decided to report her missing to the police. Prior to her disappearance, the London woman had spoken of going to see a man with long blond hair and tattoos named Peter John Peters. As reports of the tattooed madman circulated around southwestern Ontario, Charlene's best friend began to fear that they were one and the same. Coincidentally, that morning, Peters's former parole officer telephoned the authorities with similar suspicions. A twenty-eight-year-old ex-convict, Peters was known locally as "Tattoo Man" for parading shirtless through the streets of London showcasing his body art. The product of a turbulent home, his criminal record extending back into childhood included firearms-related offences and forcible confinement. Worse yet, it showed that his capacity for violence had been steadily escalating.

When police descended upon Peters's basement apartment that afternoon, each piece of the puzzle clicked to form a horrific picture. At first there seemed nothing amiss inside the flat, until investigators spied a padlocked door. After breaking the lock, they entered a large storage area to discover the nude, lifeless body of Charlene Brittain lying supine on the floor. She was surrounded by hundreds of file folders containing pornography. A plastic bag had been pulled over her head, distorting her pretty features. Autopsy results would later reveal that she had been strangled and died three days before her discovery. The investigators concluded that Charlene's murder marked a point of no return for Peters — knowing that he would be linked to the crime, he had taken off, attempting to slaughter anyone who stood between him and escape. Interestingly, the backpack abandoned at the Philip crime scene was determined to have once belonged to Charlene. Whether by intent, stupidity, or blatant disregard, Peters was leaving a trail of breadcrumbs wherever he went, allowing the authorities to connect his otherwise disparate crimes. Furthermore, the partial fingerprint lifted from Albert Philip's car matched Peters's when compared manually to a police file. Photographs of the boyish-looking suspect were sent to every major Canadian media agency, along with his name, as Ontario police prepared for one of the largest manhunts in the nation's history. Soon Peter John Peters's face was emblazoned on the front pages of newspapers across the country.

NORTHERN EXPOSURE

At noon on January 25, 460 kilometres away in Sault Ste. Marie, Peter John Peters stepped off the bus and breathed in a lungful of cold northern Ontario air. A few metres away, he spotted a woman brushing snow from her windshield — another easy target. He walked up to make her acquaintance.

"Get in the car, or I'll kill you."

The woman stood gazing back at him as if unable to comprehend his request, so he repeated himself. Again. And again. Suddenly a light of recognition appeared in her eyes, and she took off running. Realizing he had drawn attention to himself, Peters jumped into her car and slammed his foot on the gas. He headed for the cover of the back roads, but after driving for nearly an hour, found that the heavy snows were slowing his escape, and decided he needed to be armed. Ditching the vehicle, he made for a nearby house and kicked in the door, startling nineteen-year-old Brad Johnston. Peters held the knife to his throat.

"Do you have any guns?" The young man showed him to the family shotgun. Still pressing the blade to his flesh, Peters forced him to load it before taking the weapon from him. Peering out the window, Peters sighted some hydro workers inspecting his abandoned vehicle and aimed.

"They didn't do anything to you," Brad implored him. "You don't need to kill them." Incredibly, his words seemed to resonate with Peters. When Peters lowered the shotgun, Brad offered to assist him in finding another vehicle. They left the home around 2:00 p.m. to search. Farther down the road, they saw a car parked in an elderly man's driveway. Inside, Reverend Ron Hubbard of the local Pentecostal church and retired homeowner Ernie Cattley were conversing when Brad suddenly entered the dwelling with his hands in the air. Peters followed behind him with the shotgun pointed at his back.

"Just do as he says. He means business," Brad warned them. Peters asked whose car was parked outside, and the reverend replied that it was his.

"You're a cop!" Peters yelled, turning the gun on him. Fearing for his life, the reverend produced credentials from his wallet, calming Peters. The gunman demanded the car keys, and the men complied immediately. Before leaving, Peters destroyed the telephone, then took off in what was to be his fifth stolen vehicle in as many days. Once he had left, Brad Johnston, Ernie Cattley, and Reverend Hubbard sought help. Fortunately, it found them. Police cars swarmed the area, having been alerted by the hydro workers to the abandoned car. When the officers showed the three survivors a photograph of Peter John Peters, they positively identified him, but noted that his hair had been cut short.

Meanwhile, Peters continued to display a remarkable lack of driving skills, miring his car on another snowy back road. He approached a nearby residence and used his shotgun to blast the lock to pieces. Entering, he demanded the keys to a blue Ford Tempo from the terrified homeowner. Peters sped off yet again, only now his behaviour had become so reckless that he was running out of places to flee. The police had barricaded the roads and were rapidly closing in on him. While driving along a main road at around 4:00 p.m., he noticed a cruiser behind him. Exhausted, Peter John Peters did something entirely unexpected: he pulled over and exited with his hands in the air. The notorious spree killer who everyone assumed would go out in a blaze of glory lay meekly in the snow to be handcuffed. After five continuous days of fight and flight, his rampage had come to a decidedly anticlimactic finale.

SCARS AND TATTOOS

Other than his good looks, Peter John Peters hadn't been given much of a chance in life. Born to alcoholic parents, he had been raised in a dumpy green duplex on the outskirts of Wallaceburg, Ontario. His parents were more interested in drinking than raising their children, and Peters grew up in an environment of neglect, spousal abuse, and criminal behaviour. Having been completely ignored, he was understandably slow to learn at school, and dropped out before grade seven.

Instead of losing himself in books, Peters simply became lost. He found himself on the wrong side of the law in 1979, when he was sentenced to a four-year term at Millhaven maximum-security prison for pointing a firearm. While inside, the angry young man took two shop teachers hostage with a pair of scissors, earning himself an extra three years of incarceration.

By 1985, Peters was back on the streets of Sarnia, Ontario. His favourite haunts were strip clubs, where his handsome face and flirtation skills helped him bed many exotic dancers. The man with the blond hair and serpent tattoos soon earned a reputation for having a thing for handcuffs and S&M. Little did these women know the extent of his kinkiness. When he wasn't feasting his green eyes on a stripper's flesh, Peters was phoning local women and threatening to torture them and slice off their breasts. A police wiretap was put on two variety stores where female employees had received his menacing calls. Cashier Patti Armstrong remembers a voice on the other end of the phone hissing, "Women don't have the right to live." Yet Peters absolutely adored his mother — a fact which he made no secret of, whether to strippers or his fellow family members. In this way, he was like a laboratory ape, clinging to a wire substitute for nurture.

THE SNAKE SWALLOWS ITSELF

Though Peter John Peters originally refused to discuss his motivation for the London murder, police soon learned a vital clue from his former parole officer Natalie Black. For a time the two had been lovers, and she had helped him find his apartment and a position as a caretaker. Black had broken off her relationship with Peters two months before his crime spree, leaving him angry and dejected. He had attempted to temper his emotions by becoming romantically involved with Charlene Brittain. However, according to Detective Gary Harding of the London Police Service, Charlene had backed off when she learned of his criminal history. Peters pleaded with her to reconsider, but when she came over to his apartment to speak with him, they became engaged in a bitter argument. Unable to cope with the prospect of another woman abandoning him, he had decided to possess her in the only way he could: by strangling her to death. Of the Albert Philip murder, Peters said little, other than that he was in a "blind rage" and needed to steal a car.

Faced with twenty-nine charges from St. Catharines to Sault Ste. Marie, Peter John Peters travelled from one Ontario courtroom to the next, pleading guilty and recounting his frenzied crimes before a series of shocked jurors. As Peters sat in the prisoner's dock, Sandie Bellows read an emotionally charged victim impact statement that reduced the judge to tears. When he asked Sandie if there was anything else she wanted to say, she turned to Peters.

"I would like to know why. Why you did this to me, John? Why did you feel you had to do this to me?" Peters's response was surprisingly flat: "I don't know." When the dust cleared, Peter John Peters was handed three life sentences and shipped off to Kingston Penitentiary. The big bad wolf was not the only one who got what he deserved. For his bravery in rescuing Sandie Bellows, Alan Pike was awarded a citation by the Ontario Provincial Police. He was the first retired officer in the history of the organization to receive this honour.

While languishing in prison, Peters legally changed his name to John Cody, hoping to avoid notoriety in the event of his parole. He blew his chances in 2007 when, after seventeen years' incarceration, the forty-five-year-old strolled out of Ferndale minimum-security prison east of Vancouver in British Columbia. At 5:20 a.m. the following morning, he telephoned the Abbotsford police department and asked them to pick him up. Back in custody, he was transferred to a higher-level security prison, where his day passes were revoked. Perhaps the beast had come to love his cage.

Despite both being lumped under the category of "rampage murderer," Marc Lépine and Peter John Peters had drastically differing motivations. Whereas Lépine, a classic mass murderer, was determined to die and take as many "feminists" with him as possible, all but one of Peters's spree crimes occurred primarily because he wanted to escape imprisonment.

Table 3: Comparing and Contrasting Marc Lépine and Peter John Peters

Italics indicate a match.

	Lépine	Peters
Social		
IQ	High	"Slow learner"
Physically attractive	No	Yes
Sexual history with women	No, possibly virgin	Yes
Criminal history	No	Yes, extensive
Education	Some college	Grade school dropout
Nature of work	*Menial labour*	*Menial labour*

	Lépine	Peters
Psychology		
Misogyny	*Yes*	*Yes*
Abandonment issues	*Yes*	*Yes*
Name change	*Yes, when fourteen*	*Yes, after arrest*
Paraphilia	None	Scatiphilia, sadism
Attitude toward mother	Love and resentment	Adoration
Pornography	No evidence of use	Heavy use

	Lépine	Peters
Rampage		
Type	Mass murder	Spree murder
Sexual assaults	No	Yes, on one occasion
Committed suicide	Yes	No, surrendered to police
Message to society	Yes, suicide note and letters	Refusal to discuss motives

CHAPTER 2

THE PROBLEM WITH BOXES

One newspaper source consulted during the research for this book referred to **Peter John Peters** as a "sexual sadist," an individual who "derives sexual excitement from the psychological or physical suffering (including humiliation) of the victim."[25] Sadistic tendencies often develop in children who have been subjected to repeated physical or emotional agony, and who compensate as adults by inflicting pain upon another, thereby becoming the aggressor rather than the victim. Now that we have developed a clear understanding of the difference between a mass murderer like Marc Lépine and a spree killer like Peter John Peters, I will attempt to alleviate my own academic torment by irritating you with a series of "buts."

According to the FBI's *Crime Classification Manual*, the key difference between mass murderers and spree killers is the number of locations involved. The problem is that the authors do not provide a definition of what constitutes a location. Is it a room? A building? A street? City block? Neighbourhood? Small town? For this reason, some authors and criminologists have chosen to consider **Marc Lépine** a spree slayer, even though his "end game" psychology is more in keeping with that of a mass murderer.

The cases of **Rosaire Bilodeau** and **Robert Poulin** in this chapter exemplify mass murderer types whose multiple locations technically qualify them as spree killers. Rather, I refer to such offenders as "mass murderers with an overture." In the two most category-confounding cases in Canadian history, **Swift Runner** and **David Shearing** committed all three types of multicide: spree, serial, and mass murder. For further annoyance, please review the cases of **Alexander Keith Jr.** (Chapter 3), **Marcello Palma** (Chapter 6), **Dale Nelson** (Chapter 7), and "Order of the Solar Temple" members **Joel Egger, Joseph Di Mambro,** and **Luc Jouret** (Chapter 9).

Swift Runner
The Cree Cannibal

"I am the least of men and do not even merit being called a man."

Swift Runner (*Kakusikutchkin*), shackled in Fort Saskatchewan.

Victims: 8 killed
Duration of rampage: Winter of 1878/79 (difficult to classify)
Location: Sturgeon Creek area, Alberta
Weapons: Rifle, knife, hatchet, hanging

AN UNPALATABLE PALATE

In March of 1879, a hulking Cree man shambled into the Catholic mission in St. Albert, North-West Territories.* He said his name was *Kakusikutchkin*, or "Swift Runner" in the white man's tongue — the last surviving member of his family. The winter had been a

---

* Geographically the area was in the modern province of Alberta, though it was considered part of the North-West Territories until September 1, 1905.

particularly cruel one; the buffalo, already thinned by unsustainable hunting practices, had been prevented from migrating north of the American border by a vast swath of burning prairie. When ten of the once prevalent creatures were spotted at Lizard Lake in the summer of 1878, the story made headlines.

Yet, considering the famine that had claimed the lives of his wife, five children, brother, and mother-in-law, at two hundred pounds Swift Runner looked surprisingly well-nourished. Dark rumours began circulating in the Native community. Though he appeared meek in the daylight hours, Swift Runner was plagued by horrific nightmares. He drew further suspicion upon himself when he attempted to lure a group of children away on a hunting trip. Noting signs of something sinister and familiar in his behaviour — quirks that may have gone unnoticed by Caucasians — several Cree reported to a local priest that Swift Runner was a "Windigo": a cannibal killer possessed by a demonic spirit. The surprisingly open-minded clergyman contacted North-West Mounted Police Superintendent Jarvis in Fort Saskatchewan, and on May 27, 1879, Swift Runner was arrested under suspicion of murdering his family. Though he denied the allegations, the prisoner's flat affect and contra- dictory statements failed to convince his accusers otherwise. He told of how his wife had become inconsolable, shooting herself dead after learning that their son had perished from hunger. The rest of his family had starved shortly after.

Determined to get to the bottom of it, Sergeant Richard Steele organized a small party to search the area 128 kilometres north of Fort Saskatchewan where they believed Swift Runner's family had camped. Clapped in irons, the stolid Cree accompanied them along the trail in a Red River cart, his mind churning like the twin wheels through the prairie mud. As they neared their destination, he became belligerent and twice attempted escape. Rather than directing them to the camp, he seemed to be intentionally misleading them. Luckily, a guide named Brazeau had heard of Swift Runner's penchant for *muss-kee-wah-bwee* — a concoction made up of alcohol and tobacco — which they used to ply the uncooperative prisoner. As the drink slowly took hold, Swift Runner lowered his guard, and slurred *"Wahabankee keezikow,"* or, "Tomorrow I'll show you."

The skeletal remains of Swift Runner's family, brought in as evidence by the North-West Mounted Police.

The next day, the drunken captive stumbled through the bush, followed closely by the RCMP officers. Upon reaching his destination, he raised his head to the sky and let out a blood-curdling howl. Nearby they found the remains of a camp: a teepee that Swift Runner had supposedly ingested had actually been folded and concealed in the undergrowth. Empty animal traps dangled from the branches. All around them was a garden of bones, picked clean by scavengers. Though Swift Runner attributed them to ravaging bears, the discovery of a child's sock crammed into an empty skull suggested otherwise. Worse yet was the cooking pot laden with human fat. Overcome by nausea, several of the searchers hurried to empty their stomachs in the woods. The sound of vomiting was muted only by the cries of one enraged officer, who screamed a torrent of obscenities into the heavens. When the searchers had finally composed themselves, they set about the task of recovering the evidence. Swift Runner looked on drowsily as they filled their sacks with bones. What remains they couldn't take with them they buried hastily before heading back to Fort Saskatchewan. Not long after arriving, Swift Runner confessed that he had "made beef" of his family. Poking his finger into the socket of a skull on Superintendent Jarvis's desk, he muttered, "This is my wife."

TRANSFORMATION

There was a time when the "brute" had loved and been loved by his family. Born in a teepee on a blustery winter's night, probably in 1839, the babe had been named "Swift Runner" several days later by an elderly shaman. The shaman had done so at a feast to honour the newborn's arrival, during which each member of the community had taken turns cradling Swift Runner, reciting his name, and wishing him a life of happiness. For a time, fate had honoured their blessings. The child had grown up competent and carefree. As a young man he was proud of his proficiency in hunting and trapping, and his ability to craft weapons and snowshoes for wars against the neighbouring Blackfoot. Though something of an introvert, he was respected among his fellow Cree for his athleticism — combining his natural size and power with cat-like agility. While raiding a Blackfoot encampment, he had acquired a horse, a symbol of great status among his people. With his tall stature, good humour, and impressive achievements, he was able to easily woo a beautiful young woman named Sun-on-the-Mountain, and they soon fell in love. Typically there were arranged marriages in Cree society, but Swift Runner successfully broke with this convention when he brought Sun-on-the-Mountain's father the gift of a horse. Sun-on-the-Mountain presented her suitor with a pair of moccasins in return. Upon his acceptance of her offering, they were married, and her people erected a new teepee.

Much of Swift Runner's adulthood was spent in marital bliss, fathering five children by his radiant wife. He traded regularly with the white man and lived a nomadic lifestyle, hunting and tracking buffalo across what is now central Alberta. As the years went by, however, fewer and fewer of these great beasts roamed the plains. Increasingly, the confident and capable Swift Runner found himself unable to provide meat for his beloved family. There was many a night when his children fell asleep with empty bellies. The world was changing beyond Swift Runner's understanding or capacity to adapt to it, sapping his self-esteem and drowning him in the darkest depths of depression.

While food was scant, there was always an abundance of whisky. As his mood blackened, Swift Runner began to partake in the white man's poison. The alcohol redirected his internal frustrations and resentments outward, and he began to sob uncontrollably and lash out at those around him. His personal philosophy changed along with the prairie; where he had once been a revered contributor to his tribe, he now saw all men as isolated entities in constant competition for resources, and paranoia set in. The once good-natured Swift Runner developed a reputation as a violent and volatile man, and people did their best to avoid him. Voices whispered to him now in tones that only he could hear. Cruel fantasies flooded his thoughts, sweetening his resentment with visions of revenge and exacerbating his homicidal tendencies. Physically, he was numb, as if an alien entity were slowly invading his body. Hope was disappearing from his life faster than the buffalo.

By the winter of 1878, the psychological door keeping Swift Runner's murderous impulses at bay was rotten and rusted at the hinges. The cruelty of that bleak season, fuelled by whisky and self-loathing, would prove to be the blow that sent it crashing in. Camped out in the snows nearly 130 kilometres north of Fort Saskatchewan, Swift Runner had been forced to slaughter the dogs to feed his family. With his stomach aching, his memories began drifting back to the smoky fires of his youth, where tribal elders had told tales of the Windigo — a hideous monster who possessed a man's soul and drove him to cannibalism.

The presence of the Windigo seemed to grow stronger with his hunger. It was now mid-February 1879, and whenever Swift Runner went out to hunt he found himself returning empty-handed. A strange throbbing pain pervaded his muscles, and he felt something raking at his skin. No longer did he leave in search of prey — instead, his covetous eyes shifted to his own family. Of stronger resolve, his mother-in-law and brother set out looking for food, followed soon after by his wife and all but one of his children. Alone at the camp with the hapless boy, Swift Runner finally succumbed to the Windigo's maddening cries. One night as his son slept, Swift Runner approached him in a trance-like state, as if he were watching himself from afar. His head was pounding like a tribal war drum. Hefting his rifle, he fired into the boy's skull, but the shot was not fatal. Swift Runner had seemingly become so inept at hunting that he could not even murder a sleeping child. Tears streaming from his eyes, Swift Runner frantically seized a knife and plunged it repeatedly into the boy's torso, until the smell of blood pervaded the air. As the red rivers of life ran dry, Swift Runner bashed in his son's head with a club, hastening his inevitable demise. He then went to work with the axe, butchering the corpse before cooking the slices of meat over the fire. Mouthful by mouthful, he consumed the child with an animal-like neutrality, leeching the marrow from his splintered bones. In doing so, he sated his hunger and re-established an inner equilibrium — at least for the time being.

Swift Runner relaxed in front of the glowing embers, savouring the taste of blood and the smoke from his pipe. Then, leaving what remained of his first victim behind, he set out in search of the others. It wasn't long before he caught up with his wife, his favourite son Red Hawk, and his three daughters. There must have been something in her husband's demeanour which betrayed the presence of the Windigo, for Sun-on-the-Mountain lied and told him that his brother and mother-in-law had perished somewhere in the wilds. But Swift Runner saw right through her. Early the next morning, as she slept, he fired a bullet through her neck. She shuddered momentarily, then lay motionless. Hefting her body into his strong arms, he carried his dead wife into the firelight, where he carved her up like a deer. His two eldest daughters were murdered next, gazing up in terror as he rained savage blows onto their heads with his hatchet. Promising that no harm would befall him, he ordered the terrified Red Hawk to melt snow for his cooking pot, and set about chopping his daughters into meat. Together, Swift Runner and his son dined on the women's flesh. All the while his last surviving daughter, a baby, lay helpless in the darkness. Still the Windigo's belly rumbled. Cinching a rope around the infant's neck, he strung her from a lodge pole, pulling down on her little feet so she would strangle quicker. Minutes later, she joined her sisters in the cooking pot.

Whether it was hours or days later we do not know, but eventually Swift Runner followed his remaining family members' tracks and found them asleep in the forest. He crept up on them like the sun over the horizon, knife in hand. The blade tore savagely through his mother-in-law before he shattered her face with a club. So silent was the attack that it failed to rouse his brother. At point-blank range, Swift Runner aimed and fired into the man's head, killing him instantly. He eviscerated and sliced up the corpses, hanging strips of their flesh from the surrounding trees. Then he fed. Red Hawk watched passively. On the surface, Swift Runner had defied the odds, surviving the terrible winter famine. Yet so much of him had died alongside his family in those snows: his identity, his sanity, his future ...

The ducks returned with the spring, and Swift Runner and Red Hawk were soon dining on their succulence. The two were now nearing the Egg Lake (Lake Manowan) settlement, where Swift Runner expected to be found out and arrested for his horrendous crimes. It was time to dispose of the last witness. While they sat feasting around the fire, he plunged the blade into Red Hawk's sternum, observing the spark drain from the boy's gaping expression with a stony detachment. There was no need to cannibalize his son, yet he did so anyway, despite the plenitude of fowl. Forevermore, he would walk this earth as a Windigo; no flesh could ever satisfy him like that of humanity — a weak species to which he no longer belonged.

SHOEING THE DEVIL'S HOOF

On August 16, 1879, Swift Runner stood before six white jurors, charged with slaughtering and cannibalizing his family. The trial was a dull one-sided affair; Swift Runner's race and poverty, along with the grotesque nature of his crimes, made the suggestion that he could be innocent a mere formality. Within twenty minutes, the jury returned a verdict of "guilty," and the dreamy-eyed Cree was sentenced to death by hanging. After the trial, his mood turned decidedly jovial. Grinning ravenously, he ogled a particularly rotund guard nicknamed Frenchy, his pupils gleaming.

"You would make fine eating," Swift Runner held up three fingers. "There must be that much fat on your ribs."

"*Cochon* [pig], you too will make good eats *pour les coyotes*," Frenchy retorted. "But they all poisoned will be."

Over the coming weeks, Swift Runner's upbeat disposition took a turn for the worse. Confined to a cramped, malodorous cell, he began to fixate on the image of his corpse dangling from the gallows. Nightmares and headaches plagued him like the flies hovering around his face, making him lethargic and temperamental. He became convinced that the very walls and floors of his cell were gazing contemptuously upon him — signs that the first rivulets of remorse were beginning to seep into his stony heart. Piece by piece, memories of the massacre reawakened in his conscience, and though he attempted to relay these to the police, the very act of living seemed to exhaust him. He found renewed strength in Catholicism. Twenty days before his execution, the converted convict confided the sickening details of his crimes to Reverend Father Hippolyte Leduc. Weeks later, Leduc accompanied Swift Runner to the gallows, laying a reassuring hand on his shoulder as his fellow Natives beat their drums and sang the death song to hasten his passage to the "Happy Hunting Ground." When the repentant giant met his demise at the end of a rope and was buried, the Cree wondered why the executioner hadn't cremated him. Didn't he know that the only way to destroy a Windigo was to burn it? Like the buffalo, this age-old wisdom was lost in a world now dominated by the white man. Coincidentally, so was the Windigo.

Unlike schizophrenia, which is observable in numerous individuals across the globe, Swift Runner suffered from a "culturally specific" syndrome. These disorders "are generally limited to specific societies or culture areas and are localized, folk, diagnostic categories that frame coherent meanings for certain repetitive, patterned, and troubling sets of experiences and observations."[26] In laymen's terms, they are mental illnesses that occur only within certain cultures. One example is the Malaysian phenomenon of "amok," described as "homicidal frenzy preceded by a state of brooding and ending with somnolence and amnesia."[27] The "Windigo syndrome," which drove Swift Runner to devour his family in the winter of 1878/79, is confined chiefly to the Native Americans of central and northeastern Canada, though its prevalence today is practically non-existent.

Rosaire Bilodeau

Victims: 6 killed/2 injured
Duration of rampage: October 25, 1934 (difficult to classify)
Location: Quebec City, Quebec
Weapon: Revolver

ROSAIRE SEES RED

Rosaire Bilodeau served his country faithfully during the First World War, battling his way through mustard gas in the black, muddy trenches of France. Though he would survive the Germans' poison clouds, he remained tormented by its effects for the rest of his life. Upon returning to Canada, he settled in the Limoilou ward of Quebec City, the oldest district in the provincial capital. Bilodeau was on friendly terms with his neighbours and family, but remained a bundle of nerves, and never married. Despite his anxiety and health problems, he managed to secure a job as a mail carrier at the post office on 3 Buade Street (the name would only change to Rue de Buade in 2000). Rattled by the war and accustomed to the structure of military life, Bilodeau found solace and purpose in his dull routine, and in remaining close to his older sisters and extended family.

When he was laid off from the post office in 1932, the fragmented psyche he had so precariously reassembled began to collapse. He had done his duty and once again been hurt and abandoned as a result. Trying to reinvent himself as a prospector, Bilodeau travelled around the province in search of hidden riches in the earth. Yet the freedom of entrepreneurialism was ill-suited to his character, and invariably he found himself returning to the post office to beg for his job back. When his pleas were refused, Bilodeau developed a persecution complex. Like **Marc Lépine, Pierre Lebrun,** and **Denis Lortie,** he became convinced that a certain subsection of society was responsible for his personal failures and frustrations. As Lebrun would do sixty-five years later, Bilodeau focused on his co-workers — and as with Lebrun, who also suffered from visible anxiety disorders, his resentment may have been somewhat merited. However, Bilodeau's bullets would fall first upon his own family.

LOVE LETTERS

October 25, 1934, was a perfect day for a drive in the countryside, and Rosaire Bilodeau had little trouble convincing his cousins Gaston Gauvin, twenty, and Fernand Gauvin, eighteen, to accompany him on a trip to St. Therese de Beauport. Located on the northeast periphery of Quebec City, it was a place of true scenic beauty, where the Montmorency River flowed south through clustered pines over an eighty-three-metre waterfall to drain into the St. Lawrence. The thirty-eight-year-old led the two young men into a small forest far from the highway. Without warning, Bilodeau produced a revolver and gunned them down in cold blood. With their bodies concealed by the undergrowth, he calmly drove back to lure his cousin Yvette Gauvin, twenty-one, and his two older sisters, sixty-three-year-old Marie and sixty-two-year-old Rosalie, to the same wooded area. As they trod in single file along the leafy path, he opened fire, spraying the foliage with their blood.

Two hours later, Bilodeau marched into the post office at 3 Buade Street and asked to speak with J.G.L. Morin, the postmaster. Given his history of begging for his job back, there was nothing unusual about the situation, and Bilodeau was admitted to Morin's office. He entered to find Morin seated with divisional superintendent Octave Fiset and senior mail clerk Moise Jolicoeur. Before the three could process what was happening, Bilodeau pulled a revolver from his pocket and fired two shots into Morin. As the postmaster toppled to the floor, Fiset and Jolicoeur grappled with the gunman and tried to wrest the weapon from him. Bilodeau squeezed the trigger twice again, sending bullets ripping through the sixty-year-old Fiset's body, and grazing Jolicoeur. Hearing the shots, post office employees contacted the police. Constable Patrick Horrigan rushed to the scene to find Bilodeau mumbling into a telephone. Horrigan tackled the gunman, took control of the revolver, and placed him under arrest. Octave Fiset would later die from his wounds, though Bilodeau's initial target, Morin, would pull through.

By the time he reached Central Police Station, Bilodeau had calmed enough to offer a full confession to his crimes. Having notified the interrogator that he had shot five members of his family in the St. Therese de Beauport woods, he was immediately taken to the area to help the police locate the victims. They found the three murdered women soon enough, but the encroaching darkness complicated the search for Gaston and Fernand. Their lifeless bodies were finally retrieved the following evening by a joint provincial- and city-police taskforce.

Held criminally responsible for all six deaths, Bilodeau was tried only for the murder of Octave Fiset. Following a brief trial from January 24 to 29, 1935, he was found guilty of murder by a jury in the Court of King's Bench and sentenced to death by Chief Justice Albert Sevigny. The date of the execution was set for April 12, 1935. Bilodeau's defence counsel appealed the verdict on the grounds that he had been temporarily insane. Though the appeal was unsuccessful, their attempts bought their client an extra two months of life. Rosaire Bilodeau died at the end of a hangman's rope on June 14, 1935.

GOING POSTAL

Preceded only by the Australian James Hanivan, Bilodeau was an early pioneer in a phenomenon that would come to baffle Western society: going postal. In fact, the plethora of workplace killings committed by post office employees throughout the 1980s and 1990s became so unignorable that the term "going postal" actually came into widespread colloquial use to describe anyone who embarked on a rampage murder. Fox and Levin address this in *Extreme Killing*, explaining that "between 1983 and 1993, eleven separate murderous incidents occurred in postal facilities, claiming a total of thirty-four lives."[28] In her *Inside the Minds of Mass Murderers*, Ramsland gives a figure of thirty such incidents "over a ten-year period resulting in fifty-four deaths."[29] Moe Biller, president of the

American Postal Workers Union, publicly attributed the phenomenon to the postal service's "quasi-military structure and culture." Complaints levied by postal workers around the country included joyless authoritarian managers, the burden of delivering everything on time regardless of weather conditions, a disdainful public attitude toward their profession, and unstable job security.

Robert Poulin
The St. Pius X School Shooter

"I don't want to die before I have had the pleasure of fucking some girl."

Victims: 2 killed/6 injured/committed suicide
Duration of rampage: October 27, 1975 (difficult to classify)
Location: Ottawa, Ontario
Weapons: Knife; 2200 Winchester shotgun

THE MONSTER IN THE BASEMENT

Once upon a time, in the sleepy city of Ottawa, Ontario, there lived a young boy named Robert Poulin. Robert had two older sisters, one of whom still lived at home. His father, Stuart, was an elementary school teacher; while his mother, Mary, worked as a nurse. The Poulins inhabited a Tudor-style home in Old Ottawa South. Until fire trucks arrived at the two-and-a-half-storey residence on Warrington Drive on October 27, 1975, they lived an idyllic family existence. Outwardly, Robert seemed normal and well-adjusted: a reliable newspaper delivery boy who attended Catholic church every Sunday. He possessed a keen intellect which he sharpened war-gaming with friends, either in person or over the telephone. Another favourite hobby was assembling model airplanes. The military held a place of reverence in the Poulin home. Before middle age, Stuart had been a pilot in the Royal Canadian Air Force — a path that Robert wished to follow. Unlike his father, however, he was flabby, near-sighted, and pigeon-chested — incapable of fulfilling the traditional masculine roles championed by his society. While other males in similar situations learned to compensate with wit or charm, Robert was crippled by shyness. In truth, other than a stable and loving family, Robert's mind was all he had going for him. And like a sapling sprouting in inhospitable terrain, it would grow to be warped and misshapen, hunching over itself in a self-imposed prison of masturbation.

When Robert was twelve years old, Mary gave birth to a third daughter. With this new addition to the household, the Poulins decided to move Robert into the basement, where he would have more privacy. There, behind the thin curtain concealing his "room" from the rest of the cellar, the bespectacled child slowly transformed into a monster. Despite experiencing a delayed puberty, Robert obsessed over sex and developed an unhealthy addiction to pornography. He adorned his walls with Playboy centrefolds; kept photographs and ads of naked and semi-nude men and women in a scrapbook; and using a P.O. box, slowly accumulated 250 pornographic books and magazines — all of which he meticulously indexed. In a loose-leaf binder he filled eleven pages with almost a thousand "ratings" of images. Eventually, his tastes veered into the sadomasochistic, particularly pictures of women handcuffed to bedposts. "There are some girls at school that I would love to be good friends with but I know that I am still too shy to go up and talk to any of them," Robert confessed in his diary in September 1972. "I wish I could overcome this fear of women." In grade ten, at his parents' urging, Robert invited an attractive and vivacious girl named Kimberly Rabot over to his house. The two teens passed the time playing Risk, and unsurprisingly, little transpired from the encounter. Over the next three years, Kim would linger in the young man's fantasies like an erotic thorn.

Seemingly, Robert's solution to his girl problems was to resort to violent coercion. In his diary he described his plans to take a woman by force, masking his identity with a balaclava. Around this time, he purchased an ivory-handled knife and a .38 snub-nosed revolver. "I have a half hatched idea about other illegal acts besides rape … about using the gun to rob people at night," he scrawled. On April 7, 1975, Robert wrote that he was suicidal but that he didn't "want to die before [he] had the pleasure of fucking some girl." Fortunately, he had discovered a blow-up doll, retailing for $29.95 through a California mailing house, which he believed would solve all of his existential problems. "Now I no longer think that I will have to rape a girl, and am unsure as to whether or not I will commit suicide." Unsurprisingly, Robert's new inflatable bed buddy failed to satisfy his needs, and his thoughts soon returned to sexual violence. Though we cannot confirm his involvement, around this time a number of women filed complaints about indecent assaults and attempted rapes in his neighbourhood. The perpetrator reportedly fit Robert's description, and on some occasions was naked save for a balaclava.

While Robert's pornography obsession is reminiscent of the spree killer **Peter John Peters**'s, he also shared mass murderer **Marc Lépine**'s deluded military aspirations. He applied for an officer training program, lying that he was an active participant in team sports. When his deception was uncovered, he was denied admission for being "immature." Like Lépine, he did not take the rejection well. In the summer of 1975, he enlisted in the Cameron Highlanders militia as a private, receiving both militia and commando training. Though he seemed to enjoy the experience, other members recalled a wallflower who "sat alone in the camp lunch room staring into space, and … only … talked to anyone … when they talked to him." Where they laughed, he merely smiled shyly. Moreover, Robert avoided discussing his family like the plague. Privately, his suicidal fantasies had incorporated a decidedly sadistic twist, directed at his mother and father. Rambling in ink, Robert expressed his desire to burn down the Warrington Drive home before he offed himself, without ever explaining why. "I was going to make sure, though, that I burned the place down soon after payday so that they would lose the largest possible amount of money," he wrote. "I was also planning on having all my earthly possessions with me so that they won't gain one red cent from me." Amazingly, after the violence to come, his parents would remember him as "never hostile and not the kind of person who held a grudge."

YANKING THE THORN

At 8:00 a.m. on Monday, October 27, 1975, Robert Poulin left his home on Warrington Drive in search of his number one crush: Kimberly Rabot. Fifteen minutes later, he returned with the beautiful seventeen-year-old. How the awkward Robert managed to lure her into his trap is anyone's guess, but once they had entered the basement through the garage door, he took control of her. Handcuffing her to his bed, he raped her before fatally stabbing her fourteen times with a knife. At some point preceding or following the murder, Robert placed a plastic bag over her head. If Kim was still alive at the time, Robert could have used the bag as a crude torture device — depriving and providing oxygen at his own behest.

Mary Poulin had heard her son's coming and goings that morning but taken little interest. At 10:00 a.m., she entered the basement and asked Robert if she could speak with him.

"Yeah," Robert's voice replied through the closed curtain. "But don't come in."

Not wishing to invade her son's privacy, Mary explained that she had scheduled an appointment at the optometrist's for him, and returned upstairs. Robert entered the kitchen an hour later, and Mary made him a peanut butter sandwich, which he ate while blankly watching a television game show. Mary left to run some errands at 11:30, only to return two hours later to find smoke billowing from an upstairs window.

It was 2:00 p.m., and four kilometres away at St. Pius X Catholic high school, Father Robert Bedard was commencing his grade thirteen religious studies class. Just when he thought the last of his students had arrived, the door burst open to reveal Robert Poulin grinning wickedly with a 2200 Winchester shotgun in his hands. He began firing as seventy-eight students scrambled for cover. The shots ripped through their flesh, the air filling with buckshot, bellowing, and blood. Frantic, some of the students tossed chairs through the windows, clambering to safety past the broken remnants of glass. The classroom floor strewn with groaning bodies, Robert stepped back into the hallway and blew his own brains out.

When the carnage had ended, only one other student succumbed to what Robert had described as the "true bliss" of death. Shot in the neck and head, eighteen-year-old Mark Hough would later die from his wounds. Six other students suffered injuries, three of which were serious. The shotgun that had been used to maim them had been bought four days earlier at Giant Tiger for $109. Eventually, Kimberly Rabot's body was recovered from the fire; the knife that had been used to kill her taped to Robert's convex chest. His mission had been accomplished: he had died smiling.

David Shearing
The Wells Gray Gunman

"I guess I won't be as hated as Olson is. I know a lot of people who wanted to kill him."

Victims: 6 killed, 1 separate incident of vehicular homicide
Duration of rampage: Between August 6–13 and August 17, 1982 (difficult to classify)
Location: Wells Gray Provincial Park, British Columbia
Weapon: .22 Remington pump-action rifle

THE WATCHER IN THE WOODS
On a warm August night in 1982, a dark stranger stalked through the pines of Wells Gray Provincial Park toward the sound of voices. He was owl-like in appearance, hook-nosed, with round powerful shoulders hunched over the stock of his .22 Remington rifle. He had first laid eyes

on the girls a day before, when they were laughing and skipping around the old prison site in their bathing suits. They were the perfect age — like firm little peaches before ripening. Earlier, he had seated himself on a hilltop above their campground, masturbating as he fantasized about what he would do once their parents were out of the way. When the girls retired to their tent, he descended onto the main road and crept toward the camp. The clouds were hanging heavy over Bear Lake, smothering the stars. He took up position behind the camper. In the fire's golden glow, he could make out the silhouettes of three people seated, and another standing. One of the women spotted him and stood up. He stepped into the clearing brandishing the rifle.

"Don't move! I got a gun!" An adult male began to rise, but the stranger fired, hitting him in the throat. He fell back, gurgling and clutching frantically at his neck. The women screamed. As the gunman placed another bullet into the chamber, an older man made a dash for his nearby truck. He managed to reach the passenger-side door before a second shot dropped him in the dirt. The gunman took aim at a middle-aged woman scurrying in the direction of the girls' tent, and blasted her through the head. He found the fourth adult, an elderly lady, struggling to access the camper. Walking up calmly behind her, he pointed the muzzle of his rifle to the back of her skull and pulled the trigger. The gunshot thundered through the blackness, dissipating into the bucolic silence to be replaced by the drone of crickets. Now that these obstacles were out of the way, he was free to do whatever he pleased with the children. Stepping over their dead mother's body, he made his way to the tent where the two little girls lay helpless and cowering. For the first time in his twisted life, he was about to have some *real* fun.

UP IN SMOKE

In twenty years of employment at Kelowna's Gorman Mills, Bob Johnson rarely missed a day's work. On August 23, 1982, when the head sawyer failed to surface after a week's absence, his boss Al Bonar contacted the missing persons department of the local RCMP. Bonar explained that Johnson had taken two weeks' vacation to camp up north at Wells Gray Provincial Park with his forty-one-year-old wife Jackie and their

Royal Canadian Mounted Police

An aerial view of Bob Johnson's 1979 Chrysler Plymouth, camouflaged in the undergrowth.

daughters, Janet, thirteen, and Karen, eleven. The Johnsons were scheduled to meet up with Bob's in-laws, George and Edith Bentley, to spend some quality time hiking, fishing, and eating Grandma's freshly baked wild berry pies. Bob had been due back for work on the sixteenth, but had never shown up. When the investigating officers learned that nobody had heard from the Johnsons or Bentleys in weeks, the six were officially registered as missing. Frantic, George and Edith's son Brian Bentley headed to the municipality of Clearwater, just thirty-two kilometres south of Wells Gray Park, and began distributing pictures of his missing family members. Thankfully, a gas station attendant at Avola Petro-Canada remembered seeing the Johnsons and Bentleys refuelling their vehicles, and had even spoken briefly with George about berry-picking spots. Certain that the six missing people had indeed arrived at their destination, a massive search of the Wells Gray area was conducted by the RCMP, concerned citizens, local pilots, and park employees. Off-road vehicles scoured the dense thickets and slopes, to no avail.

There were no further developments until September 13. Abbotsford man Kurt Krack informed the police that he had been mushroom hunting in Wells Gray Park, around Battle Mountain Road, when he had stumbled upon the charred remains of a Chrysler — the same make of vehicle known to belong to the Johnsons. When Sergeant Frank Baruta and Constable Mike Glas searched the vicinity, they discovered tire tracks veering off into the undergrowth. Following them forty-five metres into the bush, they came across a rusted orange automobile — or what was left of it. The vehicle had been set ablaze, blowing out the windows and tail lights and scorching the surrounding soil. The tires and door handles had practically disintegrated, the roof caved inwards, and the rear bumper warped beyond recognition. An open door on the driver's side had provided the main source of oxygen for the inferno. Strangely, a collection of beer bottles and cans lay cradled in the sunken roof. Though the licence plate confirmed this had once been the cream-coloured 1979 Chrysler Plymouth owned by the Johnsons, time and fire had reduced it to just another feature of the landscape. When the investigating officers peered through the window at the molten remains of the seats, their faces paled. Blackened bones filled the interior: rib cages, vertebrae, shards of shattered femurs — it was like gazing into a makeshift crematorium.

"Mike," Sergeant Baruta said, struggling to maintain his composure, "secure the area. I've got to call Kamloops G.I. This is a homicide investigation now."

Royal Canadian Mounted Police

Eye-level views of the Johnson vehicle as seen by detectives.

By early afternoon, RCMP investigators Staff Sergeant Michael Eastham and Constable Gerry Dalen had flown up from Kamloops by chopper to conduct a thorough examination of the crime scene. To add to the irritation of the swarming flies, media helicopters hovered over the vicinity, relentlessly seeking out the location. Eastham decided to check the trunk. With the slip of a crowbar, the lid popped open to reveal a grotesque discovery: more bones, including two small skulls that could only belong to children. Their empty eye sockets gazed back hauntingly. In that moment, whatever glimmer of hope the officers had held for Janet and Karen Johnson shrunk to a pinpoint, vanishing into the abyss of those eyes. Though forensics had yet to confirm it, three generations had been slaughtered, burned, and spewed up to the heavens in a cloud of filthy smoke. To complicate matters, the Bentleys' camper and truck were nowhere to be found, and although the detectives had located the bodies, they had no idea where the family had set up camp.

COLD LEAD, FALSE LEADS

Seemingly overnight, the Johnson/Bentley murders became the focus of a national media circus. Hotels and restaurants in Clearwater were flooded with journalists, the local economy booming in the wake of one of British Columbia's most heinous tragedies. The exception, of course,

The burnt-out interior of the Johnson vehicle, in which the charred bodies of all six members of the Johnson/Bentley family were discovered.

was the campgrounds, where the now infamous Wells Gray Gunman was rumoured to lurk in search of fresh prey. Some stubbornly refused to give in to these fears, bragging that they were armed and ready to tackle any threat that came their way. What they didn't take into account was that George Bentley had kept a .410/.22 over-under rifle in his truck, which had done little to save him. Meanwhile, as detectives continued to collect evidence and canvas the public for information, a phone call from the Kamloops forensics department revealed that a melted .22 calibre bullet had been retrieved from one of the skulls. The revelation meant that George Bentley's rifle could have potentially been the murder weapon. In light of this new development, Staff Sergeant Eastham decided to employ metal detectors to search the perimeter for shell casings.*

By now, at least one hundred tips had poured in, all of which had to be checked meticulously. The remains of the Johnson's Chrysler were transported by a U-Haul cube van to Vancouver, where they would be subjected to closer examination. Further ground and aerial searches, using infrared technology, were carried out on the area in a vain attempt to uncover the missing truck and Vanguard camper. Though some posited the vehicles might be lying at the bottom of a lake or obscured by dense foliage, few among the RCMP imagined they would have left the proximity of the provincial park. That was, until a tip came in from a caller who, on August 24, had spotted an identical truck and camper with B.C. plates at a gas station in North Battleford, Saskatchewan. While dining in the Voyageur restaurant, he had seen two scruffy-looking men exit the truck and overheard them conversing in French. It wasn't until he saw an artist's rendition of George Bentley's truck and camper on television that he finally understood how they could afford such expensive vehicles. Further credence was added to this theory when a waitress in Clearwater mentioned spotting a similar pair in her restaurant.

---

* Readers of my *Cold North Killers: Canadian Serial Murder* may recall that the use of metal detectors in locating ballistics was first pioneered by detectives from the Winnipeg RCMP during their search for the "Fort Rouge Sex Maniac" Michael Vescio. Though this forensic innovation had occurred as early as 1946, Staff Sergeant Eastham claims in his gripping *The Seventh Shadow* (upon which most of this research was based) that good-quality metal detectors were still difficult for investigators to obtain in 1982. According to Eastham, if not for the high-profile nature of the Johnson/Bentley murders, he may not have been afforded this luxury at all.

Not long after these promising leads, the investigators finally got the break they were looking for. An employee at Wells Gray Park remembered noticing a truck and camper parked in a three-acre clearing at the old Bear Creek prison grounds, just before the Johnson/Bentley disappearances. Staff Sergeant Eastham and his colleagues drove immediately to the location. Within a matter of minutes they were convinced they had found the family campsite. Around the fire pit lay two sharpened sticks for roasting marshmallows, lids matching the cans recovered from the roof of the Plymouth, and perhaps most telling, three Extra Old Stock bottle caps — Bob Johnson's favourite brand. In a nearby creek, Eastham retrieved four unopened beer bottles left to cool in the icy mountain stream. Hurrying back to tell the others, he learned that in his brief absence the team had discovered six empty .22 calibre cartridges with the metal detector — one for each victim. Ballistics tests would later reveal they had likely been fired by a Ruger.

When they learned that two men who matched the descriptions from North Battleford had been hired to slash and burn bush in the area, they were sure they were onto something. Composites of the suspects were drawn up by a police artist and circulated around the vicinity of the park. Meanwhile, sightings of the truck and camper travelling east continued to trickle in from across Canada. When illustrations of the vehicles and suspects were released to the national media, the trickle became a deluge. Witnesses from Vancouver to Quebec uniformly reported having spotted the missing truck and Vanguard being driven by two dishevelled twenty-somethings. This put the detectives in a Catch-22 situation — though many privately suspected the vehicles had never left B.C., the sheer volume of sightings mandated further investigation. As Eastham brusquely explains in his book *The Seventh Shadow*, "If you don't follow up, it could bite you in the ass. If you do follow it up, and it doesn't get you anything concrete, at least you know."[30]

Unlike with the Bernardo and Homolka murders a decade later, where the unreliable account of a single eyewitness led to millions being squandered, there had been three hundred tips relating to the truck, camper, and Francophones before the rash of sightings finally dwindled in April. Ten thousand reward posters were plastered across North America offering $7,500 for information leading to the vehicle's recovery, along with

RCMP reward poster for information leading to the recovery of the Bentleys' missing 1981 Ford truck and camper, circulated nationwide. Little did the investigators know that the vehicles had never left the provincial park.

another $35,000 for any tips resulting in the conviction of the killer or killers. Detectives worked gruelling sixteen-hour days checking every record of long-distance calls made from Clearwater to Quebec; employing psychics; fielding phone calls; speaking with customs, Interpol, and

U.S. police; canvassing pawn shops; investigating every parking ticket in Canada for mention of the missing truck; cataloguing escaped convicts; and even mailing fifty thousand letters to people who had been visiting the park at the time of the slayings, asking for information or snapshots they might have taken — photographs which, in turn, would have to be scoured for details. Despite their exhaustive (and exhausting) efforts, the RCMP remained no closer to catching the Wells Gray Gunman, and the blackened remains of six innocent people weighed heavily on their minds. By now the Johnson/Bentley murder investigation had become the most expensive in Canadian history.

In an attempt to revitalize the flagging case, a re-enactment of the murders, featuring the exact model of truck, a red and grey Ford F-150, and an old worn Vanguard camper, was filmed by Global Television and aired across Canada. At the same time, Eastham and Constable Claude Oullette flew to Ontario and Quebec to conduct a media campaign. Meanwhile, Dalen and Officer Laurie Dewitt embarked on a three-week drive from Kamloops to Montreal in the same vehicles used in the Global re-enactment. Signs reading HAVE YOU SEEN THIS TRUCK? hung from the camper. The intention was not only to maintain awareness of the case, but also to test the veracity of the eyewitness testimonies that had poured in from across the country. Would the small discrepancies between these vehicles and the Bentleys' go unnoticed, and if so, how reliable were the sightings in the first place?

When summer finally arrived, campgrounds across Ontario and Quebec were inundated with information sheets and "wanted" posters featuring the composite sketches. In late August, an auto body mechanic in Windsor, Ontario, came forward with some promising information. A few months prior, two Francophones had arrived at his shop in a vehicle that he claimed was identical to the Bentleys' Ford F-150. It even sported the same modifications George had made to the bumpers and truck bed. Promising to pay him in cash, the men had brought it in to be painted overnight and mentioned that a camper had recently been detached. If that wasn't incriminating enough, they showed the mechanic a Ruger and a .410/.22 over-under rifle, asking his opinion on the best way to dispose of the weapons. No stranger to criminal activity, the mechanic had referred them to a colleague in Detroit and sent them on their way. As incredible as his story was, he had noted details of the vehicles that were hitherto unreleased to the public — intricacies extending far beyond the realm of coincidence.

Then, on October 18, as the investigation stood poised to cross over into the United States, an unexpected call came in from Clearwater. It was Frank Baruta. They had found the vehicles — dumped on a mountainside and set alight — a mere forty-eight kilometres from the murder site. Just when all of the evidence had pointed east, forcing the investigators to second-guess themselves, it turned out their gut instinct had been right. The lost pieces of the puzzle had been discarded in their own backyard. Now, the wrath of the Canadian media was about to rain down on the RCMP for failing to locate them sooner. Though the investigators were elated to have finally recovered the missing vehicles, from a public relations perspective it was a decidedly Pyrrhic victory.

BACKTRACK TO TUMBLER RIDGE

A few weeks earlier, on September 22, while driving home from his shift at the Tumbler Ridge RCMP detachment, Constable Ron German had spotted a yellow Ford pickup with three dark figures huddled inside. Along with missing tail lights, a cracked windshield, and a box loaded with expensive tools, a single cycloptic headlight glared ominously onto the road. Suspicious, German signalled for the vehicle to pull over, and blasted his off-road lights. He was just preparing to exit when a man clambered hurriedly out of the pickup's driver-side door and began stumbling toward the cruiser. He was stocky, with tousled brown curls, a droopy moustache, and a black denim jacket.

"Hey there! How are you doing tonight?" German greeted him.

"Not too bad, officer." The man shuffled nervously.

"Could I see your driver's licence?"

"Sure." The man handed German a card that read, "David William Shearing."

"So where are you heading?" German passed the licence back.

"Just back to Quadra Camp from work." Shearing's eyes flitted about, avoiding the constable's gaze. "Going to go there for a bit, then head back home."

"Okay then. So what have you got in the back of the truck?"

German and Shearing strode up to the box of the yellow Ford. Inside the cab, the two mysterious figures sat as still as statues. Shearing revealed the contents of the box: a compressor, wrenches, various impact tools — German estimated they were hauling about $40,000 worth of equipment. Knowing that construction workers in Tumbler Ridge would be readying themselves for bed at this hour rather than driving home from work, German escorted Shearing to the back seat of his cruiser and locked the door. Sensing danger, the policeman crept back to the pickup truck along the ditch, pistol in hand. As the two men squinted into the glare of the off-road lights, German snuck up. Peering through the open window of the passenger door, he spied a cocked .30/.30 rifle in one man's hands. German sprang from the darkness and pressed the muzzle of his pistol to the gunman's temple.

"Don't even think about moving," he warned. "Get your hands on the dash."

Startled, they had little option but to comply. Constable German wrenched open the door, seized the rifle, uncocked it, and removed it safely to the trunk of the cruiser. Returning, he escorted a scruffy man out of the Ford, handcuffed him, and placed him in the back seat next to Shearing. When the last of the three — the heavily tattooed passenger who had been cradling the gun — refused to leave the pickup, German wrestled him onto the hood and slapped the cuffs on. With all three suspects secured, he got whatever information he could out of them, then released Shearing and Wylen Laidenen, the scruffy man. After all, they hadn't committed any crimes he was aware of yet. Still, he made sure to list and copy down the serial numbers of the tools before letting them go. The tattooed gunman, Fred White, on the other hand, was driven up to Dawson Creek and charged with attempted murder.

The call Ron German had been expecting came the next morning from a local engineer's camp. There had been a break-in the previous night at one of the trailers, and a number of expensive tools had been stolen. The following day, Constable Mike Johnson arrived at the detachment to provide German with backup, and the two went out in a police Suburban to search for Shearing and Laidenen. They eventually found Shearing and Fred White in a clearing deep in the forest, digging a hole outside a hand-made cabin. German was astonished: hadn't he just booked White for attempted murder? Deciding that the best strategy was sudden ambush, the officers turned on the Suburban's lights and siren and drove at full speed through the bush into the glade. Startled, the two thieves dropped their shovels and took off into the woods, with the RCMP constables pursuing them on foot. When the officers' warning shots and repeated calls upon the suspects to stop failed, nature intervened, entangling Shearing and White in a thicket of thorns. It had been an epic chase, and after German and Johnson caught their breath, they cuffed the exhausted fugitives and placed them in the back of the Suburban. Unlike in their previous encounter, this time Shearing was defiant and profane, refusing to tell them where Laidenen was hiding. Nevertheless, it wasn't long before the officers found him in the cabin — taking cover under a bunk with a .303 rifle aimed at the doorway. Fortunately, German had brought Shearing along as a human shield. Laidenen cast the weapon aside and declared himself unarmed.

Once again, German found himself driving Fred White up to Dawson Creek, only this time Shearing and Laidenen were along for the ride. It was a hot, dusty, and uncomfortable journey. He charged all three men for possession of stolen property, and had them confined to cells. While there, he learned that an oblivious corporal at the detachment had decided to free Fred White on the same night German had brought him in. Apparently, he didn't feel that White should have been locked up for attempted murder simply because he was found in a pickup truck with a loaded weapon.

David Shearing was eventually released from custody and scheduled to appear in court on November 21 to face the stolen property charges. Laidenen and White, wanted on other counts, were jailed. Comparatively, their criminal records made Shearing look like a boy scout. Then again, nobody knew about the crimes he hadn't been caught for. If they had, Laidenen and White might have pointed their guns at him. Stealing and bar fights were one thing — but molesting and killing two little girls was disgusting, even in the eyes of many hardened criminals.

HIDDEN IN PLANE SIGHT

The fire had scorched the red and grey Ford bare, rendering it indistinguishable from the surrounding foliage. Only remnants of the camper remained. It was no wonder that, despite the frequent air searches of Trophy Mountain, they had gone undiscovered for so long. Later, much to the investigators' chagrin, they would learn that an aircraft using infrared technology had passed by the area, but had run out of videotape. Two forestry workers had stumbled upon the burnt-out wreck while traipsing along a skidder trail, at an altitude of 1.43 kilometres. When they informed the Clearwater RCMP of the licence plate — 483 6FY — the police immediately identified the vehicle as belonging to the late Bob Johnson. Whoever had stolen the truck and camper appeared to have been steering them toward a nearby canyon, but had become stuck on a log and abandoned them. As nobody unfamiliar with the area would have known about this hidden route to the gully, the police surmised the killer had to be local. The truck was promptly removed to Vancouver to undergo intensive forensic examination. Investigators had already discovered a bullet hole in the passenger-side door.

Confident that the killer resided or had once resided in the Clearwater area, the team of twenty local detectives, along with Mounties from Vancouver, began going door to door within a thousand-square-mile perimeter, questioning every man, woman, and child. They also examined thirteen thousand tips to see if any viable suspects emerged. Sometime during this period the name David Shearing first surfaced. An unidentified telephone informant explained that Shearing had been implicated in a hit-and-run fatality on the Wells Gray Highway but was never charged. When, coincidentally on the same day, a waitress slipped an investigator a piece of paper reading, "David Shearing," the twenty-three-year-old became a high-priority suspect. Residing within a few kilometres of the Bear Creek campground, Shearing and his family had already been interviewed by police. Reports indicated that he had expressed outrage over the massacre and cursed the perpetrator but hadn't seen anything suspicious. Though he came from a respectable family, with a brother who was a sheriff, Shearing was something of a lone wolf, known for driving under the influence, abusing drugs, and fighting. More sinisterly, he was rumoured to prefer his feminine company on the young side — as in thirteen years old. Shearing may have dressed like a cowboy, but he seemed much closer to John Wayne Gacy than John Wayne.

At the time of the murders, Shearing's employment would have taken him past the crime scene at least twice a day. Currently, he was working in the logging town of Tumbler Ridge, northeast of Prince George near the Alberta border. The investigators' suspicions only deepened when, during a routine police interview the following day, a local woman asked her husband whether he was "going to tell them about what David Shearing said about re-registering that truck with the bullet hole in the door." Staff Sergeant Eastham made the decision to contact his old friend Ron German at the Tumbler Ridge RCMP detachment to feel things out.

"Mike! I guess you're pretty busy with that family murder case," German greeted him over the telephone. "Look, I've got a bit of a weird duck up here. He said he used to live in Clearwater, and I figured I could ask him some questions if you want me to. His name's David William Shearing." Flabbergasted, Eastham informed German that they were looking at Shearing as a suspect in the Johnson/Bentley murders, and requested that they keep tabs on him. German was already ahead of the game — for weeks he had been surveilling Shearing to ensure he didn't skip out on his court date.

First by plane, then by jalopy, on Friday, November 18, 1983, Mike Eastham and Gerry Dalen battled their way north through a raging blizzard to Dawson Creek. The next morning, German approached a tired and hungover David Shearing in Tumbler Ridge, and requested that he come up to Dawson Creek of his own volition to answer some questions. Having just seen his drinking buddy Jason Harwood arrested for outstanding warrants acquired in Ottawa, and realizing that German would be forced to arrest him if he didn't comply, Shearing agreed. On the drive north, the two began chatting about hunting, and German brought up the fact that he was fond of shooting grouse with his .22 Cooey. Shearing responded by detailing the accuracy of his father's superior .22 Remington in hunting deer. Little did he know what lay in store for him at Dawson Creek.

Once they reached their destination, German escorted Shearing into the local police station, where he introduced Staff Sergeant Eastham and interrogation expert Ken Leibel. Shearing's reaction was one of barely concealed terror. Clearly he was familiar with Eastham's name and his involvement in the Johnson/Bentley investigation. As Shearing was taken to the downstairs interrogation room, German offered some tips to his old friend Mike Eastham regarding Shearing's body language and the fact that he had claimed to own a .22 Remington.

COWBOYS DON'T CRY

David Shearing's chain-smoking put Eastham's to shame. Thick cancerous clouds hung around them like fog over the pines. With his arms and legs crossed, brow creased, and body tensed, it was obvious that he was already on psychological lockdown. To loosen him up, Eastham and Leibel started by throwing him softball questions about his childhood. They learned that Shearing had been born on April 10, 1959. After attaining his high school diploma, he took a six-month heavy mechanic's course at college before travelling around British Columbia and Alberta working odd jobs — from cabinetmaking to fertilizer manufacturing. He had a thirty-seven-year-old brother named Greg, who until recently had worked as a sheriff, and a sister. His mother was still alive and living in a nursing home in Clearwater; but he noted somewhat sadly that his father, a former prison guard, had succumbed to cancer in the spring of 1982. Following the death, Shearing had begun to drink heavily and have regular run-ins with the law. When Eastham asked him if he had ever spent time behind bars, Shearing's green eyes started to shift about — a sign that he was uncomfortable with the line of questioning. However, when they changed tack and began talking about cars, guitars, and fishing, the suspect's arms unfolded. He was beginning to open up to them. After a little more friendly banter about the negative effects of his alcohol abuse, including a drunken accident where Shearing had fractured his pelvis, Eastham decided it was time to take things up a level.

"Do you know what we're doing here, Dave? Considering the distance we came, we must be here for a good reason."

"No." Shearing averted his gaze. "I'm not sure. I don't have anything to hide, you know. I'm an honest guy."

Eastham reassured him that they would be fair, but professional, and reiterated his rights to remain silent and to an attorney. He explained that they were investigating a serious crime. Simultaneously, he hinted that guilty men used lawyers, manipulating Shearing into thinking everything would be all right if he just kept talking. In reality, the innocent often become loud and indignant about wanting an attorney. David Shearing was acting completely the opposite, and by now, Eastham was smelling blood.

"Are you guys investigating the Johnson/Bentley murders?" Shearing asked.

Eastham took his time answering, letting the silence gnaw at Shearing's conscience. "Did anyone talk to you about it last year?"

"Yeah. Some cop talked to me briefly about it before, last year sometime."

Eastham asked Shearing if he knew about Trophy and Battle Mountains, and that they had found the vehicles there. He did. Eastham explained they were getting a lot of help from the community, even from bikers. Shearing squirmed, seeking comfort in cigarettes.

"I want to see if you are an honest guy. I'm going to start back a couple years ago, and see what you will do. Remember, you can leave at any time. We discovered that a kid was killed that summer on Wells Gray Road. It was a hit and run, or criminal negligence, or whatever. The guy didn't stop. I know all about it, otherwise I wouldn't be up here in Dawson Creek on a weekend."

"I know." Shearing breathed a sigh of relief. Eastham struggled to contain a smile as he saw the suspect's body relax. It was working — by making Shearing think they were investigating the fatal hit and run accident, they were lowering his guard. Once they had learned everything they needed to know about the vehicular manslaughter, Eastham and Leibel would move in for the kill. Recounting that night in 1980, Shearing recalled that he and a friend, Doug Elliot, had been drinking heavily, and were cruising at about eighty kilometres per hour on the Wells Gray Road when a shape suddenly appeared in his headlights. Before Shearing could react, the car slammed into Dave Carter, lurching as all four tires crushed the life from his body. Suspecting that Carter was already dead, and since Shearing had been drinking, he and Elliot had agreed to keep their mouths shut.

When asked how he felt about it, Shearing replied that it made him feel "upset." Eastham handed him a pen, paper, and coffee so that he could document his own account of what had happened that night.

Between fits of crying, smoking, and sipping coffee, Shearing eventually finished and signed his two-page confession in just over an hour. It was 6:39 p.m., and they had already got him to admit to one homicide — only six more to go.

"Okay, David," Eastham continued, "you understand everything we've done. I told you when we started that we know a lot about you. We wouldn't be here, especially on a weekend, unless there was a good reason. When we started, we gave you a warning: anything you say can be used as evidence on everything. I also told you we were investigating the Johnson and Bentley murders, and this is where this all stems from. The warning we gave you still stands. As long as you realize that." Shearing indicated that he did, and Eastham took some time to peruse his statement. When he was finished, the two discussed the possible outcomes of the confession, whether Shearing would be going to jail, and the likelihood that his passenger, Doug Elliot, would face legal action. After some conversation about religion and morality to soften Shearing up, Eastham finally made his move.

"David, what do you think about the Johnson and Bentley murders? What do you think of them being killed in your front yard, so to speak?"

"Well it was pretty bad for the community." Shearing's cigarette wobbled.

"Do you know where the car was found?" Eastham asked.

"Yeah."

"You know where the truck was found?"

"Yeah."

"You also know where they were killed?"

"Bear Creek," Shearing replied, his face suddenly dropping. Eastham felt his heart beat like a victory drum. Never mind Bear Creek: Shearing had just put himself up Shit Creek without a paddle. Unlike the sites where the vehicles had been found, the whereabouts of the murder scene had never been disclosed to the public. The only person outside of the RCMP who could have been aware of the location was the killer himself.

"I think I need to speak to a lawyer now," Shearing chimed in.

TRUTH AND JUSTICE

As David William Shearing's trial drew near, the investigators were over-joyed to learn that their case was so airtight that his lawyers were opting to enter guilty pleas on all six charges, without any legal wheeling and dealing. On the morning before he was scheduled to appear in court — Monday, April 16, 1984 — Shearing received an unexpected visit from Staff Sergeant Eastham. They exchanged brief pleasantries before Eastham got to the point.

"You told me once that you might tell me the whole story one day, and I left it at that. Well, David, the day you're sentenced I'm going to come and collect. Think about it, David. I'll be back."

Later that day, Shearing stood before Justice Harry McKay in the red-brick Kamloops courthouse, clad in a brown suit and striped tie. There he plead guilty to all six counts of second-degree murder, his law-yers proclaiming he had done so to spare the victims' family and his own family the anguish of a lengthy trial. Before sentencing, it was necessary to consider the defendant's character, and over the next few hours, the story of David Shearing was revealed to those in attendance.

Born to the children of prairie farmers in New Westminster, B.C., Shearing had relocated with his family to Clearwater at the age of five. His home life had been happy and stable, and he held a deep reverence for his father, an erudite conservationist whose interests extended from ancient history to photography and stamp collecting. Shearing gradu-ated high school with a 70 percent average. Letters from officials at the institution described him as a "good average student ... a very quiet per-son who responded politely and respectfully." He had gone on to attend Cariboo College, where he won an award for his aptitude in the heavy machinery program. A left-brained thinker, Shearing was forever reading about mechanics, science, and chemistry as well as sci-fi novels. He also enjoyed the simple pleasures of country life: dogs, hiking, and twanging out country-and-western tunes on his electric guitar. Testaments from friends and neighbours portrayed a shy, helpful young man who could be funny when he opened up to people.

Unfortunately, everything seemed to fall apart in March 1982, when lung cancer claimed his beloved father. Shearing was devastated. Having already established a predisposition for binge drinking in his teens, he turned increasingly to alcohol to cope with the sixty-seven-year-old's death. Approximately four months later, he gunned down the Johnson/Bentley family at Bear Creek. After, he claimed that on multiple occasions he had climbed to the top of a mountain, intent on committing suicide. Perhaps the most powerful argument for the defence was a letter from Shearing's brother, Gary, a former sheriff. Soon after the reading of the letter, Judge McKay declared that the prisoner be remanded until 10:00 the following morning.

But the dawning of a new day would bring no light for David Shearing. The twenty-five-year-old was ordered to stand as Judge McKay's voice boomed down at him from the bench: "What we have here is a cold-blooded and senseless execution of six defenceless and innocent victims for no apparent reason other than he possibly coveted some of their possessions." A wave of shock and relief rushed over the courtroom as Judge McKay handed down a maximum sentence of twenty-five years with parole for each of the six murders, to be served concurrently. At long last justice had been served. The truth, on the other hand, remained elusive, and Staff Sergeant Mike Eastham was determined to get to the bottom of it.

The next time Eastham visited Shearing behind bars, the policeman's friendly facade had disappeared. Shearing was less than affable himself: unsurprising, considering the unprecedented severity of his second-degree murder sentence.

"You know why I'm here, David. There's a couple things that don't sit well with me, and you know what they are," Eastham began. "What's gnawing at me right now is, I think you sexually abused those girls before you killed them."

Shearing asked for his lawyer.

Defence attorney Fred Kaatz arrived on the scene and was greeted by Eastham's steely glare. Kaatz knew only too well who was holding the cards, and if he denied Eastham this opportunity, Shearing could expect no future co-operation from him. The lawyer entered the room to speak with his client, and left soon after. Eastham re-entered to find Shearing sitting blank-faced, as if deep in thought. He took a seat across from the convicted murderer.

"All right, Mike. You got it," Shearing sighed.

Over the next few hours, he admitted to having spotted little Janet and Karen on his way home from work, and had made up his mind that he would have them at any cost. Sometime between August 6 and 13, he had ambushed the adults at night, shooting them dead. Ripping open the door of the girls' tent, he found them lying propped up on their elbows. They wanted to know what all of the noise was, so Shearing had spun a tale of the camp being attacked by bikers. The adults had left in search of help, he explained, leaving him to guard Janet and Karen from the "bad men."*

Once he had them convinced, he returned to where Bob Johnson lay gargling blood, and silenced him with a second bullet. Then, one by one, he carried the bodies to the back seat of the Chrysler, stacking them neatly on top of each other. Laying a blanket over them, he quickly cleaned up before returning to the tent where the two Johnson girls lay cowering. The details of the subsequent sexual assault have never been made public, though Eastham has stated that Shearing's account left him "breathless" and glad that he was unarmed. When Shearing had finished with the girls, he redressed himself in clothing smeared with their family's blood, and ordered them to help him collapse the tent. They had asked where their parents were, and he had repeated the lie that they had gone to find help. By the time he had instructed them to climb into the front seat of the Chrysler, there would have been no way that Janet and Karen could fail to notice their family's corpses, blanket or not. The floor would have been swimming in blood.

Pulling the car onto Wells Gray Road, Shearing drove them to his ranch, then forced them to erect the tent and remain inside it. Returning to Bear Creek on foot, he then piloted the truck and camper back to the ranch and secreted it in the forest by the tent. He warned the Johnson girls not to stray or the wolves, bears, and bikers might get them. Shearing strolled back to his house, climbed into bed, and fell into a deep sleep.

---

* Eastham doubts the veracity of such claims, proposing that the gunshots and screams would have caused the girls to react much less passively. He believes that Janet and Karen had seen the entire massacre unfold and probably took off running. Shearing would have chased them through the forest, caught up, and scared them into submitting to his twisted demands.

The next morning, he awoke and went to work. He continued to visit the girls' tent every night, almost certainly subjecting them to more sexual abuse. Then, on Friday evening, he marched them through the dark, rainy, black forest toward a fishing cabin. They did not reach their destination that night, and camped under a plastic sheet strung between trees. By Saturday they entered the little hut by the water, but an unexpected visit from a prison guard at Clearwater Correctional Institute, who was supervising inmates fishing on the river, spooked Shearing. The guard had not seen the girls hiding behind the cabin door, and when the opportunity arose, Shearing forced the exhausted sisters to hike back up to the ranch. When they finally made it, he lured Karen away from her sister to where his .22 rifle lay stashed. Shearing faked urinating, and when Karen turned away, he fired into the back of her head. Leaving her body in the woods, he returned to the camp and explained to Janet that he had bound her sister to a tree. They spent the night together in the camper, allegedly "talking" because "Janet was a virgin, and didn't know a lot about sex at all." The next day he used the same ruse on the thirteen-year-old, and shot her dead in the woods. With these final witnesses to his crimes eliminated, Shearing stuffed the bodies in the trunk of the Chrysler, and went to sleep.

When he climbed into the driver's seat the next night, the stench of rotting bodies was overpowering. Under cover of darkness, he guided the Chrysler up to Battle Mountain, turning off-road into the pines, where the vehicle became stuck. He dowsed it from front to back with gasoline, set it ablaze, and stood watching it burn. Later, following the reports of the disappearances on the August 23, Shearing attempted to drive the Bentleys' truck and camper off the canyon on Trophy Mountain. Yet the heavy rains mired the vehicles in the mud, leaving him no option but to torch them. As the last traces of evidence vanished into the roaring flames and smoke, Shearing trudged home wearily through the pitch-black woods.

Not long after hearing the confession, Mike Eastham stopped by the little cabin on the river and spoke to Don Gordon, a prison guard, who confirmed that he had encountered Shearing on the day in question. Inside the structure, police discovered the initials DS+JJ carved crudely into the wood. Yet David Shearing had never loved Janet

Johnson — instead, he had wanted to own her. By repeatedly sexually assaulting her and extinguishing her life, he had ensured that he would be the only man she knew carnally.

One would think that Shearing's cruel and pathetic behaviour would repel any woman from ever falling in love with him. This was not the case. While exchanging letters with Shearing in prison, a woman named Heather fell for him. Sometime in the vicinity of 1994 they were married, and today she is one of his most vocal supporters: "I have a hard time believing this man could kill a fly. He feels remorse. I've watched him cry. This has hurt everyone. The time has come for him to work his way back."*

While in prison, Shearing followed in the footsteps of fellow rampage murderers **Marc Lépine** and **Peter John Peters** (Chapter 1), and changed his surname to his mother's maiden name, Ennis. As of 2012, David and Heather Ennis live in the hope that he will be paroled. None of his six victims were granted a second chance.

Many crimes dubbed spree killings, like those of **Rosaire Bilodeau** and **Robert Poulin**, actually bear a closer resemblance to mass murder, in that they generally end in a public place where the offender decides to make his last stand. They are usually marked by one or more earlier incidences of murder occurring within twenty-four hours of the subsequent massacre, and often directed toward a victim who is related to or knows the perpetrator. "Mass murder with an overture" is perhaps the most fitting designation. Unfortunately, rather than considering the spirit of the killings, many authors and academics focus too strictly on the "single location" criteria associated with mass murder, labelling the likes of Charles Whitman and Seung Hu Cho as spree killers. We'll take a further look at spree killers in Part C. First, let's examine the earliest examples of rampage murders in Canadian history.

---

* Dialogue used in this case was drawn entirely from Mike Eastham's *The Seventh Shadow*, as it is assumed to be a true and accurate account of what was said during the investigation and interrogation.

CHAPTER 3

THE FIRST RAMPAGE KILLERS IN CANADIAN HISTORY

Canada's first two mass murderers emerged within the boundaries of what is now Ontario; the third and fourth surfaced farther east, in the Maritime provinces of New Brunswick and Nova Scotia. All of the perpetrators were first-generation immigrants from Scotland, Ireland, or the United States, and fire was involved to varying degrees in each of their crimes. **Thomas Easby** and **Henry Sovereign** were early examples of Family Annihilators, a subtype of mass murderer we will explore in Chapter 8. Though **Patrick Slavin** also slaughtered an entire family, it was not his own, and he did so purely for material gain. **Alexander Keith Jr.** shared Slavin's motives, but their methods diverged greatly. Where the working class Slavin used an axe to bludgeon his victims, the privileged Keith relied purely on his intellect, and could not stomach the sight of blood.

Thomas Easby

"Justice has been done."

Victims: 5 killed
Duration of rampage: One day in early December 1828 (mass murder)
Location: Drummond, Upper Canada (Ontario)
Weapons: Bludgeoning/suffocation from fire

FATHER'S GAME

Aside from the numerous state-sponsored massacres of Canada's indigenous population, the nation's first known mass murder occurred in Drummond, Upper Canada — roughly seventy kilometres southwest of present-day Ottawa. It is prescient that, as with many of our subsequent mass murders, fire was involved and the victims were the killer's own flesh and blood.

In 1828, Thomas Easby — a former Scottish crofter turned immigrant — and his family inhabited a log house in Lanark County where he farmed his own land. One fateful night in early December, flames consumed the home, taking Thomas's pregnant wife, Ann, and four of his five children with it. An inquest into the fire determined that the victims had suffocated to death in their sleep. Their remains were laid to rest, and the members of the small rural community did their best to console the gigantic widower and his surviving four-year-old child, Joseph. Everything was wrapped up neatly. The quiet, sober Thomas went back to work, while Joseph was fostered out to the neighbouring Richardsons until his father got back on his feet. Though his foster family had several children, Joseph was withdrawn and preferred to play alone. Reasoning that the boy was probably grieving, Mrs. Richardson allowed him his space, all the time keeping tabs on his emotional well-being. The accounts of what happened next differ. In their *Encyclopedia of Mass Murder*, Lane and Gregg claim that, upon seeing his foster family building a fire, Joseph exclaimed, "That was what Daddy did to Mammy!" A more plausible account comes from local author Susan Code, who writes that Mrs. Richardson observed the boy striking the ground with a stick while reciting the names of his dead brothers and sisters. After several weeks of this strange behaviour, she had asked Joseph if she was allowed to play the game with him, to which the youngster replied that it was his "father's game" and only he could play it.

Joseph's actions alerted the Richardsons to the possibility that Thomas Easby may have been responsible for his family's deaths. They divulged this information to the police, and the Easby bodies were exhumed. Before a second inquest could occur, Thomas admitted murdering his wife and four children to a jailer. Easby was arrested on February 2, 1829. Upon re-examination that same month, indications of bludgeoning were observed on the skulls. By evidence and his own admission, it seemed obvious that Thomas Easby had bashed in his family's heads and ignited the blaze. When asked why, his manner was aloof and evasive. Though Susan Code has proposed that Easby was a glutton who slaughtered his "bairns" because they were eating his food, in truth, he never provided a motive for his monstrous acts.

THE BIG EASBY

Thomas Easby took rather well to life behind bars, gorging on supplies of pork, flour, and butter shipped in fresh from his farm. His girth grew astronomically to match his status as Perth Jail's most notorious inmate. The months he spent awaiting his day in court may have been among the happiest of his life.

By the end of his trial in August 1829, the jury deliberated for a matter of minutes before reaching a guilty verdict. Days later, Thomas Easby stepped onto the gallows as angry onlookers jeered at him drunkenly in the hot noon sun. When asked if he had any parting words, Easby simply replied, "Justice has been done." With that, a hood was placed over his head so that the crowd would be spared the unpleasantness of witnessing his bulging eyes and tongue. The gallows yawned under his colossal weight as Easby slowly strangled to death. His bloated corpse was interred in a local Anglican cemetery, but soon after was dug up and dissected by a Dr. Wilson and his students for medical research. Those expressing outrage at the retail of modern "murderabelia" should note that Easby's hide was tanned and diced into squares which sold for $2 each. Often these were fashioned into wallets. Juxtaposing this with the controversy over true-crime trading cards, the idea of a moral decline is laughable.

Henry Sovereign

"I am afraid they have murdered my family."

Victims: 8 killed
Duration of rampage: January 23, 1832 (mass murder)
Location: Waterford, Ontario
Weapons: Jackknife/bludgeoning

RAIN CHECK ON A STRETCHED NECK

Henry Sovereign, born in 1790, almost never made the history books. Convicted of "knowingly, willfully, and maliciously shooting a horse" in August 1819, the New Jersey–born farmer was sentenced to hang in accordance with the British Criminal Code. However, due to the public outcry over the severity of his punishment, Sovereign was granted clemency by Justice James Buchanan. By 1821, he returned to farming and shingle-making in Windham County in southwestern Ontario, setting up his home on Lot 1 along Concession 5. Judging by the events of January 22, 1832, it would have been better if he had mounted the gallows.

On the dark winter's morning of January 23, Ephraim Serils responded to an unexpected hammering on his door. He opened it to find his niece Polly's husband, Henry Sovereign, dripping blood from his arms and chest. The frantic caller explained that two strangers with "blackened faces" had broken into his home, a farm northwest of Waterford, and attacked his family. He had escaped to find help. Arming himself, the relative hurried to the dwelling along with Sovereign and another neighbour. As they approached, Sovereign stopped short in his tracks.

"I am afraid they have murdered my family," he exclaimed.

About eighty metres from the house, they came across the lifeless bodies of his wife, Polly, and his twelve-year-old son. Sovereign's seventeen-year-old daughter lay similarly butchered a few metres away, along with two more of his offspring. Entering the house, they found the corpses of two children — the youngest burning in the fireplace. A third was discovered alive but badly wounded, and died soon after. The wailing of two-year-old Anna Sovereign — the lone survivor of the massacre — resounded through the blood-soaked dwelling.

The aptly named Constable John Massacer was summoned to the scene and, deciding to track the killers immediately, began searching the surrounding area with Henry Sovereign. Interestingly, neither of the alleged intruders had left prints in the snow. However, against its unblemished white blanket, a broken knife handle stood in stark contrast. The weapon's bloodstained blade lay nearby. Upon observing the instrument of murder, Sovereign noted that it had belonged to his son. Something in the bereaved father's manner stoked Constable Massacer's suspicions. He was well aware of Sovereign's reputation for violence when drinking — the alcoholic shingle-maker had abused his wife and children and threatened their lives on several occasions — so he ordered Sovereign to empty his pockets. When the suspect complied, Massacer discovered a jackknife caked in dried blood. Later, a beetle or maul used to bludgeon several family members to death was discovered secreted in a straw and feather mattress. Articles of Henry's clothing, sullied with blood and brain, were also retrieved from the crime scene. Most tellingly, there were strands of his hair still clenched in Polly's fist. An examining physician, Dr. John Crouse, determined that Henry Sovereign's own injuries were superficial and, most likely, self-inflicted. The suspect was placed under arrested and taken to London jail.

By August 8, 1832, Sovereign was standing before Justice James Buchanan once again. Throughout the proceedings, he stuck to his story of the home invaders, claiming the blood on the jackknife was his own. For what it's worth, Ephraim Serils testified that the accused had seemed completely sober on the night in question. Before the jury deliberated his fate, Sovereign calmly addressed them, declaring, "The thought of murdering my family never once entered into my heart. I had always taken good care of them and loved them as a father and husband should do. God knows, if I die for the act, I die an innocent man." Ultimately, the nine jurors disagreed, finding him guilty in less than an hour.

Henry Sovereign finally adorned the rope necklace atop London's gallows on August 13, 1832. He protested his innocence before a crowd of three hundred astonished onlookers. As with **Thomas Easby**, following his execution Sovereign's body was donated to a medical school for dissection — his death bringing more benefit to mankind than the totality of his wretched life. His eldest children, absent on the day of his massacre, would go on to start families of their own. To this day, the Sovereigns are a respected family in the London area, although time has yet to erase the memory of the drunkard who murdered his wife and children. Along with the 2006 massacre of eight Bandidos motorcycle club members in nearby Shedden, the Sovereign familicide ranks as the worst mass murder in Ontario's history.

Patrick Slavin

"When I went in I saw Mrs. McKenzie sitting by the fire and the four children beside her. I struck her on the head 10 or 15 times. I killed them all. They did not cry much."

Victims: 6 killed
Duration of rampage: October 24, 1857 (mass murder)
Location: Mispec, New Brunswick
Weapon: Axe

BUTCHERED AND BURNED

Robert McKenzie left his native Scotland in the mid-nineteenth century, settling outside Saint John, New Brunswick, in the Mispec area. Blessed with a shrewd business sense and determined work ethic, he rose quickly from tailoring to success in real estate, money lending, and chair manufacturing. By 1857, McKenzie had amassed a small fortune, and occupied a large house on Black River Road with his wife and children.

Unfortunately, word of his wealth fell upon the wrong ears. On the morning of Sunday, October 25, 1857, a visitor arrived at the McKenzie home to find only smoking black ruins. Soon after, the lifeless bodies of Mrs. Effie McKenzie and one of her babes were pulled from the ashes. In a burned outbuilding, searchers discovered Robert McKenzie's torso — his head and arms severed and missing — along with three of the couple's four children. Instantly, what had seemed like a tragic accident transformed into a full-fledged murder investigation. One didn't have to look far for a motive; among the debris were the charred remains of a money chest that had been emptied prior to the blaze. Saint John police learned that a Mr. Williams had reportedly visited the McKenzie home in the days before the fire to inquire about working for Robert as a labourer. Having been hired on the spot, Williams had left on Friday, promising to return Saturday evening with his wife and personal belongings. When the enigmatic "Mr. Williams" came under closer scrutiny, investigators learned that he also went by the surnames Breen, Green, and McGuire. Furthermore, rather than returning to his wife that Friday, Williams had stopped at the home of Patrick Slavin in Simonds Parish, where he had been living sporadically for the past month.

Like Robert McKenzie, the middle-aged Slavin was an immigrant. During the potato famine of the 1840s, he had relocated from Ireland to New Brunswick, where he found employment as a railroad construction worker and labourer. But while Robert McKenzie had found wealth in the new world, Slavin remained impoverished, sharing a tiny log hut in Loch

Lomond with his wife and three sons. Not only was the cabin a mere five kilometres from the crime scene, but Slavin's neighbours reported spotting his children playing with a suspiciously large sum of cash. Speaking with Slavin's wife, the investigators ascertained that the man who had visited the McKenzie home was actually named Hugh Breen. Though Mrs. Slavin acted oblivious to any of her husband's misdeeds, one of her children admitted overhearing Breen and his father discussing the murders. According to the boy, they had left Saturday with his brother Patrick Slavin Jr., only to return later with darkened demeanours and an abundance of coin.

Putting two and two together, police obtained a warrant to arrest Slavin, Breen, and Patrick Slavin Jr., who was believed to be an accessory to the murders. The three suspects were soon found hiding in a woodland sixteen kilometres from Simonds Parish, and were taken into custody. During the coroner's inquest, Slavin Sr.'s youngest son, Jamie, formally testified that his father, brother, and Mr. Breen had left the house together on the evening of October 24, 1857. Later they had returned with a substantial amount of money and stolen property. This account was corroborated by additional witnesses. Indeed, the police had uncovered a stash of eighty sovereigns, prompting the jury to reach a verdict of willful murder.

LIKE FATHER?

Patrick Slavin Sr. was officially charged with the slayings of Effie McKenzie and her unnamed child. Caught red-handed, he and Breen entered guilty pleas at their November trial. Only Patrick Slavin Jr. pleaded not guilty. Throughout the proceedings, the jury heard testimony from each of the three men. Breen admitted to masterminding the crime, but placed the blame for the murders squarely on the shoulders of Patrick Slavin Sr.:

> I went to the house and asked McKenzie to come down as my wife had come. Old Slavin said not to make a fire, and after it was made we put it out. McKenzie came down with a candle in his hand and old Slavin took the axe used for chopping wood out of my hand. His son was there. There were two or three in the house. Slavin was in one place and McKenzie in another. When McKenzie came in, Slavin

came out and said "She is on hand" (this was referring to my wife's coming). He had the axe in his hand and hit McKenzie on the breast. He said "Dead dogs tell no lies." He hit him on the breast with the back of the axe. McKenzie groaned but did not speak. We put him into the cellar and old Slavin afterwards brought him up when we went to the upper house. Slavin asked me if I knew the house; he told me to go in and watch the door till he got a view of her. He then went in and Mrs. McKenzie was sitting at the fire with a child in her arms. She asked if she was coming (meaning my wife). Slavin then struck her with the axe on her head and she fell over the edge of the stone; he then struck her three blows on the body. He then struck the children who were standing round their mother crying, he killed the whole of them; the children cried, but Mrs. McKenzie did not. Prisoner [Slavin Jr.] and me took no direct part in the murder; we were standing in the porch at the time.[31]

Though he took full responsibility for the slayings, Patrick Slavin Sr.'s account of the events cast Breen in a slightly darker light:

We went up to the house, Breen and I. I was first. Breen showed me the way. I did not take the axe. There was one at the door, Breen gave it to me. When I went in I saw Mrs. McKenzie sitting by the fire and the four children beside her. I struck her on the head 10 or 15 times. I killed them all. They did not cry much. We searched the house and found over 100 pounds of money. It was myself that ransacked the chest, the money was in gold. It was in a yellow bag, like the one in Court. There was a purse also and portmanteau. The boy was knocking about keeping watch. We had something to eat. We thought it best to set fire to the houses. Breen and I both did it.

In an "extraordinary" turn of events, both the prosecution and defence called upon Patrick Slavin Sr. to testify on their behalf. The

Crown sought to establish that even though Slavin Jr. had not wielded the axe, he had entered the home to collect loot and was therefore, under English criminal law, as guilty as his father. Simultaneously, the defence attempted to use Slavin Sr.'s account as evidence of his son's diminished mental capacity and subsequent lack of culpability:

> I have three boys: Pat Slavin, 15 to 16, Johnnie Slavin, 10 to 11, and Jamie Slavin, 6 to 7. Pat knows right from wrong; I have sometimes been too severe to him. He did not know when we left what we were going to do; if he had refused to go, I would have made him. He is a tender hearted boy and has not looked the same since. It was I that killed them all. I am aware that the sentence of death will be passed on me. I have told the truth....

Slavin Jr.'s supposed lack of agency was buttressed by the testimony of several witnesses who referred to him as "simple," and a neighbour who admitted that though the younger Slavin lacked common sense, he was far from a "bad boy."

Despite their efforts, prosecutor Charles Fisher wasn't buying it. Not only did he effectively dispute the implications that Patrick Slavin Jr. was mentally impaired, he even labelled the teen as having "a most diabolical nature, and not fit to let loose on this country."[32] As the trial neared its ending after three days, an emotional Judge Robert Parker dismissed the coercion defence, and informed the jury that they were to concentrate on Slavin Jr.'s ability to discern right from wrong. In the meantime, he sentenced Patrick Slavin Sr. and Hugh Breen to hang on December 11, 1857. Both men accepted his decision with stony faces.

Eventually, the jury concluded that Patrick Slavin Jr. was guilty, and he too was condemned to the gallows. Judge Parker penned an elaborate justification for his decision, qualifying it with a recommendation that the executive government reduce the younger Slavin's sentence of capital punishment to a term of incarceration in a provincial penitentiary. If they didn't, the teenager would be dangling at the end of a rope by March 4 of the following year.

SLIP SLIDIN' AWAY

Meanwhile, the elder Slavin and Breen's date with death was fast approaching. On a Sunday evening five days before the scheduled execution, a Mrs. Doherty visited Hugh Breen in his cell at around 6:30 p.m. Twenty minutes after she departed, a Miss Creighton came to see him, but was alarmed when he didn't receive her. She summoned a priest, who arrived just before 7:00 p.m. to find Breen kneeling in his cell "suspended by an old yellow silk handkerchief from a small piece of wood, one end of which rested on a shelf and the other on a cleet [*sic*]. A bit of wood, which had a hole bored in it and fitting on the stump of an old nail, assisted in the support of the cross stick."[33] As there was no point in the room high enough from which to hang himself, Breen had stood on the tips of his toes, leaning the full weight of his body against the ligature until he slowly strangled to death. He was taken down and subsequently interred in the Almshouse Burying Ground.

Evidently in less of a hurry to be cast into hell, Patrick Slavin Sr. kept his December 11 appointment with the hangman. Riflemen from the British garrison were deployed to maintain order, as a crowd of five thousand onlookers gathered around the platform outside the county jail. At 10:10 a.m., Slavin ascended onto the gallows with his priest Reverend Sweeny, High Sheriff Charles Johnston, and a Constable Pidgeon. Sheriff Johnston secured the noose around the prisoner's throat, and the constable pulled the mask over his visage. Then, joining Reverend Sweeny in prayer, Slavin stepped onto the trap. Sheriff Johnston severed the support, and Slavin plunged through the gallows. In less than a second, the rope went taut, snapping his neck. With that, the Irishman who had murdered the McKenzies in cold blood became the second conspirator to pay for his crimes. Interestingly, just weeks later, Slavin's wife made news by wedding a man who had been acquitted of rape that same year.

Fortunately for Patrick Slavin Jr., on the recommendation of Judge Parker, his sentence was commuted to life imprisonment in a Courtenay Bay penitentiary. After fourteen years of incarceration, he managed a daring escape, crossing the border into Maine. As there was no extradition treaty with the United States at the time, Slavin lived the rest of his life in freedom, albeit constantly looking over his shoulder.

Staatsarchiv Bremen

Alexander Keith Jr.
The Dynamite Fiend

*"What I have seen today,
I cannot stand."*

Victims: 81 killed/50 wounded/committed suicide
Duration of rampage: December 11, 1875 (serial mass murderer?)
Location: Bremerhaven, Germany
Weapon: Time bomb

WHOOPS

In December 1875, the fledgling German nation was truly coming into its own. Prussia's crushing victory over France in 1870/71 had laid a strong foundation upon which to unite the German principalities into a formidable European power. Under the guidance of that genius of *realpolitik* Otto von Bismarck, Germany had prospered, industrializing and forging an empire that would ultimately challenge Britain for supremacy in the First World War.

Docked in the port of Bremerhaven, the transatlantic steamship *Mosel* represented the height of Germany's engineering brilliance and affluence. On December 11, 1875, a crowd of passengers huddled on the dock waiting to board, their breath like smoke on the frosty sea air. Using a winch, a group of stevedores was hoisting a large wooden barrel onto the ship, when suddenly the keg slipped and plummeted, landing on the dock. A fiery blast tore through the ropes and metal, evaporating the snow and blowing charred bodies in all directions. Twisted iron shrapnel and shards of glass flew like stray bullets, shredding flesh and ripping clothing from the dead and maimed. The *Mosel's* bow caved as smoke billowed from a hole blown in the vessel.

In his cabin below the deck, a portly bearded man calling himself W.K. Thomas sat down at his desk. The smell of schnapps hung heavy on his breath, the numbing elixir doing little to steel him against the images of screaming amputees and blackened corpses — a grotesque scene he had never intended to witness. Pressing the tip of his pencil against the paper, he jotted out a terse farewell to his wife: "God bless you and my darling children, you will never see my [*sic*] to speak to again. William." His second letter, to the ship's captain, was much longer:

> To the captain of the Steamer Mosel Please Send money you will find in my pocket — 20 pounds sterling 80 marks German money My wife resides at 14 Residenze Strasse Strehlen by Dresden What I have seen today I cannot stand W K Thomas[34]

Then, after removing his jacket, he planted his sizable girth on the divan and drew a revolver. Two pathetic gunshots rang out, mere pin drops in comparison to the thunderous boom that had shaken the harbour minutes earlier. Nobody noticed. Only later, when a rescue crew boarded the *Mosel*, was an anguished moaning heard emanating from the cabin. Breaking down the locked door, the rescuers found the balding and bloodied Thomas unconscious on the floor, presumably injured in the explosion. Yet his cabin had been locked from the inside. An inspection of the room revealed a revolver with four bullets in its chamber lodged under the couch. The strange passenger had fired twice into his head, one shot tearing through his cheek and embedding itself in his right cortex. Paralyzed on his left side, he was like a beached whale helplessly awaiting death. The medics rolled him onto a stretcher and struggled to carry him to the harbour barrack. There they laid him alongside the scores of debilitated and dying passengers.

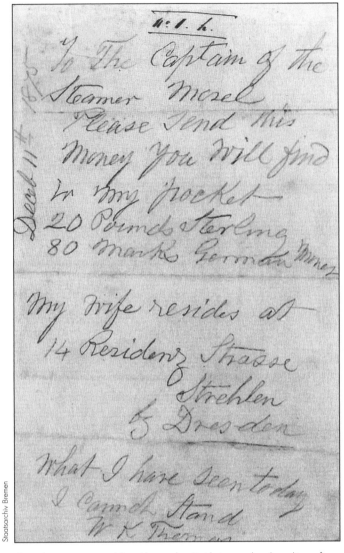

Staatsarchiv Bremen

Suicide note penned by Alexander Keith Jr., under the alias of W.K. Thomas.

Little did they know that the man they had strained their backs to save was the cause of all this anguish. Thomas's botched suicide was merely an echo of his greater foible: an elaborate time bomb, inadvertently triggered too soon. He had concealed the device in a wooden barrel, much the same way he masked his true identity. In time, the corpulent package that was W.K. Thomas would also be destroyed, and the villainous Alexander Keith Jr. would return to the public conscience, not just as a Confederate spy and con man, but as the worst mass murderer of the nineteenth century.

THE NEFARIOUS NEPHEW

Since the opening of his Nova Scotia brewery in 1820, Canadians have associated the name Alexander Keith with the comforting flavour of hops and malt — widely regarded as a top-shelf India Pale Ale by laymen, and a poor imitation by connoisseurs. In 1817, twenty-two-year-old Alexander Keith Sr. immigrated to Halifax from Scotland. Within two decades, he had established himself as the most powerful and industrious man in the city. Apart from owning what would become one of North America's oldest breweries, Keith was also elected mayor on three occasions, served for thirty years as a member of the legislative council, and acted as Provincial Grand Master of the Maritimes for the Freemasons. Unfortunately, his nephew and namesake, Alexander "Sandy" Keith Jr., shared his uncle's ambition but lacked his work ethic and delight in public service. Sandy, thus called for his red-tinged hair, was born in Halkirk, Scotland, on November 13, 1827. With the economic downturn of the early 1830s, his father, John Keith, took his wife and three children on a gruelling six-week ship voyage to join John's wealthy brother Alexander in Halifax. Sandy first set foot on Canadian soil at the age of nine. In 1838, John Keith decided to place himself in direct competition with his older brother, opening the Caledonia Brewery, an unimpressive wooden building on Lower Water Street. John's aspirations were bold, but in reality, he stood little chance against Alexander's clout. Perhaps the first indication of young Sandy's Machiavellian leanings was his decision to forsake his struggling father and work in a clerical position for his successful uncle. To add further insult, Sandy added "the Younger" to his name, in an effort to pass himself off as his uncle's son. Later, as he grew older and more rotund, he would actually assume "the Elder's" identity when it suited him.

Knowing that his cousin Donald was heir to the Keith dynasty, the avaricious Sandy sought to gain his fortune any way he could. Initially he tried his hand at forgery, but by the age of twenty-nine he had switched to

Staatsarchiv Bremen

A young Alexander Keith Jr. posing, circa 1865.

what would become his standard modus operandi: money scams involving fire. In 1834, Sandy was suspected of throwing a muslin bag drenched in turpentine and stuffed with wood shavings, charcoal, cotton, and wadding through the window of a warehouse he had insured. Though the crude contraption did little more than scorch the floor, had it ignited, the residents of the boarding house upstairs would have been roasted alive.

Sandy's first foray into bombing on August 14, 1857, was marked by a meteor shower — a grim omen of the fires to come. Shortly after midnight, the merchants' powder magazine, containing the whole stock of gunpowder in Halifax, exploded, destroying five houses in the city's poverty-stricken north suburb. The government magazine and barracks were similarly devastated, along with several houses, causing an estimated $100,000 in damages. One man was killed in the blast and fifteen others wounded. The town's alderman concluded that a stray meteor must have struck the building, but his theory was soon disproved when a farmer in a nearby field happened upon a stone from the barracks embedded ten inches into the dirt. The projectile was caked in gunpowder and wax with a three-inch wick protruding from it. Investigators concluded that an unknown rogue had carefully crept into the magazine and placed a candle with a lengthy wick inside. After igniting it, the intruder would have had sufficient time to flee before the explosion tore the neighbourhood to shreds.

If not for his social connections, Sandy Keith would likely have been charged with the crime. At the time, he was working as a civil engineering agent, and frequently visited the magazine. Coincidentally, the magazine keeper, Samuel Marshall, had been bedridden with illness for six weeks leading up to the explosion and had entrusted the only key to him. Sandy also had a motive. His uncle, Alexander Keith, had poorly organized and invested in the construction of a railroad running west from Halifax to Windsor, Ontario. Foolishly, he had employed Sandy to manage his contractors, all of whom needed access to gunpowder. His nefarious nephew was charged with transporting it by wagon from the magazine to the railroad lines, where he would supposedly sell it at twenty-five cents a pound. However, railway investors suspected Sandy was purchasing the powder at half price from other contractors so that he could retail it at the regular price and pocket twelve and a half cents from every sale. The destruction of the Halifax merchants' powder magazine had conveniently obliterated all evidence of the surplus gunpowder that Sandy claimed to have sold. The few merchants who dared insinuate that Sandy was responsible for the explosion and demanded financial compensation for their losses were quietly paid off by the Keith family. In Alexander Keith's Halifax, saving face was more important than seeking justice for the man his nephew had murdered and the scores of working-class Haligonians he had left crippled and destitute. Sandy seems to have taken the lesson to heart: little people — the poor, the enslaved, even the bourgeoisie — were disposable. Life was war, and only the ruthless became rich and powerful.

AN EVIL EXISTENCE

Leading up to the explosion of the *Mosel*, Alexander Keith Jr.'s legacy of crimes and inhumane acts is enough to fill an encyclopedia. Halifax had long prospered as a midway point between southern cotton plantations and British textile mills, so when the American Civil War broke out in 1861, it was in the interest of most Haligonians to support the Confederacy. Sandy Keith, a notorious racist and opportunist, went a step further, aiding and abetting blockade runners and pirates. He opened the Halifax Hotel to house them while they were in port, and spent many an evening puffing cigars and clinking champagne glasses with fine southern gentlemen, whose style and attitudes he learned to emulate perfectly. Sandy also collaborated with Confederate agents on (usually botched) terrorist attacks launched from Canada, including one particularly vile plan to send clothing infected with yellow fever to Yankee cities. Considering that the disease was spread by mosquitos, the operation was doomed to failure. If we are to measure a man by his intent rather than his success, it is clear that Alexander Keith Jr. had no compunction about using biological warfare on civilian populations.

When his father died in July 1863, Sandy left his uncle's employment. A variety of reasons for his departure have been given: Alexander Keith Sr. pressuring him to marry his spinster cousin; Keith Sr.'s support for the American federal army; disagreements with his uncle's business manager; and most likely, his constant shaming of the Keith family name with his sordid reputation. Ideology and loyalty always came second to profit on Sandy's list of priorities, and it wasn't uncommon for him to charge his Confederate allies top dollar for goods only to fill ships bound for Dixie with spoiled food stuffs. In fact, such was his selfish duplicity that he took to sleeping with a revolver under his pillow, lest one of the countless men he had swindled come seeking revenge.

One of Keith's favourite cons became insuring goods to be transported by vehicle, then manipulating events so that they would be lost or destroyed, and making a fortune in compensation. Confederate blockade-runner John Smoot groomed Keith for a smuggling operation in which Keith would purchase two train engines in Philadelphia for $85,000, then sneak them past Yankee customs officials into Dixie, where Smoot could use them to transport cotton from Virginia to the ocean. It would have been a lucrative enterprise for Smoot, but Keith twisted the southerner's trust to his own advantage. Under the identity of A.K. Thompson, he travelled to Philly, and on July 7, 1864, ordered the engines from the Norris Works company for $25,000. However, he had convinced the Petersburg Steamship Company and George Lang's quarrying business to also invest $20,000 and $40,000 respectively in the same engines. By mid-August they were ready, and, under the surveillance of customs agents, placed on a ship bound for Halifax. But instead of honouring his word, Keith informed the War Department that the engines were actually heading south, and they were seized. Keith returned to his investors with a sob story about how the authorities in Philadelphia had learned he was an infamous Confederate agent and taken the contraband. Having no idea that three separate entities had entrusted him with money to purchase them, the individual investors reluctantly shrugged off their financial loss as a casualty of war, and Sandy Keith came out of the situation with a $60,000 profit. Eventually, all three investors would learn they had been duped, but only Luther Smoot swore vengeance and meant it.

In August 1864, Confederate disbursing agent Major Norman Walker gave Keith $40,000 to purchase pork from New York to be distributed to starving southerners. Keith returned with only sixty pounds of meat, blaming customs agents for confiscating the rest. He pretended to become embroiled in a legal battle to win back his client's pork, keeping Walker's money under the auspices of paying for his lawsuit. Eventually the wealthy Walker resigned himself to defeat, and Sandy Keith pocketed the money once again.

Around 1864, Keith's modus operandi seems to have evolved further, switching from seeking compensation for lost cargo to sunken ships. That year, he tricked South Carolina dry-goods merchant H.W. Kinsman into entrusting him with the ownership papers for his ship, the *Caledonia*, which had sunk off the coast of Nova Scotia en route to Nassau. Keith collected the $32,000 in insurance, passing himself off as the true owner. Kinsman was furious, but without the paperwork to back his claim, he was legally impotent. The next to fall prey to Keith's insatiable greed was his associate, Montreal businessman Patrick Martin, who was known to dabble in the blockade-running racket. Martin was an associate of the reputed southern actor, and later presidential assassin, John Wilkes Booth. As part of an elaborate scheme to kidnap Abraham Lincoln, Martin had promised Booth he would ship his wardrobe past the Union blockade to the south. Along came good old Sandy, who convinced Martin of the benefits of heavily insuring both the vessels and cargo — sound advice which he took, even allowing Sandy to make the arrangements on his behalf. True to form, Martin passed the papers into Sandy's trust along with power of attorney in case of his untimely demise. The fat Haligonian then had another great idea for his gullible friend: Martin should sail one of the two schooners to Dixie himself! The fact that it was November, a particularly dangerous time to sail, replete with whiteouts and freezing gales, did not seem to register with Martin, though his family begged him to reconsider. His first vessel, the *Marie Victoria*, was shipwrecked near Bic before even leaving the St. Lawrence. Though the crew swam to safety, Booth's theatrical costumes sank into its murky depths, much like his dreams of a Confederate state. Patrick Martin disappeared with his flagship, never to be seen again. Sandy received $100,000 in insurance payouts, and refused to give his colleague's widow one red cent, plunging her into poverty.

With the American Civil War drawing to a close, Sandy took the opportunity to swindle as many of his Haligonian friends as he could, before sneaking across the border to eventually settle under the alias "A.K. Thompson" in New York City. He brought his lover Mary Clifton, a former chambermaid at the Halifax Hotel, with him, and the two enjoyed a life of luxury. However, Sandy was as blundering at legitimate business ventures as he was deft in illicit ones, and he soon lost $100,000 on the stock market. Having made enemies practically all over North America, he became a nervous wreck, obsessing over the notion that they would come seeking their revenge. New York City may have been colossal, but many of his foes had connections there. He told Mary that he was leaving for St. Louis, Missouri, and would soon send for her. Of course, that was the last she ever saw of him. After discovering she was pregnant, she was forced back to the role of lowly chambermaid in order to buy her passage back to Halifax. There she gave birth to Sandy's twins, and later attempted to commit suicide.

A.K. Thompson, as Sandy Keith now liked to be known, stepped off the train in St. Louis in January of 1865, and booked a room in the Southern Hotel. He wasn't long there before detectives and other men out for his head began showing up in the city. Sandy decided that unless he wanted a knife in his back, he would have to not only avoid the lavishness of city life, but relocate far away from the railroad. His solution was to move to the middle of nowhere, or more specifically Highland, Illinois: a bucolic community accessible only by coach, which harboured a large Swiss population. He arrived in the spring of 1865 and checked in for a long-term stay at the Highland House. Living off his immense wealth and enjoying what luxury he could in this remote location, Sandy began taking German lessons. While socializing one night in a beer garden, he was introduced to a dark French beauty by the name of Cecelia Paris. The twenty-year-old was a cultured milliner, fluent in several languages, with immaculate taste and manners. Though Sandy had always aspired to move seamlessly among the elite, he had never shed the crassness of his brewer's roots, and saw Cecelia as his chance at a more refined existence. He won her spendthrift heart instantly, flashing $75,000 in bonds. The two courted briefly before marrying in the summer. Amazingly, their union seems to have been a happy one for a time. Sandy, who was in the habit of waking up terrified of assassins by his bed, reluctantly confided in Cecelia that he had been involved in blockade running. Yet everything else he told his new bride was either a lie or gross distortion. To our knowledge, she never learned his true identity.

Things took a turn for the worse in the days before Christmas, when the couple were awakened at night by an unexpected knocking on their door. Dressed only in his nightclothes, Sandy opened it to discover Luther Smoot along with a U.S. marshal with a warrant for his arrest. Smoot had finally tracked his old nemesis through Mary Clifton, from whom he had learned that Sandy had absconded to St. Louis. Without uttering a word of explanation to Cecelia, Sandy allowed himself to be taken to St. Louis, where he was imprisoned in the local jail. While in the city, Smoot tried to convince an unlikely friend, General William Tecumseh Sherman, to have federal troops intimidate Sandy into reimbursing him. Sherman replied that he could not oblige his friend. Frustrated, Smoot finally reached a grudging compromise with Keith: Sandy would give him $10,000 in bonds in return for his freedom. Sandy was loosed from his cage in 1866, and travelled with Smoot to the local bank, where he handed him the bonds. Before he left, Smoot sternly admonished Sandy to repay his creditors or there would be further trouble down the road. Specifically, he mentioned the name H.W. Kinsman, and warned Sandy that he would not cover for him.

When Sandy returned to the distraught Cecelia at Highland House ten days after his arrest, he was a nervous wreck. He informed her that he was being hunted by bad men, and that they had to leave for New York. On January 13, 1866, the "Thompsons" watched from the deck of the *Hermann* as the American coast grew smaller and smaller, until it was swallowed by the horizon. Sandy was about to put his German to good use.

THE DARLINGS OF DRESDEN

Twelve days later, the Thompsons landed in the Germanic port of Bremerhaven, and travelled by train to the historic city of Dresden in Saxony. Here, Sandy altered his alias to William King Thompson, and he and Cecelia adopted the guise of a southern gentleman and his New Orleanian belle. Through his dealings with Confederate bluebloods in Halifax, Sandy had learned to emulate their accents, style, and cultural airs surprisingly well, even compiling their personal stories into a fake biography for himself. With $45,000 — roughly $1 million in today's currency — still in their possession, coupled with the romanticized image of the southern plantation owner, the well-to-do Thompsons mixed easily with European aristocrats and wealthy American ex-pats alike. They joined the exclusive American Club, where Sandy enjoyed all of the pleasantries he had become accustomed to over his life: brandy, cigars, euchre, and nepotism. He and Cecelia hosted teas and threw extravagant parties, cementing their high-society status in Dresden and the surrounding area. Things were going so well that in 1868 the couple started a family, producing Blanche, William, and Klina within four years. Given Sandy's ineptitude in legitimate business, their extravagance would not last forever. Had either he or

Cecelia opted to live more frugally, they might have enjoyed a comfortable life in Dresden until their deaths. Yet they chose opulence and admiration over common sense, and by the end of 1872, Sandy had a meagre $2,500 in his bank account. Defaulting to his criminal ways, he decided that the solution was to blow up a steamer to collect the insurance money. To do so, he would need a special kind of time bomb.

Sandy approached one of the finest clockwork engineers in Europe, J.J. Fuchs of Bernberg, to inquire whether it was possible to build a spring-loaded device capable of running silently for ten days before releasing a lever. Though Thompson would provide no details of his intended use for the mechanism, Fuchs nevertheless accepted the challenge. However, secretly he questioned Thompson's seriousness and, as a result, put the project on the backburner, eventually forgetting about it. Meanwhile, Sandy and Cecelia had been forced to move into a new home, which they dubbed Villa Thomas — a dwelling so inferior to their previous one that they struggled to find servants to work for them. It was 1863, and the holdings in Sandy Keith's bank account now stood at $1,600. He pleaded with Cecelia to rein in her spending, but she laughed at his attempts. One day, when he received an astronomical milliner's bill, he flew into a rage and beat her. Cecelia took to bed, refusing to speak with him. Desperate, Sandy approached two Viennese clockworkers with his idea, but after several attempts to construct the mechanism they were unable to produce a lever that struck with the necessary force. Reluctantly, Sandy returned to Fuchs's workshop with the thirty-pound Viennese prototype and informed the clockmaker that he required a similar, more forceful device that would release a lever after twelve days and stay intact even while in motion. Unaware that he was about to be an accomplice to the worst mass murder of the nineteenth century, Fuchs fashioned the mechanism to perfection.

Soon after, Sandy Keith procured some dynamite, and headed to Bremerhaven. There he decided upon a target — the *Mosel* — scheduled to sail from Bremerhaven to Southampton, England, before continuing on to New York. Sandy booked passage on the vessel as W.K. Thomas, and attempted to insure twenty-seven chests to be loaded onboard, reneging after learning that the premium was too high. In the end, he settled for 3,000 marks (the equivalent of £150) for a barrel of caviar. His plan was to sail with the *Mosel* to Southampton, disembark, and return to Dresden,

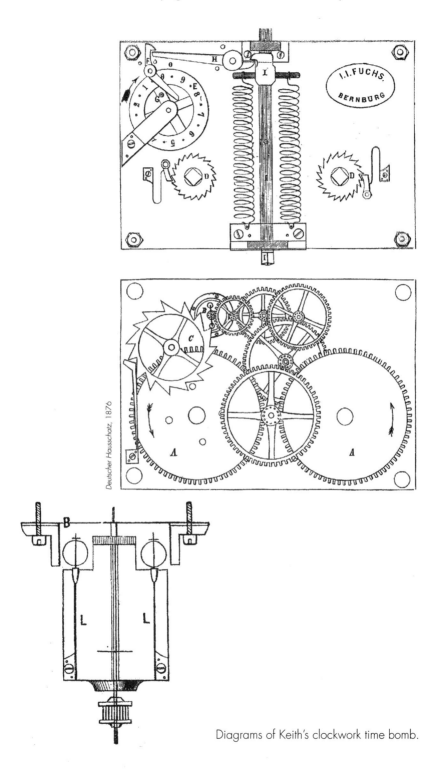

Deutscher Hausschatz, 1876

Diagrams of Keith's clockwork time bomb.

where he would await the news that the steamer had been lost at sea, and collect his insurance money. He had become so greedy and callous that he was now willing to sacrifice the lives of hundreds of people to gain a mere £150 and to see whether his "infernal machine" actually worked.

On December 11, he presented his passport and went to his first-class cabin on the *Mosel*. Less than an hour later, eighty-one people were dead, and Sandy attempted to join them by shooting himself. Unfortunately for Sandy Keith, he wouldn't get off that easily.

AFTER THE *MOSEL*

Alexander "Sandy" Keith Jr. made two catastrophic mistakes on December 11, 1875: prematurely blowing up the *Mosel*, and failing to competently blow off his own head with a pistol. For rather than escaping into the unknowing bliss of death, he awoke to find himself in a makeshift hospital, surrounded by the agonized moans of his victims. Having suffered neurological damage, he had lost all feeling on the left side of his body,

Nineteenth-century illustration of the steamer Mosel in harbour, immediately before its explosion.

Deutscher Hausschatz, 1876

and his faulty eyes now saw the world in a permanent blur. Suspicious, the doctors began questioning him about the reasons for his attempted suicide. Yet the bullet had not eliminated his tremendous capacity to deceive, for that lay at the very foundation of the man's character. Therefore Sandy competently maintained the guise of W.K. Thomas, lying that he had shot himself because he could not bear to be bankrupt. In a vain attempt to appeal to his conscience, the incredulous doctors notified him that he was dying and had only limited time to confess. When that didn't work, police interrogators soon arrived, and used wine to loosen his tongue. They brought along two ace cards: the insurance broker, and one of the clockmakers, a man called Bruns. Nevertheless, Sandy's poker face never faltered. Chief Inspector P.J. Schnepel then reminded Keith about the precarious future of his children, and something inside his cold heart stirred. He began a confession of sorts, laden with lies and half-truths. He told them that he was really a German-born blockade runner raised in Virginia, and went by the name of William King Thomson. To escape his sordid past, he had adopted W.K. Thomas as a pseudonym. He blamed the explosion on a broker named Skidmore — a man who had shipped the barrel containing the time bomb to him along the Rhine. Though that was indeed true, Sandy attempted to paint himself as Skidmore's unknowing accomplice. He added that he felt no remorse and wasn't a bad man, which, given his bogus story and suicide note, is difficult to understand.

Four days after his botched suicide, Sandy was caught trying to peel away his bandages in the hope of bleeding out, rather than admitting the truth. That it was he whose power over life and death now rested firmly in the hands of others is poetic justice. The doctors had no intention of letting him croak before he fessed up. Increasingly, journalists and rubberneckers gathered around the dying man to hear his incoherent and incongruent accounts of the bombing. Given the testimonies of the insurance broker and three clockmakers, the only person Sandy Keith was fooling was himself. The media had already deemed him guilty, labelling him the Dynamite Fiend, as many attributed his crimes to demonic possession. Newspapers across Europe and North America ran article after article, expounding theories of his criminality, analyzing the mechanical efficiency of his time bomb, and decrying the immorality of this new scientific age that would surely bring the world to ruin.

Alexander Keith Jr. after death.

Eventually, investigators at Bremerhaven learned the identity and whereabouts of Sandy's wife. As Cecelia languished in Villa Thomas, distressed over Sandy's disappearance, she received a visit from a detective who informed her that her husband had attempted to take his own life. He escorted Cecelia to Bremen by train. Upon arriving, she was told of Sandy's involvement in the explosion. As she struggled to digest this information, local investigators launched into a full-scale interrogation. At some point during the questioning, Cecelia stumbled and referred to her husband as Alexander. Realizing her slip, she demanded to speak with John Steuart, the American consul in Leipzig and a close personal friend. Sensing a change in the tide, the investigators switched tactics, offering to take Cecelia to Bremerhaven to see her dying husband. There were two stipulations: police officers were required to be present, and any conversation between the couple had to be in German. By the time they permitted Cecelia to visit her husband, Sandy was lingering at death's door. Observing his wretched state, Cecelia begged the doctor to kill him. She pleaded with her husband to repent so that one day they would be reunited in heaven, but Sandy remained defiant. When she left him, he was barely alive. It is fitting that, having lived his whole life in deceit, the last words to escape his lips were lies: "I have been a thick-head. The fellows in New York are guilty."

Despite his efforts to maintain the facade of W.K. Thomson until his dying breath, Sandy's elaborate deception inevitably came unravelled when world-renowned detective Allan Pinkerton was hired onto the case. In early 1876, he sent a report to Detective Schnepel containing a wealth of evidence indicating that the mysterious W.K. Thomas was in fact Alexander Keith Jr., the nephew of a famous Canadian brewer. Satisfied, Schnepel gladly paid Pinkerton's fee of $642.42, and at long last revealed the identity of the Dynamite Fiend to excited newspapermen across the globe. With his body buried in a pauper's grave and his name quickly fading from the headlines, all that remained of Alexander Keith Jr. was his head — severed from his body post-mortem. From the breweries of Halifax to preservation in a large bottle of alcohol, Sandy had come full circle. In a final ironic twist, his head was obliterated during an Allied bombing of Bremen in the Second World War. The distant, mechanized methods of destruction Sandy had ushered in to make him a "somebody" were the same weapons that erased all trace of his corpse. Among numerous other crimes, he is also suspected of sabotaging Patrick Martin's ships bound from Montreal, as well as the lost *City of Boston* in 1870. Though never convicted of homicide, in all likelihood Alexander Keith Jr. was the worst permutation of predator: a serial mass murderer.

PART B

PERSONALITY DISORDERS

Following an incidence of multiple murder, the general public invariably asks, "Why?" How could somebody ruin the lives of so many innocent people with such callous disregard? Our political leaders throw up their hands in apparent frustration, labelling the murders "senseless" and beyond our collective understanding. Whether their words are sincere or a dubious attempt to feign identification with the average Joe, the fact is that over the past two hundred years, criminologists and mental health experts have uncovered a plurality of explanations for these heinous acts. The stories contained here will examine just some of the mental disorders found among criminals who have been convicted of multiple murders. Among them are narcissistic and anti-social personality disorders as well as psychopathy.

The fallout from the December 14, 2012 massacre at Sandy Hook Elementary School necessitates a clarification before we dive in.

Compounding this recent tragedy, the American news media placed undue emphasis on the fact that gunman Adam Lanza suffered from Asperger's Syndrome. The resulting stigmatization of this condition prompted the Autistic Self Advocacy Network to issue a statement clarifying that the mentally disabled were "no more likely to commit violent crime than non-disabled people." For the most part, this is true; in fact they are statistically more likely to become victims. Unfortunately, we cannot say the same about narcissists, antisocial personalities, and psychopaths. To quote the forensic psychiatrist Dr. Michael Stone:

> Certain personality disorders are distinctly over-represented in the annals of violent crime. Besides narcissistic personality or traits thereof — which underlie almost all types of violent crime, antisocial, psychopathic, sadistic, paranoid and explosive-irritable types are particularly common in this realm.[*]

Nevertheless, it is crucial to understand that the majority of people diagnosed with these conditions *do not go on to kill*. The presence of one of these personality disorders simply elevates the likelihood that violence will occur. Human beings are too complex for there to be a single explanation for our behaviour. This does not mean that rampage slayings are incomprehensible, merely complicated. By learning the basics of the three personality disorders commonly found in multiple murderers, we begin to take small steps toward a greater understanding. For an example of a Canadian mass murderer suffering from paranoid personality disorder, please consult the case of **Pierre Lebrun** (Chapter 10).

Caution: Though well-versed in the subject matter, the author is not a trained mental-health professional, and is theoretically unqualified to make a formal diagnosis. Please keep this in mind when reading the following assessments.

---

[*] Michael H. Stone, "Violent Crimes and Their Relationships to Personality Disorders" in *Personality and Mental Health* 2 (2007), 150.

CHAPTER 4

NARCISSISTS, ANTI-SOCIAL PERSONALITIES, AND PSYCHOPATHS

Andre Kirchoff

Valery Fabrikant

"I know how people get what they want. They shoot a lot of people."

Victims: 4 killed/1 wounded
Duration of rampage: August 24, 1992 (mass murder)
Location: Montreal, Quebec
Weapons: Snub-nosed Smith & Wesson .38-calibre pistol, semi-automatic Meb pistol, semi-automatic Bersa pistol

SELF-ENTITLEMENT

On a cold December day in 1979, a diminutive balding man shuffled into the Department of Mechanical Engineering at Montreal's Concordia University. In a deep Slavic monotone, he introduced himself as Valery Fabrikant, and asked to see the chair of the department about applying for a position. Though he was undeniably awkward, behind the lenses of his Coke-bottle glasses his eyes showed a cold intelligence. When Fabrikant was informed that it was university policy to not conduct job interviews without first scheduling an appointment or checking the applicant's background, he returned every day until the chair of mechanical engineering finally agreed to speak with him. Sitting down with T.S. Sankar, a specialist in solid mechanics, Fabrikant explained that he was a Jewish dissident from Minsk who had fled the Soviet Union, where he had once been an associate professor and the author of numerous scientific publications. Furthermore, he had been once been a student of a scientist whom Sankar profoundly respected. By the end of the interview, Sankar was impressed enough to offer Fabrikant a $7,000-per-year position as his research assistant. He began work on December 20, 1979. If Sankar had bothered to check the thirty-nine-year-old applicant's credentials or references, he might have thought twice about hiring him. Though Fabrikant's record in academia was exceptional, he had lied about being a political refugee. Instead, the enigmatic doctor had been fired from numerous positions in the U.S.S.R. due to severe behavioural misconduct.

Shortly after obtaining his position at Concordia, Fabrikant became embittered that the Soviet Union was dragging its feet in sending him a few thousand dollars he had inherited from his late father. In response, he sent a letter to the Canadian Ministry of External Affairs calling for the immediate suspension of grain exports to the U.S.S.R. Here was a man who seriously believed that he could single-handedly disrupt trade between Canada and the Soviet Union in order to hasten the transfer of his inheritance. This was merely the beginning of Valery Fabrikant's deadly delusions.

When his application was shot down by the University of Calgary in 1981, he travelled to an academic conference solely to belittle the professor who had signed his rejection letter. Fabrikant also wrote angry dismissals to the editors of academic journals who, according to standard practice, had questioned his "ingenious" work. Dr. Sankar received several complaints regarding his colleague's bizarre behaviour, but ignored them, viewing the world of academia as a necessary haven for brilliant eccentrics. Furthermore, Fabrikant had published a total of twenty-five papers in less than four years — more than double the standard output for his field. As chair of the department, Sankar appeared as co-author on every one. Perhaps this is why he used the department's research grants to fund the created position of research associate for Fabrikant in 1980, increasing his annual salary to $12,000; then the $23,250-per-year "research assistant professor" in 1982. In Sankar's eyes, his inclusion as a co-author on Fabrikant's publications was simply a standard way for his colleague to repay his generosity. For the narcissistic Fabrikant, it was "academic prostitution."

ARROGANT, HAUGHTY BEHAVIOUR

In 1982, through mutual friends in Brooklyn, Fabrikant met and married a fellow Slav, Maya Tyker, with whom he would father two children. In his new role as research assistant professor, he was teaching a probability and statistics class, even though he had failed to provide his mandatory three letters of reference. On the surface, Fabrikant's life was improving, yet his aggressive behaviour only worsened. Students and co-workers alike were taken aback by his constant aggression. One female student even came forward with allegations that he had violently raped her, dislocating her shoulder in the process. Terrified of him, she persuaded the ombudsperson not to disclose the information. The matter was never pursued any further.

In early 1983, Fabrikant began attending a non-credit French class, but took an immediate dislike to the instructor. He routinely disrupted the class to complain about her smoking, teaching methods, and manner of speaking the language. So rude and frequent were his interruptions that the instructor warned her supervisor that she would quit unless action was taken. Fabrikant was subsequently informed, both verbally and in writing, that he could no longer attend the class. Predictably, he showed up anyway, read the supervisor's note aloud, ripped it to pieces, and sat through the lesson in open defiance. When an official higher up on Concordia's food chain issued a warning, he complied, insisting that the university give him $1,000 to pay for classes at another institution. After months of hemming and hawing, the administration finally refused.

Fabrikant was incensed. His arrogance was now beginning to affect his professional capacity for upward mobility. Dr. Sankar recommended that Fabrikant be given the position of research associate professor, but the vice-rector academic, John Daniel, expressed grave concerns. Seemingly oblivious to his colleague's severe emotional problems, Sankar wrote to Daniel in protest, citing Fabrikant's "truly outstanding" publication history: "I was always under the impression that we took decisions on promotions, reappointments and salary ... increases purely on the basis of scholarly achievements and academic excellence rather than on the individual's behaviour.... I hope my understanding is still valid."[35] With the promise of a major breakthrough impending, Daniel acquiesced, and the insidious Dr. Fabrikant scuttled up the ranks once more.

When the university's mechanical engineering program invented CONCAVE — the Concordia Computer-Aided Vehicle Engineering Centre — in 1985, Fabrikant was hired on as a research associate professor at $30,000 per year under the direction of Tom Sankar's brother, Sheshadri. Secure in his employment for the first time, Fabrikant now included only his own name on his papers unless he deemed that someone else had made a significant academic contribution.

Two years later, Tom Sankar was no longer the chair of the mechanical engineering department owing to some "discrepancies" in his bookkeeping. Nevertheless, he retained a position as professor at the university. When, in 1988, Fabrikant's position at CONCAVE came up for review, he was confident that his eight years of service to the university would be rewarded. Contrary to his expectations, Fabrikant learned from Sheshadri Sankar that the university would be renewing his contract for one more year, after which he would be made redundant. The forty-eight-year-old father of two was utterly devastated. Fabrikant decided he had been let go simply because he had ceased including his colleagues' names on his publications. In order to prove this, he clandestinely tape-recorded conversations with fellow academics, including Tom Sankar himself. Fabrikant demanded details of the scientific contribution the former chair had made to their co-authored paper, *On the Method of Fabrikant, Sankar and Swamy*. Sankar answered that they had "discussed" some of the ideas in the publication.

"Discussion is not a contribution," Fabrikant replied. "Contribution is contribution." He then asserted that Sankar had made no contribution to thirty-three additional essays, and asked Sankar whether he agreed. Rather than address the question directly, Sankar claimed that he had never requested that his name appear on any of the writings, saying that Fabrikant had listed him as a co-author of his own volition. These secretly taped discussions were merely the first battle in the Belarusian's one-man war against the department. Behind closed doors, school administrators desperately discussed ways to deal with the hostile force that had infiltrated their mechanical engineering department, and even solicited a psychiatrist for guidance. In the meantime, Sheshadri Sankar attempted to placate Fabrikant by granting him a contract to work at CONCAVE for another two years. It was the wrong move. The more they submitted to his bullying, the more Fabrikant saw intimidation and manipulation as weapons to be employed whenever he didn't get his way. Worse, now the university was stuck with him until 1990, and he was hell-bent on seeking tenure. Rather than being mollified, Fabrikant escalated the nature of his verbal threats from legal action to violence.

"I know how people get what they want," he once told Catherine MacKenzie, the executive assistant to rector Patrick Kenniff. "They shoot a lot of people." She informed the university's conflict resolution specialist, Grendon Haines, who spoke with Fabrikant on several occasions. Fabrikant indicated that he owned a gun and was planning to take Kenniff hostage and shoot several people, including the hated Sankar brothers. Soon after, Fabrikant was put under private surveillance, while bodyguards were stationed around the Kenniff home. When consulted by the university, psychiatrist Warren Steiner advised them that Fabrikant's behaviour was clearly indicative of a personality disorder. Steiner admonished Concordia to inform Fabrikant in writing that he had gone too far and required professional help. Furthermore, the professor's campaign of intimidation could no longer be tolerated. Fabrikant never received the letter; rather, they rewarded his aggression with salary increases, and by the end of December 1989 he was earning $54,430 annually. He began looking into the possibility of obtaining a tenure-track position. While visiting the department chair,

Sam Osman, Fabrikant positioned his fingers as if firing a gun and explained that if he did not get on the tenure track he might choose to deal with it "the American way." Osman assured him he would do his best. He was so used to Fabrikant's grandstanding that he took these threats with a grain of salt.

In February of the following year, a committee for the mechanical engineering department reviewed Fabrikant's many publications, student evaluations, grant records, and supervision of graduate students, and recommended that he be promoted to the position of research associate professor. Letters of support for his work poured in from mechanical elasticity experts, claiming he was among the world's top ten researchers in the field. Despite the department's unanimous approval, the administration shot down Fabrikant's promotion because the rank of research associate professor did not formally exist. It didn't help that Rose Sheinin, Concordia's newly appointed vice-rector academic, had been threatened by Fabrikant a month earlier. Nevertheless, in September, Osman submitted Fabrikant's name for one of three new tenure-track positions, which the committee approved. He was now an associate professor on a two-year probation. There was no mention of his habitual antagonism.

Unsurprisingly, by 1991 Fabrikant was back to his old habits. Some co-workers installed panic buttons in their offices and secured the doors with extra deadbolts. Rose Sheinin was chilled one night to hear his voice on her home answer machine warning, "You know who I am and you know what is going to happen." Unlike other faculty members, however, Sheinin was not about to bow to Fabrikant's will. She consulted Concordia's legal counsel to learn about the process of firing a non-tenured professor, and learned that if his actions continued after two clearly worded written warnings, he could be dismissed. Sheinin had also met with Dr. Steiner, who reiterated that Fabrikant suffered from a personality disorder and needed to be shown boundaries. Steiner added that Fabrikant's aggressive behaviour would continue because it had worked in his favour, though he doubted the professor would resort to violence. Rose Sheinin did what no other staff member had dared to do: she wrote Valery Fabrikant a letter of condemnation:

> [T]he frequency of [your] telephone calls, the tone which you use, your warnings that you intend to tape record … conversations, etc., are totally unacceptable. The veiled threats conveyed through my staff and through Grendon Haines must stop immediately [or] I will be left with no alternative than to seek protection through the University's policies concerning discipline.[36]

Fabrikant replied with a half-hearted apology through Grendon Haines, denouncing his own behaviour. Sheinin wasn't so easily fooled. From now on, she informed the senior faculty of the mechanical engineering department, they were to keep records of Fabrikant's unruliness. Furthermore, she asked them to drop their tenure-track recommendation. Amazingly, they refused to comply with her wishes. Osman suggested that giving Fabrikant a tenure-track position would "bring out the best in him."

A memo from Sheinin arrived on rector Patrick Kenniff's desk on November 16, 1990, stating:

> [Though] all members of faculty were adamant that Dr. Fabrikant was an asset … none of them wanted to work with or near him.… Whatever problems we have been presented with by Dr. Fabrikant will continue.… My gut feelings tell me that he should not be taken onto the full-time faculty.[37]

Kenniff didn't listen, and Sheinin explained that if they hired Fabrikant he was their problem. When she reluctantly drafted his two-year contract for $59,677 annually, Sheinin included a rider stating that Fabrikant would have to wait three years before being considered for tenure. In the autumn of 1991 there would be a review to see if the contract should be extended.

Rather than being made redundant, Fabrikant was given a merit increase in spring 1991 to reflect the quality of his research and teaching. Never satisfied, he promptly requested a four-month paid leave from Sam Osman so that he could pursue a $4,500-per-month fellowship in France. Predictably, he was denied. By July, Fabrikant claimed to have been offered a $10,000 grant from NASA to work on a project, and told Sheshadri Sankar that he would like to abandon CONCAVE for the time being. Apparently, contracts and laws were meaningless unless they worked to his benefit. An example of the latter occurred in October, when Fabrikant wrote Osman asking if he could buy his way out of being a teacher with his $7,000 research grant. Osman was aghast: both university and federal regulations expressly forbade it. He called Fabrikant and explained.

"Are you trying to scare me?" the voice on the other end of the phone croaked. "I am not scared. I wrote a letter and I want a written reply." Incensed, Osman did reply to him in writing, curtly stating that such requests were illegal. Furthermore, he demanded Fabrikant submit him a detailed report outlining his plans for teaching. Instead, Fabrikant insisted on an apology, claiming that Tom Sankar had allegedly purchased a leave from his teaching duties. He also flaunted his merit award as if it were indestructible armour, announcing that he would be spending his next year on sabbatical. Osman began to suspect there was something fishy about this enigmatic Belarusian, and requested proof of Fabrikant's academic qualifications.

"How can a scientist like YOU, ask a scientist like ME for proof of my credentials?" came Fabrikant's seething reply. The mechanical engineering department finally decided that enough was enough. Sixteen senior members assembled on October 25 and enthusiastically passed a motion for both the university and department to take action against Fabrikant. When, days later, they reconvened to discuss Fabrikant's history of hostility and whether it should affect the extension of his contract, they discovered him snooping outside the conference room, and had him removed by security guards. Considering his bizarre personal conduct and growing disinterest in working with the students, they voted against renewing his contract. They had finally done the right thing, but now Fabrikant's potential for violence hung over them like a guillotine.

GRANDIOSE SENSE OF SELF-IMPORTANCE
So deep-rooted were the fears of Fabrikant's retaliation that members of the committee held an emergency meeting with an intervention team on November 1 to discuss prevention. Eventually they concluded that a professor's "capacity to teach and carry out research activities" did not outweigh his interpersonal conduct, and the bellicose Belarusian should be suspended immediately from his position using emergency measures. This

recommendation was not acted upon. Later that day, Fabrikant entered a university senate meeting carrying an artist's portfolio under his arm. Remembering his threat to "solve things the American way," associate vice-rector Catherine MacKenzie became concerned that the portfolio could be concealing a gun. She quietly ordered security to call the authorities, and sat down next to Fabrikant to conduct the meeting. Officers from the Montreal police arrived to search him, only to discover he was unarmed. Fabrikant smiled. He played head games like Kasparov played chess.

Having learned about the plot to oust him from Concordia, Fabrikant wrote a letter to the dean, Srikanta Swamy, asking how his situation could have changed so drastically in seven months. Had he not been awarded the highest merit increase in the department? If his behaviour was so nefarious, why had nobody filed a formal complaint? Swamy had no answer for him.

The most baffling aspect of the Fabrikant affair was the lack of any record of his improprieties: the alleged rape, his harassment of the French instructor, his countless run-ins with the faculty and administration — nothing, zip, zero. This information should have been stored in the dean's office, but Swamy and the Faculty Personnel Committee found no paper trail whatsoever. Understandably, when faculty members began recounting the history of Valery Fabrikant's unruliness in November 1991 and asked for the non-renewal of his contract, the committee was completely taken aback. Without evidence of his poor conduct, Swamy and the committee voted against the department's recommendations, and renewed Fabrikant's contract for an extra year on four conditions: 1) he would teach advanced classes in mechanical engineering; 2) he would supervise more graduate students; 3) his research must fall in line with the goals of the department; and 4) he would conform to the predetermined course of the curriculum development.

Fabrikant would not allow a "genius" like himself to be bossed around. In February 1992, he began a concerted campaign of email harassment, accusing the faculty association of betraying him. He dismissed Rose Sheinin's warning that he was abusing the communication system by stating that there were no rules forbidding his activities. His emails, including transcripts of conversations he had secretly audiotaped, began flooding the inboxes of bewildered academics everywhere. Professors who had never even heard the name "Valery Fabrikant" were now drawn into his one-man war against his colleagues, whose alleged crimes ranged from conflict of interest to fraud. He repeatedly baited the university to take legal action against him. In one email, Fabrikant wrote, "I am no longer afraid of anything or anybody. We all have to die one day. Whenever I die, I shall die an honest person. I cannot fight all the crooks in the world, but I shall not rest until the bogus scientists in this university are exposed"[38]

That March, workplace violence expert Frema Engel advised the executive assistant to the rector that there was "reason to be concerned and I would take [Fabrikant's] behaviour very seriously.... The worst-case scenario is that he would act out his anger, become violent and either harm a member or members of the university or himself." The executive assistant would later testify that she forwarded this letter to Rose Sheinin — a claim that the vice-rector academic would dispute. In fact, Sheinin had mailed a letter to Fabrikant himself, reading, "You have made very serious allegations against members of the University community, thereby causing significant disturbance.... You shall ... immediately cease and desist from making these types of unsubstantiated allegations by any means." Fabrikant rebutted the warning via email, accusing Sheinin of breaching due process by not including a standard complaint from the dean. Sheinin responded by doing just that.

Valery Fabrikant's twisted behaviour had now seeped from the confines of academia into the local media. He was quoted in the *Montreal Gazette* as declaring that, after living in Canada for twelve years, he had not met a single honest Canadian. This wider exposure caused the alleged rape victim from 1982 to contact Sheinin and inform her that Fabrikant was capable of horrendous violence. Terrified, she refused to go on record, and died of a brain embolism two years later.

In early April, Tom Sankar and Srikanta Swamy received letters from Fabrikant threatening to sue them. Sankar's letter read:

> You are listed as co-author [of 35] publications of mine though your scientific contribution to them was zero.... I hereby request that you write ... letters of retraction that you did not make any   scientific contribution to those publications.... Failure to do so will result in a legal action against you.[39]

The worst employee in the history of mechanical engineering made good on his threats, filing lawsuits against both men. Tom Sankar was surely cursing the day he had warmly invited the pitiful little "dissident" into his office.

FANTASIES OF UNLIMITED POWER

At the end of the winter term, Sam Osman discovered that Fabrikant had artificially raised his students' grades by eight percent. By now, Fabrikant had become so consumed with his personal vendetta that he was nearly completely neglecting his academic pursuits. On June 23, he filed a request with Osman's secretary to carry a pistol on campus, which was understandably rejected. Fabrikant had likely never expected his wish to be granted, and wanted to scare people. Having learned of Fabrikant's sinister request, Sheinin and several other members of the administration wrote to Kenniff:

> [Valery Fabrikant] presents an immediate and continuing threat to members of the University community.... We suggest that he be suspended indefinitely and that he be forbidden to enter any University buildings until such time that the suspension is lifted. As a condition for reinstatement in the University, Dr. Fabrikant must be required to produce a statement from a psychiatrist (chosen by the University) attesting to his mental stability.[40]

Astonishingly, Kenniff refused to use his emergency powers, citing a lack of evidence of Fabrikant's misconduct. Later he claimed to have tried to contact the administrators to suggest an alternative course of action, but had learned that they had gone on holiday. Whatever the case, this breakdown in communication would prove to be deadly.

When Fabrikant sent out an email accusing two co-workers of being parasites, then followed up with lawsuits claiming they had forced him to name them as co-authors on his articles, the university administrators put their collective foot down. He was given a clear warning that if he did not restrain himself immediately, there would be consequences. To a narcissist of Fabrikant's calibre, this was like attempting to douse a fire with gasoline: the flames of his hatred roared to new heights. Little did he know that he was burning himself in the immolation.

When it became obvious that there was an unwillingness to terminate Fabrikant's position, the administration offered him the prospect of early retirement with two years' salary. The fifty-two-year-old responded by asking for ten. When they upped it to three he countered with thirteen. Obviously, there was no possibility of negotiating with Fabrikant. He thrived on confrontation. Instead, in August, the university went on the counterattack. After sending out defamatory emails directed at Quebec Supreme Court Justice Alan Gold, Fabrikant was charged with being in contempt of court, and ordered to stand trial on August 25. Lawsuits stung him like hornets, and he responded by filing more. To cap it off, he no longer had any support whatsoever from the faculty association. Instead, they had installed video cameras in the offices of the Concordia University Faculty Association to keep tabs on him.

Like fellow narcissistic bully Adolf Hitler, Fabrikant's ambitions of power and conquest had fallen short of his strategic abilities, and his nerves were beginning to suffer. In the week leading up to August 24, 1992, Fabrikant was bombarded with numerous threats and court orders. He received a second cautionary letter from Rose Sheinin on Wednesday, August 19, concerning his harassing emails. On August 21, Concordia's external legal counsel sent Fabrikant a formal notification that his job was at risk. Whether he saw the letter or not is unknown; however, that same day he ranted about his upcoming court hearing over email: "[V]ery soon I might be in jail for contempt of court. I have dared to say publicly that the court is lawless and corrupt. If you hear that I have committed suicide in jail or was a victim of an accident, do not believe [it]."[41] Meanwhile, Fabrikant's wife, Maya Tyker, obtained two pistols that same afternoon, entrusting them to her husband. She had purchased them through a catalogue, ostensibly to practise shooting at a local range. Ultimately, the targets they would be pointed at were flesh, blood, and bone.

LACKS EMPATHY

On Monday August 24, 1992, Valery Fabrikant made good on his threats. Just before 2:30 p.m., he strode into the Henry F. Hall Building dressed in sunglasses, a dark suit, and a white shirt and carrying a briefcase. Fabrikant took the escalator to the engineering department on the ninth floor and searched the vicinity for Sam Osman and Dean Swamy. Unable to locate them, he proceeded to his own office to await a scheduled visit from Michael Hogben. The fifty-three-year-old president of the CUFA arrived on time for their appointment, and was reaching to pass a letter to Fabrikant when the nutty professor produced a .38-calibre pistol. He fired three times, striking Hogben in the head, neck, and back, dropping him to the floor. Fabrikant switched the .38 for a German-made Meb 7.65-millimetre semi-automatic pistol, and then hid a Belgian Bersa 6.35-millimetre in his belt.

Hearing a male voice shout from nearby, Fabrikant stepped into the corridor to search for the source. He found his colleague Aaron Jaan Saber in his adjoining office, and shot the forty-six-year-old through his skull and side, causing fatal injuries. Exiting, he fired at sixty-six-year-old secretary Elizabeth Horwood as she fled, winging her thigh. Fabrikant made his way across the ninth floor to the office of Phovios Ziogas, chair of the electrical and computer engineering department. Ziogas, who was engaged in a conversation with Otto Schwelb, looked on in surprise as Fabrikant unleashed two bullets at him. One of them tore through Ziogas's abdomen, severing two major arteries and permanently damaging his kidney. As the injured Ziogas clung to Fabrikant, Schwelb grappled the gunman, disarming him. Fabrikant fled, and Schwelb immediately turned his attention to his wounded colleague. Ziogas would later die from his injuries.

Retrieving the Bersa from his belt, Valery Fabrikant set off for Srikanta Swamy's office. When civil engineering professor Matthew Douglass attempted to talk him out of it, the gunman reciprocated by blasting him four times through his head and raised hands, killing him. Finally, with the hallways of the ninth floor all but empty, Fabrikant shepherded a security guard and professor into one of the offices, locking the door behind him. Picking up a telephone, he dialled 911 and proudly proclaimed that he had "made several murders." He demanded to speak with a television reporter. Over the course of his hour-long phone conversation, Fabrikant dropped his guard, and placed the pistol down momentarily to switch the position of the phone. His captives seized the opportunity, the professor kicking the firearm away while the security guard wrestled Fabrikant to the floor.

Upon entering the building, the police immediately took the gunman into custody. Searching the crime scene, they discovered the lifeless body of Michael Hogben in Fabrikant's office, the letter still gripped in his hand. Blood had sullied the paper, staining its feckless formality with the reality of unchecked primal aggression. If Fabrikant had bothered to read it, he would have learned that the CUFA had decided to limit his access to its offices because he was causing "considerable distress" to its employees. Words on paper. Over the thirteen years Valery Fabrikant had terrorized Concordia with threats of violence, the university had sent him many such documents, trusting that the pen was mightier than the sword. Fabrikant's philosophy was much more flexible; depending on the situation, he would assert his will with words or bullets. Now his options would be limited to the former, though this would by no means slow him down.

In a pathetic and untimely display, Patrick Kenniff finally fired Fabrikant seventeen days after the massacre, writing:

> Events before, on, and subsequent to August 24, 1992, demonstrate clearly that you constitute an immediate and continuing threat to this university, its faculty, staff and students…. Furthermore you are no longer accomplishing your duties as a faculty member.[42]

Apparently the university didn't think much of Kenniff's leadership abilities, and he was also fired from his position of rector, taking a $580,000 severance package along with him. Ironically, the gunman had been right all along: Concordia in the early nineties was a haven for injustice. In their 1994 report *Integrity in Scholarship*, an independent committee of inquiry appointed by the school's Board of Governors found significant violations in Concordia's academic integrity and "confirmed the validity of a number of Dr. Fabrikant's more specific allegations."[43]

Valery Fabrikant stood trial in 1993 on four counts of murder in what would be arguably the most bizarre and eccentric trial in Canadian history. Found in contempt of court on six occasions, and after firing ten attorneys, Fabrikant opted to act as his own defence lawyer. He repeatedly raised pedantic and frivolous points throughout the proceedings, much to the annoyance of the judge. One observer noted that Fabrikant would often glance around excitedly at the onlookers whenever he said something "clever." Five months later, he was convicted on every count, and sentenced to life imprisonment. Valery Fabrikant is currently incarcerated at the Archambault institution in Sainte-Anne-des-Pleines, Quebec, where he continues his academic pursuits and maintains a website devoted to his personal war against the system. Declared a vexatious litigant by the Quebec Superior Court in 2000, his status as such was upheld during a 2007 review.

Valery Fabrikant's court appearances, prison writings, and lawsuits are so plentiful that they would necessitate an entire book to detail. As tempting as it is to describe his abundance of eccentricities, I will instead refer you to several online links that will be infinitely more useful.

Web Links (for further info)

Fabrikant's trial (audio only): *www.youtube.com/watch?v=AwfqxZ35iEU*
Fabrikant's personal website: *http://fabrikant.webs.com*
Integrity in Scholarship: A Report to Concordia University (independent inquiry explores veracity of Fabrikant's claims): *http://archives. concordia.ca/sites/default/files/uploaded-documents/pages /2011/07/26/Arthurs_report.pdf*

NARCISSISTIC PERSONALITY DISORDER

According to the *Diagnostic and Statistical Manual of Mental Disorders: Fourth Edition* (DSM IV), the diagnostic criteria for narcissistic personality disorder are "a pervasive pattern of grandiosity (in fantasy or behavior), need for admiration, and lack of empathy, beginning by early adulthood and present in a variety of contexts, as indicated by five (or more) of the following:

	Fabrikant
1) Has a grandiose sense of self-importance (e.g., exaggerates achievements and talents, expects to be recognized as superior without commensurate achievements)	Yes
2) Is preoccupied with fantasies of unlimited success, power, brilliance, beauty, or ideal love	Yes
3) Believes that he or she is "special" and unique and can only be understood by, or should associate with, other special or high-status people (or institutions)	Yes
4) Requires excessive admiration	Yes
5) Has a sense of entitlement (i.e., unreasonable expectations of especially favourable treatment or automatic compliance with his or her expectations)	Yes
6) Is interpersonally exploitative (i.e., takes advantage of others to achieve his or her own ends)	Yes
7) Lacks empathy: is unwilling to recognize or identify with the feelings and needs of others	Yes
8) Is often envious of others or believes others are envious of him or her	Yes
9) Shows arrogant, haughty behaviours or attitudes"	Yes[44]

Considering that Valery Fabrikant qualified for every single one of these criteria, the unspecified "personality disorder" that Dr. Steiner proposed he suffered from was most likely narcissistic.

Robert Raymond Cook

Victims: 7 killed
Duration of rampage: June 25, 1959 (mass murder)

Location: Stettler, Alberta
Weapon: Shotgun

CONDUCT DISORDER

Robert Raymond Cook came screaming into the world of Hanna, Alberta, on July 15, 1937, the first-born child of eighteen-year-old Josephine Cook and her husband, twenty-eight-year-old Raymond Albert Cook. The marriage was a turbulent one, with Josephine constantly accusing Raymond of philandery. To complicate matters, she suffered from a number of illnesses, including a weak heart, and on September 16, 1946, died during reparative surgery on a twisted bowel. In the blink of an eye, nine-year-old Bobby found himself motherless and the sole object of Raymond's attention. This claustrophobic emotional bond with his father lasted until the summer of 1949, when Raymond wed Bobby's grade school teacher, Daisy May Gaspar. A son, Gerald, followed in February 1950 (the Cooks would go on to have four more children). That same year, the family relocated to the rural community of Stettler, 170 kilometres north of Calgary and 145 kilometres south of Edmonton. This sudden shift in family dynamic and location seemed to have a profound effect on the thirteen-year-old Bobby, who began showing signs of conduct disorder, a prerequisite for anti-social personality disorder. Though he was fond of breaking and entering, his crime of choice was hot-wiring cars to take on joy rides for "the excitement and adventure."[45] Such was his knack for automobile theft that, at the age of fourteen, Bobby was sent to Bowden Reformatory. The institution did not live up to its name, and between the ages of thirteen and twenty-one, Bobby earned nineteen separate convictions, landing himself in Lethbridge Jail, then Stony Mountain Penitentiary. There, the 155-pound convict was groomed to be a welterweight boxer. Rather than earning himself a professional fighting career, Bobby ended up in Saskatchewan Penitentiary.

Fortune intervened on his behalf. To celebrate Queen Elizabeth II's royal tour of Canada, one hundred non-violent inmates at the Saskatchewan facility were granted amnesty. On Tuesday, June 23, 1959, Robert Raymond Cook was among sixty prisoners released back into the public, and rode the bus from the Prince Albert penitentiary to Saskatoon, where he went bar hopping with prison buddy Jimmy Myhaluk. The next morning they caught a Greyhound to Edmonton, where Bobby slept off his hangover at the Commercial Hotel and Jimmy left for his parents' home. Before heading to the Myhaluks' for dinner, Bobby stopped by Hood Motors, where his car-coveting eyes fell upon a brand new white Chevrolet Impala convertible, its red upholstery beckoning like a pin-up girl's lips. Entranced, he spoke with salesman Carl Thalbing about the possibility of exchanging a 1958 station wagon for the object of his desire. Bobby knew just where to find one.

CONSISTENT IRRESPONSIBILITY/FAILURE TO PLAN AHEAD

Two days later, at 8:00 a.m. on Friday, June 26, Bobby returned to Edmonton in his father's station wagon. At South Park Motors he attempted to trade the vehicle for something fancier, but was unable to successfully negotiate a deal with salesman Arthur Pilling. By 11:30 he tried his luck once more at the Hood dealership. Posing as his father, Raymond, who had a record of steady work experience, Bobby conned salesman Len Amoroso into letting him take the Impala for a test drive in exchange for the station wagon, a $40 down payment, and the promise that he would be back by 5:00 p.m. to fill out the necessary documentation. Of course, he had no such intentions.

Thirty hours and 720 kilometres later, Robert Raymond Cook was coasting through downtown Stettler when he was pulled over by Constable Allan Braden. Taken to the RCMP detachment, the young car thief came face to face with Sergeant Tom Roach. Hood Motors had contacted the Stettler police to inform them that a local man named Raymond Cook had bought a shiny new Chevy convertible and had forgotten to sign the paperwork. Well aware of Bobby's criminal history, Sergeant Roach suspected he had impersonated his father and stolen the vehicle, but decided it was best to speak with Raymond himself before leaping to conclusions. Contacting the elder Cook by telephone proved to be more difficult than expected.

While searching the Impala, Roach discovered two suitcases stuffed with nightclothes, along with a metal box containing the Cook children's birth certificates, Raymond's bank book, and his marriage licence.

Bobby explained to Sergeant Roach that his family had taken a trip to "somewhere in British Columbia" in hopes of purchasing a garage. Before they left, his father had instructed him to exchange the station wagon for the Impala. As Bobby had no identification, Raymond had lent him his own. Bobby assured them there was no cause for concern: everything would be satisfactorily explained when his father returned. Suspicious, Roach confined Bobby to a holding cell, anticipating that he would soon be charged with false pretenses. In the meantime, he drove to the Cooks' four-bedroom bungalow, a mere two blocks from the station, but noted no signs of disturbance. Still, Roach had a nagging feeling that something was terribly wrong. At half past midnight, he returned to the dwelling with Constable Al Morrison. The two entered, scouring the darkness with their flashlights. They noticed that while the children's shoes remained neatly under their beds, the sheets had been removed from the mattresses. If the Cooks had left for British Columbia, why had they done so barefoot and stripped the linens?

Intent on getting to the bottom of the mystery, five RCMP officers arrived at 11:00 a.m. to search the premises. The late-morning sun through the windows cast light upon the shocking truth: the walls and beds were caked with blood. Shards of a broken shotgun butt were mixed among clumps of brain, bone, and hair. The only trip the Cook family had taken was a screaming departure from this world. But where were the bodies? That answer came half an hour later, when the officers entered the adjoining garage at the back of the bungalow. Somebody had flattened a number of cardboard boxes, laying them like tiles across the filthy floor. Beneath the cardboard, the investigators discovered a second layer of wooden boards placed over a grease pit. Pulling away the planks, they gagged at the stench of decay rising from below. Among the discarded clothing, bedding, used car parts, and other junk, the bloated corpses of Raymond and Daisy Cook lay stacked upon their dead children — like seven sardines crammed into a two-by-four-foot oily tin. Raymond's chest had been blown open by buckshot, while only fragments of Daisy's skull remained — the remnants of a shotgun blast to the head. In a sickening twist, the children had each been bludgeoned to death with the butt of the weapon, as if sparing their suffering hadn't been worth the ammunition. All seven victims had been slaughtered in their pajamas, their bedclothes lacquered to their green-blue bodies with grease. Whether they knew it or not, the men from the Stettler RCMP were gazing down upon Alberta's worst familicide of the twentieth century.

Table 4: Victims of the Cook Family Massacre

Name	Age	Cause of Death
Raymond	51	Shot multiple times
Daisy	37	Shot in the head
Gerald	9	Skull fractured by shotgun butt
Patrick	8	Skull fractured by shotgun butt
Christopher	6	Skull fractured by shotgun butt
Cathy	4	Skull fractured by shotgun butt
Linda Mae	3	Skull fractured by shotgun butt

DECEITFULNESS/FAILURE TO CONFORM TO SOCIAL NORMS

The horrified officers got to work immediately. An inspection of the premises revealed Bobby's bloodstained blue prison uniform concealed beneath a bed. The killer had made an unsuccessful attempt to scrub the spattered walls clean. Judging by the bloody mattresses, Raymond and Daisy had been shot fatally in their beds, before the boys — Gerald, Patrick, and Christopher — were battered to death. The lack of blood on Kathy's and Linda's linens implied the girls had fled their room when the gunshots began, but that their assailant had followed them into the living room, clubbing them to death like baby seals. He had then rolled all seven corpses into the filthy mass grave along with various other junk, and made a half-hearted attempt to conceal them. The pathologist estimated that the murders had occurred within the last twenty-four to seventy-two hours, placing the time of death between noon on Thursday, June 25, and noon on Saturday, June 27. However, the failure of Raymond and the children to show up for work or school on Friday seemed to indicate that they had been slaughtered either the previous evening or during the wee hours of Friday morning.

Further investigation revealed that a couple named Jim and Leona Hoskins had visited the Cooks until 9:00 on the night of Thursday, June 25. A witness named Arnold Filenko claimed to have seen Raymond give Bobby a lift soon after. It seemed an open and shut case: Robert Raymond Cook had arrived at his family's home Friday night, mercilessly slaughtering them to steal their station wagon, which he then traded for the Impala. But Bobby had an explanation for everything. He had cadged a ride to Stettler with Walter Berezowski early on Thursday, June 25, arriving at 1:00 p.m. There he had loitered around town until 9:00 p.m., when his father came to pick him up. Robert and Ray went for a beer at a local bar, where their conversation soon turned to the possibility of buying a garage in British Columbia. Having agreed that it was an excellent idea, they parted ways. Bobby returned to the family home at 9:30 p.m., where the two men proposed their plan to Daisy, who seems to have got on board immediately. Bobby handed his father his blue prison-issued suit and approximately $4,000 in cash that he had dug up from a hiding place in Bowden the previous day, keeping a few hundred aside for himself.* This money was to be his contribution to the purchase of their garage. Raymond reciprocated by lending his automobile, wallet, identification, and car keys to Bobby so that he could swap the station wagon in Edmonton for the Impala. When the exchange was complete, Bobby was to drive the convertible back to Stettler and await a telephone call from his father with instructions to collect the rest of the family. Bobby claimed that when he left the house for Edmonton at 10:30 p.m., his father, stepmother, and siblings were alive and well. The following day, he successfully traded the vehicles and drove to Camrose, Whitecourt, and then back to Camrose again on some kind of aimless road trip. On Saturday he had been ticketed for driving with an open bottle of liquor in his car, before finally heading back to Stettler. At 7:00 p.m., he arrived at the little bungalow to find his family had left without him. Lingering for an hour or so, he drove downtown, where he was eventually stopped by Constable Braden. Unfortunately for Bobby, the police weren't buying his story.

---

* The exact amounts he claimed to have unearthed, given his father, and pocketed changed on three separate occasions.

Charged with his father's murder the following day, Robert Raymond Cook was sent by Magistrate Fred Biggs to be psychiatrically evaluated over a thirty-day period. While he was held at Ponoka Mental Hospital, Cook's seven deceased family members were buried in a single grave in a Hanna, Alberta, cemetery on July 2 — his requests to attend denied. Then, on July 11, Bobby tore through a wire mesh window and escaped. Thus commenced one of the largest manhunts in Alberta history; with seventy-five police officers, two hunting dogs, and a light spotter plane searching the hillsides and farm fields around Ponoka. The authorities sensibly cautioned the public against picking up hitchhikers, but thumbing rides was hardly the fugitive's m.o. Later that same day, a car Cook had supposedly stolen from the Ponoka area was found overturned in the tiny hamlet of Nevis, along with evidence of a break and enter at the town hall. Accompanied by a second spotter plane, a hundred RCMP patrollers spent Sunday searching the seventeen kilometres between Nevis and nearby Alix. It wasn't until Monday that they picked up the fugitive's trail, discovering a second stolen vehicle outside of Bashaw. Judging by the evidence, the police deduced that Robert had fled southeast to Stettler before veering north. By now, sixty soldiers from the Canadian Army Provost Corps were on his trail in jeeps and helicopters. When a farmer's wife telephoned police around 3:00 p.m. Tuesday to report a shadowy figure lurking behind her barn, two police cruisers sped to her home. The property owner, Norman Dufva, greeted them upon arrival and led them to the area where his wife had sighted the trespasser. As they approached, a starved and dishevelled-looking Bobby Cook stepped out from his hiding place and surrendered. A consummate criminal failure, he had been on the lam for a mere seventy-four hours before being handcuffed and carted off to Fort Saskatchewan Jail.

Between November 30 and December 10, 1959, Robert Raymond Cook was tried for the murder of his family in a Red Deer courthouse. As the case against him was entirely circumstantial, Justice Peter Greschuk reminded the jury that, in order to convict, the evidence had to be consistent with guilt and not with any other rational explanation. Nevertheless, they deliberated for a mere hour and a half before finding Cook guilty of capital murder. Judge Greschuk sentenced the twenty-two-year-old to hang on April 15, 1960. Shocked by the surprise conviction, Cook's defence team filed for an appeal from the Appellate Division of the Supreme Court of Alberta. Their request was granted, and a second trial commenced in Edmonton on June 20, 1960, under Judge Harry Riley. Ultimately, the jurors reached the same verdict in a fraction of the time, and after the Appellate Court denied him a third trial, on November 15, 1960, Robert Raymond Cook became the first man to be executed in Alberta since 1952, and the last in the province's history. In accordance with his wishes, Cook's cadaver was donated to the University of Edmonton to be used for medical research. Whether the recipients of his transplanted eyes ever learned what horrors they had once fallen upon is unknown. Then again, there were many who did not believe that Bobby Cook was responsible for the murders at all.

HARMLESS?

One need not look any further than Bobby's implausible tale of the days surrounding the murders for indications of his guilt.

1. Alberta's greatest salesman: If we are to believe Bobby's account, within an hour and a half this compulsive criminal had not only managed to convince his father and stepmother to go into business with him, but also to uproot to British Columbia with their five children ... immediately.

2. Leave it to the convict: Instead of travelling to Edmonton to swap the vehicles himself, for some reason Raymond Cook had chosen fraud, entrusting a habitual car thief with the transaction.

3. Paperwork — why not? Rather than completing the necessary paperwork and returning promptly to Stettler with the station wagon, Bobby had embarked on a drunken joyride through Camrose and Whitecourt, inexplicably neglecting to fill out the documentation in Edmonton. If he had intended to turn over a new leaf, why would he do this, knowing it would eventually cause problems down the line?

4. Conveniently overlooking carnage: On Saturday Bobby had spent an hour in his family home, and found it unexpectedly vacant. Yet somehow he failed to notice the bloodstained mattresses and walls, along with the remnants of broken skull and shotgun.

5. Mr. Dressup or Jack the Stripper? Finally, if the killer was anyone other than Bobby Cook, why was the blue prison-issued suit secreted under a mattress? Raymond had been found in his bedclothes, so unless the perpetrator had stripped him of his bloodstained suit and redressed him, Bobby's father could not have been wearing this article of clothing. It seems even more unlikely that the murderer would have donned the suit himself, exterminated the family, changed his apparel, then concealed the bloody clothes. In both cases, there would be no purpose for these elaborate and time-consuming actions. Is it not more feasible that Bobby himself had committed the massacre while wearing his own suit, which as a result became bloodied? Surely if he had left the house spattered in gore, he would have put himself at great risk of being detected. Given the options, the quickest way for Bobby to solve this problem was to change his clothes and hide the evidence.

Some mental health professionals doubted that Bobby was capable of slaughtering his family because of the lack of violence in his history. Then again, **Valery Fabrikant**'s past was similarly free of bloodshed. Others have argued that Cook did not qualify for the type of major personality disorder that would lead a man to cull his entire family. These assessments were wrong. Though it is obvious that Cook was not psychopathic, there is ample evidence to suggest he was governed by anti-social personality disorder. In DSM IV, anti-social personality disorder is diagnosed as "a pervasive pattern of disregard for and violation of the rights of others occurring since age fifteen years, as indicated by three (or more) of the following:

	Cook
1) Failure to conform to social norms with respect to lawful behaviors as indicated by repeatedly performing acts that are grounds for arrest	Yes
2) Deceitfulness, as indicated by repeated lying, use of aliases, or conning others for personal profit or pleasure	Possible
3) Impulsivity or failure to plan ahead	Yes
4) Irritability and aggressiveness, as indicated by repeated physical fights or assaults	No
5) Reckless disregard for safety of self or others	No
6) Consistent irresponsibility, as indicated by repeated failure to sustain consistent work behaviour or honour financial obligations	Yes
7) Lack of remorse, as indicated by being indifferent to or rationalizing having hurt, mistreated, or stolen from another	No[46]

This disorder, paired with the inconsistency and improbability of Cook's account and the mountain of circumstantial evidence against him, suggests that the juries who convicted him of murder were correct. A possible explanation for the massacre was that Cook had developed an overwhelming desire for the Impala, and after days of neglecting to visit his family, realized how they might be useful to him in this acquisition. When he had approached his father on Thursday, June 25, about trading the family station wagon for the Impala, Raymond had declined the offer. Not only would he have been a fool to trust Bobby, he probably sensed that he was being used. Enraged that the father who had once doted on him now cared more about his step-siblings, Bobby had entered the home after 9:30 on Thursday night and massacred them one by one. After concealing the bodies in the grease pit, he had absconded with the station wagon. Unlike Robert's execution, the massacre had been a poorly planned and hot-blooded affair. He had been as incompetent at murder as he had been at theft: in the end, he gained nothing but pain.

Up to 50 percent of Canadian prison inmates may harbour anti-social personalities just as Bobby Cook did. The psychopath, with whom ASPs are often confused, is a much rarer entity. The notorious case of Mountie murderer **James Roszko**, a terrifying and utterly ruthless character, reflects the significant difference between the two.

James Roszko

*"If I ever have to go, I'm taking a
hell of a pile of them with me!"*

Victims: 4 killed/committed suicide
Duration of rampage: March 3, 2005 (mass murder)
Location: Mayerthorpe, Alberta
Weapon: Hechler and Koch .308 automatic assault rifle

SHARK TANK

March 2, 2005: 3:00 p.m. Bailiff Robert Parry's car horn broke the snowy Alberta silence. Beyond the chain-link fence, two large Rottweilers emerged from the Quonset hut, baring their fangs. Predictably, the debtor, James Michael Roszko, was not co-operating; now it was simply a matter of how aggressively he would resist. Outside the padlocked pipe gate barring the driveway, fellow bailiff Mike Hnatiw scoured the 1.2-kilometre-square enclosed property. Roszko had built himself a small fortress. Within the prison of paranoia, Hnatiw spotted three granaries, a mobile home, and a white 2005 Ford F-350 truck. After discovering irregularities in Roszko's credit history, Kentwood Ford Sales of Edmonton had requested that the bailiffs travel 120 kilometres north of the city to repossess the truck. Given Roszko's legendary animosity toward authority figures, it was like asking them to dive into a shark tank. On a previous occasion, he had used hidden spikes to flatten a visitor's tires. There were also rumours Roszko had threatened people with guns. Hnatiw attempted to gain entry through the gate, but one of the Rottweilers raced toward him, prompting him to blast it with pepper spray. Deciding that it was too dangerous to proceed, Hnatiw returned to Parry's vehicle and advised him to contact the RCMP. As they sat outside the compound awaiting the police cruisers, a runtish man in a ball cap, dark jacket, and jeans emerged from a building, entered the truck, and revved the engine.

"Mr. Roszko!" Hnatiw hollered. Parry blasted the horn again. The man drove over to two gates on the south side of the property, alighted, opened the first, and then began to fiddle with the second. Clambering back inside the truck, he drove north toward the chain-link gates and opened them. Before re-entering his vehicle, he turned to the bailiffs and shouted, "Fuck off." Hnatiw and Parry watched as one of the most dangerous men in Alberta accelerated rapidly to the north and veered west down a hill, leaving his compound behind him. Not long after, the RCMP arrived. Hearing the bailiffs' account, several officers drove north in search of Roszko, while others helped Hnatiw and Parry safely infiltrate the property. Hnatiw damaged his gate cutters trying to snip through the padlock, but eventually gained access using a pry bar on the gate, warding off the dogs with more pepper spray. The bailiffs and RCMP officers entered the Quonset to find an auto-theft chop-shop, a stolen generator, and an illegal cannabis-growing operation consisting of between 192 and 280 marijuana plants and $8,000 in cultivation materials.* Realizing that they would now require a *Criminal Code and Controlled Drug and Substances Act* search warrant, RCMP Corporal James Martin ordered his officers to vacate the property, leaving Constables Julie Letal and Trevor Josok to watch over the Roszko farm. He returned to the Mayerthorpe RCMP detachment with Constable Peter Schiemann to obtain the warrant. At 6:30 p.m., bailiffs Mike Hnatiw and Rob Parry posted seizure documents on the door of Roszko's mobile home and departed.

Back at the detachment, at 7:40 p.m. Corporal Martin faxed the warrant request to Queen's Counsel Robert Philp in Edmonton, and within fifteen minutes received approval to search the Roszko property over a

---

* Multiple sources contradict the exact number of plants. They fall into this range.

twenty-four-hour period, beginning at 8:00 that evening. Martin then telephoned the RCMP Edmonton Auto Theft Unit to request their help in identifying which auto parts had been stolen. They agreed to send Constables Garrett Hoogestraat and Stephen Vigor sometime after dawn. In the meantime, the RCMP Edmonton Operational Communications Centre had issued a BOLF ("Be on the Lookout For") for Roszko. As Corporal Martin descended upon the farm with his warrant and six officers, police vehicles continued to patrol the surrounding area, their eyes peeled for any sign of the fugitive. At 11:30 p.m., members of the Edmonton Police Service's Green Team arrived to assist with the search. The team included a forensic identification specialist from Edson and a tow truck driver to remove the stolen parts. According to CBC's *The Fifth Estate*, items seized over the next day included the following:

- Evidence of marijuana cultivation, stolen and suspected stolen property, namely, marijuana lamps, pots containing seven marijuana plants and 88 hanging harvested plants, and notes pertaining to the maintenance and harvesting of marijuana from the residence at the location.
- One hundred and ninety-two growing marihuana [*sic*] plants complete with pots, irrigation and lighting systems from the quonsit [*sic*] at the location.
- A Warmac generator, the property of Trident Exploration reported stolen on the 16th of February, 2005.
- A newer Sierra 2500 truck, red in colour, with the vehicle identification numbers removed from the door frame and dashboard.
- A newer model grey Ford truck which was partially disassembled and the interior stripped. This vehicle contained a vehicle identification number plate which appeared glued on the dashboard and thus is suspected to be from a different vehicle.
- A Honda 400R dirt bike with serial numbers altered.
- Pick truck [*sic*] box containing newer truck seats, truck grilles and various other new model truck parts.
- Firearms ammunition of assorted calibers.[47]

Eeriest of all was the handwritten list of officers from the Mayerthorpe RCMP detachment, along with the call signs and cellphone numbers of their respective cruisers.

MOUNTIE MURDERER

Early the next morning, Constables Peter Schiemann and Brock Myrol paid a visit to a local veterinary clinic where they acquired Xylazine, Acepromazine, and a syringe. At 8:00 a.m., Auto Theft Constables Hoogestraat and Vigor arrived from Edmonton to find less than a handful of Mounties patrolling the Roszko property. They witnessed Schiemann and Myrol feeding sedative-injected meat to two Rottweilers in a shed. While Hoogestraat and Vigor changed into their coveralls and prepared their equipment, Schiemann, Myrol, Constable Anthony Gordon, and Constable Leo Johnston walked over to the Quonset hut. Schiemann, who had intended to go to Edmonton to purchase camera equipment, was both unarmed and clad in civilian clothing. Upon entering, Myrol, Johnston, and Schiemann walked to the middle of the structure, while Gordon lingered in the doorway. Suddenly their conversation was interrupted by gunshots. The three officers turned to see Gordon topple to the ground, struck twice in the head at point-blank range. Hidden behind three plastic barrels to the left of the door, James Roszko turned his Hechler and Koch .308 automatic assault rifle on them and pulled the trigger. All hell broke loose. Schiemann and Johnston were cut down before they could react. Myrol ran for the cover of two sheds at the back of the hut, but the bullets caught him. In seconds, James Roszko had committed the single worst massacre of RCMP officers in the past hundred years.

Outside the Quonset, Constable Stephen Vigor heard the sounds of gunfire and screaming, and told his partner to radio for help. Vigor, with pistol drawn, made his way to the doorway of the hut, which was obscured by a jumble of police cars. Without warning, Roszko casually walked out of the Quonset, gripping an assault rifle. A .300 Magnum rifle was slung over his shoulder and a semi-automatic pistol tucked in his waistband. Spotting Vigor, a look of surprise came over Roszko's face, and he fired twice. Both bullets missed their mark, the first pinging off a nearby police cruiser and the second shattering its mirror. Constable Vigor returned fire, striking Roszko in the thigh and hand. Dripping blood, Roszko staggered back inside the Quonset. Constable Hoogestraat pulled his vehicle in front of Vigor to shield him from further bullets. Hoogestraat took up position next to his partner, and both men nervously awaited round two of the shootout. From where they were standing, neither one could see inside the hut. They called out to Roszko and the other officers, but received no reply. The tension hung like frost in the cold Alberta air.

Over the next few hours, backup and emergency response teams arrived at the scene. Nobody would risk entering the Quonset lest Roszko have any tricks up his sleeve. It wasn't until 2:00 p.m., when a Remote Mechanical Investigator (a robot with a camera attached) was sent in, that they learned of the horror that had unfolded. James Roszko lay dead among the corpses of all four constables. Wounded and outgunned, the outlaw had chosen to end his life by firing a pistol into his heart. A cop hater to the end, he hadn't wanted to give them the satisfaction of finishing the job.

As Canada mourned the loss of four dutiful young RCMP officers, questions regarding the Mayerthorpe Tragedy inevitably emerged. Had the police taken the proper precautions? Could anything be done in future to prevent a similar incident from occurring? And underpinning both questions, who was James Michael Roszko?

WICKED DEVIL

When pressed by reporters to comment on his son Jim, eighty-year-old William Roszko replied that he hadn't exchanged words with the "wicked devil" in almost a decade. Other Mayerthorpe-area residents referred to Jimmy Roszko as a walking time bomb. Unlike **Valery Fabrikant** and **Robert Cook**, who were liked or respected by some people, it seems there wasn't an honest soul who could attest to a single virtue in Roszko's character. Though his final body count numbered nowhere near that of **Alexander Keith Jr.** or **Marc Lépine**, he may be the most morally reprehensible Canadian rampage murderer in this book.

The second youngest of the Roszko children, Jim grew up in the Alberta countryside, 130 kilometres northwest of Edmonton. Both his father and brother have claimed he went astray in his early teens, when he began using drugs. This early experimentation should be viewed as symptomatic rather than causal. When an autopsy was conducted on Roszko following the Mayerthorpe tragedy, the medical examiner found no traces of any drugs or alcohol in his body whatsoever. Drugs hadn't made him a monster: embryo psychopathy, an over-indulging mother, and a fanatically religious father had.

Like many who have made the Canadian prairies their home, William Roszko and Stephanie Liwczak were of Ukrainian stock. The two had met when William was a twenty-five-year-old farmer and Stephanie the seventeen-year-old daughter of a Catholic deacon. In November 1950 they married and settled down to work the land. Their first child, Billy, followed soon after in 1951. During an argument, Stephanie said that she was going to leave William, and attempted to wrest Billy from his hands. William responded by punching her in the mouth, chipping her tooth. "After that she never forgave me," he moaned fifty-five years later. "She's so stone-hearted." William Roszko claimed that he never laid a hand on her again, and as a result she got "spoiled" and did "whatever she felt like." Though William's act was obviously barbaric, his son George corroborated that Stephanie never missed an opportunity to bring it up whenever they argued. Yet, despite their dysfunctional marriage, the Roszkos continued to have babies annually from 1953: Josephine, Pauline, George, John, Joseph, and on November 8, 1958, James.

Within months of Jimmy's birth, William began to express irrational beliefs that the end of the world was drawing near. By 1960, he was plagued by dreams of Armageddon and final judgment, becoming convinced that God was using his dreams as a conduit to send him visions. In his diaries he wrote: "A very dark cloud began to come from the West, a terrible storm, and with great noise like rushing waters, with thunder and roaring that I have never seen nor heard of in my life. And I heard the sounds of Angels' trumpets. I thought it cannot be anything else but the end of the world." Much to his wife's embarrassment, William grew his beard to biblical proportions and began preaching of a 1961 apocalypse. His constant religious diatribes alienated their closest friends, many refusing to come over lest they be subject to one of his sermons. Even around his buddies at the bar, William would speak only of doom and prophecy. Whereas others could escape his constant proselytizing, his wife and children were forced to listen as he read scripture aloud for hours. By January 1960, Stephanie had reached her breaking point: she attempted suicide and had to have her stomach pumped at Mayerthorpe hospital. William finally tired of his apocalyptic obsession in 1961 (presumably because it didn't come true), though his wife remained wracked with depression and anxiety. The couple had their seventh and final child together, Mary Ann, that same year.

Jimmy Roszko was a particularly adorable infant, coddled by almost everyone around him. Whether he was bouncing gleefully on a relative's knee or being ferried around the countryside by his siblings in an old washtub, he must have felt like the centre of the universe. If Jimmy wanted something, he would throw an ungodly squealing tantrum until he got it. Instead of teaching him restraint, Stephanie would project the blame onto others: "You showed him that! You give it to him!" Also, unlike the other Roszko children, Jimmy never did chores, and inevitably, their lovable little brother transformed into a spoiled brat to be avoided at all costs. Jimmy was even spared the harsh discipline of his father's strap.

"He'd somehow get away with his ways," William later recounted. "One time, he hit one of the boys and I couldn't catch up to him. He was such a sneaky, zigzagging person."

As Jimmy's elder brother John would later say in a CBC interview: "Those preschool years, that's when the framework is built for the rest of your life. If you grow up out of your diapers thinking that everything is your way, and everything you feel is right, well, what do you think is going to happen?"

Stephanie continued to give Jimmy preferential treatment well into adulthood, even when it risked the safety of her other children. Doug, her younger son by another man, once testified under oath that Jimmy "was always kicking the shit out of me in the yard. We would be working on something and he would get mad, throw wrenches around, grab me, kaboof in the head. Mom never said anything." On one occasion he showed Stephanie a crack in the bedroom wall where Jimmy had thrown him, and she allegedly replied, "What crack? I can't see no crack?" When, in 1994, a grown man charged Jimmy with repeatedly sexually abusing him in the late 1980s, Stephanie openly challenged the victim's story: "If it really happened, why didn't you say something then?" Privately she admitted to another son that she knew Jimmy was guilty and had "problems."

In the company of others, Jimmy learned to mask his self-centred nature, presenting himself as the perfect little boy. The Roszkos had a good reputation at school for being polite, well-behaved children — an "ideal family" who did everything together. Though not unintelligent, Jimmy lacked focus and achieved average grades. His parents' turbulent marriage was likely the source of much distraction. In May 1969, when Jimmy was ten, William Roszko began to suspect Stephanie of infidelity. On the advice of a social worker, Stephanie attempted to leave her husband, but he refused to grant her a divorce on the grounds that it violated God's commandments. A modern woman, Stephanie would not abide his attempts to control her, and abandoned him in February 1970 for a farmer named Marvin Prosser. Left with little choice, William finally consented to divorce. The ensuing court battle was an ugly, spiteful affair. Stephanie admitted committing adultery, but accused William of physically abusing her on a number of occasions. She also alleged he raped her when he was drunk, and that in 1969 he had pulled a gun on her when he suspected her of cheating on him. William maintained that Stephanie had fabricated these charges until his dying breath. For his part, he told the court that his wife was prone to drinking in town and would return in the evening acting surly and argumentative. Stephanie denied his accusations.

The level of animosity between his parents, coinciding with the onset of puberty, should have had a dramatic effect on Jimmy, although William said in court that he had "never seen him cry once." Nevertheless, in November 1970, Jimmy visited his mother and her new lover, and decided he wanted to stay with them. Stephanie couldn't resist taking a potshot at her ex-husband in court during her custody appeal: "He [William] pumped him so much [full of poison, that] I can't control the child.... I need discipline from a man on this twelve-year-old child.... When [Marvin Prosser] just speaks to the child, he can get scared of the man." Considering that in 1978 Prosser beat Stephanie within an inch of her life, this was unsurprising.

Always quick to figure people out, Jimmy moved back in with William. His father wanted the children to go back to church, but Jimmy refused. By now he was a highly disturbed grade nine student, who slumped over his desk staring at the floor. He appeared two years younger than his actual age; his complexion was pallid and his physique frail. When William caught the fourteen-year-old Jimmy with marijuana, he not only reprimanded him, but also contacted the RCMP. Jimmy flew into a rage, attacking his father in a wild fury until William had to physically drag him to the floor. Around the same period, Jimmy was lining his pockets by selling drugs and homemade moonshine. On one occasion he broke into a firearms store with some friends and made off with a rifle. An accomplice was nabbed for the burglary and squealed on them. That day, a man wearing the proud red uniform of the Royal Canadian Mounted Police knocked on William's door to collect the rifle. From that day forth, James Roszko began developing a pathological enmity toward policemen, one that would ultimately culminate in his own demise. In the words of his lawyer, whenever Jimmy spoke of the RCMP his eyes lit up with fire.

BAD THINGS, SMALL PACKAGE

After the gun theft, William Roszko gave up on his son and avoided arguing with him altogether. Disciplining Jimmy became the sole responsibility of the police. Social workers intervened and fostered the wayward teen out to the Ziemmers — local farmers with a solid reputation. It wasn't long before the patriarch, Herbert Ziemmer, realized that the "quiet, ordinary boy" entrusted into his care was absolutely self-absorbed. Jimmy denounced his brother John as a "square" when Herbert praised his sibling's work ethic. Eventually, Jimmy unleashed a torrent of obscenities at the other Ziemmer children, and was sent back to live with his mother, her second husband, and Jimmy's newborn stepbrother Douglas. However, while Stephanie had once been overjoyed at having traded dour old Bill for the tall, handsome Marvin, she now found herself wed to an even worse wife-beater who obsessed about her carrying on affairs with other men. On one occasion, Marvin battered her so severely that he fractured her skull, and Jimmy had to drive her to the hospital. According to William, his son began to fantasize about killing his stepfather. Fortunately for Prosser, Jimmy let him live. After Jimmy dropped out of high school in grade eleven, he divided his time between petty crime and legitimate labour, trying his hand as an oil worker.

Jimmy's criminal record began in earnest in November 1975 and continued until his death. Of all the surviving policemen who had run-ins with him over the years, veteran RCMP officer Mike Statnyk knew the depths of Jimmy's evil better than any. In 1993, Roszko filed a formal civilian case against Statnyk for investigating him in the alleged sexual assault of several teenagers. Even though Statnyk was removed from the case, Jimmy continued to harass him, driving by his family home at all hours, and even conspiring to assassinate him. "Jimmy was always willing to step it up one. Jimmy crossed the line," recalled Statnyk. "You know most criminals will respect a person, a member's family ... there's boundaries that you as a policeman have, but there's also boundaries that ... criminals have. And ... they know where to step and not to step.... I thought there would come a time when it would be a likelihood that I would probably have to shoot Mr. Roszko on my property out of fear for my life or my family's life or safety...." Statnyk echoed the statements of Jimmy's stepbrother Doug and those of William and John Roszko: "Jimmy wasn't used to being told.... He was used to getting his way." Following the murders at Mayerthorpe, Alberta Justice Minister Ron Stevens requested that Gordon K. Wong, QC, conduct a review of Roszko's past criminality. Wong's *Report on James Michael Roszko: Prosecution History*, presented on September 23, 2005, reveals a versatile and extensive criminal career:

Table 5: The History of Criminal Charges against James Roszko[48]

Date	Charge	Result
February 18, 1976	Two counts of break, enter, and theft	Convicted on one count of break, enter, and theft and one count of possession of stolen property. Fined $150 on each charge and a one-year probation order imposed
November 19, 1976	One charge of theft under $200	Convicted. Received a fine of $250
January 24, 1978	One count of possession of stolen property, and a further count of break, enter, and theft	Pled guilty to possession of stolen property, and acquitted on the break and enter charge. Given a suspended sentence and a probation order of eighteen months

April 5, 1979	One count of making harassing telephone calls. Three counts of breaching conditions of his probation order	Convicted. Sentenced to thirty days jail on the harassing telephone calls charge. On one of the breach of probation order charges, received fifteen days jail to be served consecutively. On the other two breaches of probation order charges, received fifteen-day jail sentences to be served concurrent to the others
December 17, 1981	One count of obstructing justice	Acquitted
December 5, 1990	One count of uttering threats to cause death or serious bodily harm	Convicted after trial. Fined $200
March 3, 1993	Two traffic violation tickets. One for not wearing a seat belt and one for having tinted windows. On the same day, charged with causing a disturbance by use of obscene language	Pled guilty to the two violation tickets and to a violation ticket for failing to wear a seatbelt on October 18, 1992. Fined $25 for each. The Crown called no evidence on the cause of the disturbance charge, resulting in acquittal
September 28, 1993	One count of assault	Stayed
September 28, 1993	One count of impersonating a peace officer	Acquitted
December 1, 1993	See "Bradley" story	At preliminary inquiry, discharged on the counselling to commit murder charge, and discharged on the breach of recognizance charge at the invitation of the Crown. At trial on remaining charges, the Crown calls no further evidence. Acquittal on all counts
March 11, 1994	Speeding ticket	Convicted. Conviction appealed. Convicted again at second trial
March 27, 1994	Breach of a condition of a recognizance. Two counts of obstructing justice	Discharged of obstructing justice at preliminary inquiry. Acquitted on breaching condition

March 29, 1994	One count of sexual assault. One count of sexual touching	Found guilty at trial, sentenced to five years. Conviction appealed, new trial ordered. Found guilty at second trial, sentenced to two and a half years
January 1, 1995	See "Edward" story	Charges of assault and possession of prohibited weapon were stayed at trial; the remainder were withdrawn because they arose from the same facts
April 5, 1999	Charged under the *Federal Employment Insurance Act*	Acquitted
September 9, 1999	See "Harold and Gregory" story	Crown called no evidence, resulting in acquittal
December 29, 2004	Two counts of mischief	Withdrawn after his death

Among some of Roszko's more serious offences were those allegedly committed against his friend "Bradley," a handyman on the farm. While driving together near Drayton Valley in late May of 1993, Bradley claimed that Roszko repeatedly demanded to see his penis. When he refused, Roszko pointed a loaded 9-millimetre Beretta to his head. Then, on July 12, 1993, Roszko paid a visit to Bradley's home. Once inside, he pushed Bradley onto a bed, and pressed the same pistol against his head, insisting that he "had a job to do." The sudden arrival of a friend of Bradley's prevented Roszko from doing his job; however, when the friend left, their physical confrontation resumed. Bradley stabbed Roszko in the chin with a knife, and later drove him to the hospital. The "fool me twice, shame on me" proverb does not seem to have been part of Bradley's lexicon, as Roszko justified his acts and the two let bygones be bygones. A few months later, he allegedly offered Bradley $10,000 to kill a man using Roszko's own rifle. Bradley refused, and the two didn't speak for a month. When they bumped into each other in Whitecourt on December 1, 1993, Roszko convinced the handyman to drive up to his farm with him to examine a vehicle. Bradley agreed, on the condition that a friend be allowed to follow in another car. Roszko easily shook Bradley's escort from their tail, and once back at the homestead, pulled a shotgun on Bradley, forcing him to handcuff himself. Roszko began aggressively questioning the handyman: why had he been avoiding him;

what had he said; who had he talked to? At one point Roszko hit Bradley. Eventually he released him so that they could have a "fair fight." When the dust cleared, Roszko demanded that Bradley consent to having pornographic photographs taken of him so that he wouldn't talk. Thus the evening ended with Bradley performing fellatio on Roszko while a camera snapped lurid stills on a timer.

There was also Roszko's alleged September 28, 1993, attack on "Arthur" for spreading rumours about Roszko's homosexuality. While Arthur was seated in the back of his friend's car, Roszko struck him in the face, breaking his glasses. Later that day, Roszko received a telephone call from a Mayerthorpe-area resident about the assault. Determined to obtain the caller's number, he contacted an AGT security clerk under the guise of being an RCMP officer and requested that the call be traced.

In March 1994, "Edward" came forward, accusing James Roszko of routinely sexually abusing him from January 1983 to December 1989, beginning when Roszko was twenty-four and Edward eleven. These sexual assaults progressed from fondling to oral sex, and even one failed attempt at forcible sodomy. After the charges were laid, Roszko followed Edward to a Whitecourt bar on New Year's Eve and blasted him with pepper spray, clearing the establishment. On April 12, 2000, Roszko was convicted of sexual assault charges and sentenced to a two-and-a-half-year prison term, throughout which he continued to deny responsibility.

Before he served time behind bars, on the night of September 9, 1999, Roszko took a drunken vandal named "Harold" hostage with a 12-gauge shotgun, after catching him on his property. Binding the intruder's hands with rope, Roszko marched him over to Harold's truck, where fellow vandal "Gregory" was hiding nearby. Not one to be fooled, Roszko called out for Gregory to surrender, which he did. Roszko began escorting the two back toward his property. Along the way he supposedly said, "If Wiebo Ludwig can get away with it, then so can I.... I got you where I want you." Sensing that death was imminent, Gregory told Roszko to either shoot him or he was going back to the truck. When Gregory turned to do so, Roszko fired, but only grazed his target's left arm and face. Roszko told Gregory and Harold to climb into the truck's box so he could take them to the hospital. They complied, but he only drove farther onto his property. When Roszko stopped, Gregory and Harold managed to wrest control of the shotgun, and bludgeoned Roszko into submission, shattering the stock. Leaving him severely beaten, they sped off to the hospital and later informed the police of the incident.

Considering everything we know about the tumultuous childhood, personality, and criminal acts of James Roszko, the fact that his own father labelled him a wicked devil is understandable — for he most certainly was. But in a less hyperbolic, more clinical sense, can we accurately diagnose him as a psychopath?

PSYCHOPATH

Among the many professionals brought in to make sense of the Roszko murders was trained RCMP psychologist Matt Logan, a member of British Columbia's Major Crimes Unit. His assignment was to perform a "psychological autopsy" on the gunman, in an attempt to learn what Roszko "thought, felt, and did before death, based on information gathered from personal documents, police reports, medical and coroner's records, and face-to-face interviews with families, friends, and others who had contact with the person before the death." Logan determined that the attack had been premeditated, and not an instance of a man suddenly flipping his lid. In fact, he believed that Roszko might even have masturbated to the thought of slaughtering policemen. While searching Roszko's trailer, Logan found evidence of extreme deviance and violent fantasy. A newspaper clipping with a photo of cop killer Albert Foulston had been taped to a sideboard by a sink. Moving into the bedroom, he discovered two magazines, both heavily featuring firearms. One in particular contained an article about Harris and Klebold, the Columbine High School shooters. Logan suspected that given Roszko's history of sexually abusing young men, he would be harbouring a stash of pornography. He eventually found it sealed in a plastic package and stowed behind a loose panel in the closet. Inside were photographs of Roszko administering alcohol to two adolescent males and then sexually assaulting them. In his essay "No More Bagpipes," Logan claims to have identified Roszko as a psychopath in the ninety-first percentile of offenders, along with the presence of paranoid, schizotypal, and sexually deviant traits. Likewise, I have run Dr. Robert Hare's PCL-R on Roszko to determine if he meets the criteria for psychopathy.

Factor 1: Personality — Interpersonal/Affective

Trait (0 – Does not apply; 1 – Applies somewhat; 2 – Fully applies)	Roszko
Glibness/superficial charm	1
Grandiose sense of self-worth	1
Pathological lying	1
Conning/manipulative	2
Lack of remorse or guilt	2
Shallow affect (genuine emotion is short-lived and egocentric)	2
Callousness; lack of empathy	2
Failure to accept responsibility for own actions	2

Factor 2: Case History — Socially Deviant Lifestyle

Need for stimulation/proneness to boredom	2
Parasitic lifestyle	1
Poor behavioural control	2
Lack of realistic long-term goals	2
Impulsivity	2
Irresponsibility	2
Juvenile delinquency	2
Early behaviour problems	1
Revocation of conditional release	0
Criminal versatility	2[49]

Traits Not Correlated with Either Factor

Promiscuous sexual behaviour	1
Many short-term marital relationships	0

According to my PCL-R test assessment, James Michael Roszko scored thirty points: the minimum cut-off for psychopathy. Of all the Canadian mass murderers reviewed thus far in *Rampage*, he is the only offender who I can, with all confidence, label psychopathic.

PART C

SPREE KILLERS

In Chapter 1 we differentiated the concept of spree killing from mass and serial homicide. We also addressed some major problems arising from this definition in Chapter 2, such as what constitutes a "location" or a "cooling-off" period. At the FBI's first Serial Murder Symposium, from August 29 to September 5, 2005, in San Antonio, Texas, a panel of 135 experts reached the conclusion that spree killing should henceforth be considered a subcategory of serial murder. The subsequent report, *Serial Murder: Multi-Disciplinary Perspectives for Investigators*, explains the reasoning behind this proposed departure from the original categories:

> According to the definition, the lack of a cooling-off period marks the difference between a spree murder and a serial murder. Central to the discussion was the definitional problems relating to the concept of a cooling-off

period. Because it creates arbitrary guidelines, the confusion surrounding this concept led the majority of attendees to advocate disregarding the use of spree murder as a separate category. The designation does not provide any real benefit for use by law enforcement.[47]

Having addressed this issue at length with some of the symposium's attendees, I submit that if we are to accept these new parameters, offenders like **Rosaire Bilodeau** and **Robert Poulin**, whose crimes were detailed in Chapter 2, should be considered mass murder subtypes. The offenders presented in this chapter, however, would qualify for the spree killer subtype of serial murderer advocated at the FBI symposium.

Unlike mass and serial murderers, there has never been an adequate classification system devised for spree killers. In the following chapters I propose categories for the three spree killer types that I have noted in Canadian criminal history: Utilitarian, Exterminator, and Signature. Though admittedly this is merely a first step, I believe this system provides a solid heuristic foundation which may be improved and expanded upon. I have noted the need for a fourth category, tentatively called Marauder. As there are no Canadian examples of these types of spree killers, I have been unable to include a chapter on them. The personalities and crime scenes corresponding to the Utilitarian, Exterminator, Signature, and Marauder spree killers are listed here.

Table 6: Preliminary Typology System for Spree Killers

	Utilitarian	Exterminator	Signature	Marauder
Personality Traits				
Relationship status	Usually single, though they may have recently been involved in a relationship	Usually single	No pattern	Usually single

Employment	Unemployed or in menial work. Cannot hold down a long-term job	Yes, menial work or student	"Hands on" work, if employed at all	Usually menial work, student, or unemployed
Introverted/ extroverted?	Extroverted	Introverted	Usually introverted	Introverted, or extroverts who lack social skills and are shunned for being "weird"
History of suicide attempts?	No	No	Possibly	No
Reaction at end of spree	Will allow themselves to be captured	Half commit suicide or suicide by cop	Half commit suicide or suicide by cop	More than half commit suicide or suicide by cop
What sparks rampage?	Usually has trigger event	No trigger event. Planned in advance	Can have trigger event, but not always	Can have trigger event, but not always
Psychopathic?	Usually	No	Usually	No
Uses vehicle(s) in spree?	Yes, frequently steals victims' vehicles	Yes	Sometimes, though many killers will walk or rely on public transit	Yes, some steal vehicles
Substance abuse?	Yes	No	Usually, to varying degrees	No pattern
Possible motivations	Escaping justice; criminal notoriety; excitement	Political — hate crimes	Sadism; deviant sexual desires; criminal notoriety	Psychosis or other severe mental health problems; anger; revenge
Warning signs	Criminal history, usually in robbery, burglary, and/ or substance abuse	Express hatred for targeted group before spree and belong to (typically) right-wing extremist organizations or forums	Criminal history of violence, sex crimes, aggression, among many others	Mental health problems; obsession with firearms; non-serious criminal history

	Utilitarian	Exterminator	Signature	Marauder
Crime Scene				
Weapons used	Firearms and/or hand weapons. Hand weapons tend to be used on first victim	Firearms and bombs exclusively	Hand weapons on primary victims. Firearms on incidentals	Firearms usually, but in rare cases will employ hand weapons
Spend time with victims?	May spend hours with some, and no time at all with others	No	Typically	No
Moves body?	Not usually	No	Possibly	No
Robs victim?	Yes	No	No	Only of vehicles
Victimology	Other than first incident, victims are typically selected at random	Has ideal victim type. May stalk victims beforehand	Has ideal victim type, or is acquainted with victim	Initial victims are known, while later victims are generally selected at random
Act or process focused?	Act focused	Act focused	Process focused	Act focused
Sexually assaults victim?	May do on occasion, but this is not the driving motivation of his spree	No	Primary victims will be sexually assaulted or subject to a criminal signature	No
Signature at crime scene?	No, though sometimes overkill is present	No	Yes: rape, object penetration, necrophilia, mutilation, overkill, evisceration, etc.	No
Canadian examples	Jesse Imeson, Gregory McMaster, Peter John Peters	Stephen Marshall, Marcello Palma	Dale Merle Nelson, Jonathan Yeo	
International examples	Billy Cook, Gary Gilmore, Charles Starkweather	Anders Breivik, Mark Essex, John Salvi, Benjamin Smith	Anthony Arkwright, Gordon Cummins, Daniel Gonzalez, Mark Rowntree	Mark O. Barton, Derrick Bird, Michael Ryan, Maksim Gelman, Michael McLendon, Martin Bryant

CHAPTER 5

THE UTILITARIAN

The utilitarian spree killer is a natural-born criminal and wouldn't have it any other way. Arrogant and self-entitled, he eschews the stability of marriage or a career in favour of the excitement of living his life outside the law. Often he is an angry young man, whose murder spree begins when he uses violent means to solve a situation that causes frustration to his inflated ego. Once he knows that a felony offence will be linked to him, he flees the hand of justice, murdering and robbing anyone who has the misfortune to cross his path. Accordingly, his first victim may be an acquaintance or family member, while subsequent victims are strangers whom he seeks to use for his own gain. The utilitarian spree killer usually kills to eliminate witnesses, thus the majority of his murders are quick and impersonal — a few quick blasts from a firearm. At times he will take a situation more personally, stabbing, bludgeoning, or strangling his victims, though these occurrences are rarer. Suicidal behaviour is atypical of the utilitarian spree killer because he is not ashamed of his criminality; rather, he embraces it as a virtue. He may even enjoy the media attention when he is finally brought to justice. The case of **Peter John Peters** examined in the first chapter constitutes a spree murder who occasionally incorporated sexual assault. We will now take a look at two additional Canadian examples: the killer hitchhiker **Gregory McMaster**, and **Jesse Imeson**.

Kay Feely

Gregory McMaster

*"I wanted someone
held accountable."*

Victims: 4 killed
Duration of rampage: July 27 to August 2, 1978 (spree killing)
Locations: Quebec, Canada; Ontario, Canada; Manitoba, Canada;
Minnesota, U.S.
Weapon: Sawed-off .22-calibre rifle

KILLER ON THE ROAD

In late July 1978, American tourist Gregory McMaster travelled through
Quebec, Ontario, and Manitoba, seeing more of our home and native
land in six days than most Canadians will in a lifetime. Tragically, the
twenty-one-year-old thug left a legacy of pain along the way. A native
of New Haven, Connecticut, McMaster was a substance abuser awaiting
sentencing in the United States for assault, weapons offences, and burglary. Not pleased at the thought of going to prison, he decided to skip
bond and flee across the border with his girlfriend, Lori-Ann Sidbury.
Somewhere in eastern Canada, Lori-Ann absconded with most of their
money, leaving McMaster alone and furious. When his clunky Toyota
broke down, McMaster's rage finally consumed him. With only a thumb
and a sawed-off .22 rifle at his disposal, he took to the highways, hitch-
ing rides from helpful strangers. But things were moving too slowly for
McMaster. On July 27, he stepped onto the shoulder of the Trans-Canada
Highway, sweating as the blazing summer sun blanched the farm fields of
rural Quebec. Soon after, a red Chevrolet Blazer pulled up in a cloud of
dust, and McMaster hopped inside. The driver, seventeen-year-old Louis

Bertrand, was a gentle giant who resided in nearby Drummondville. According to one source, the two men went for drinks at a Drummondville bar. Within hours, McMaster showed his gratitude by shooting Bertrand eleven times and hiding him by the roadside.

Stealing Bertrand's truck, McMaster frantically drove west to Ontario. Thirty kilometres southeast of North Bay, he stopped to give a lift to fellow hitchhiker Marcel Girard. The nineteen-year-old had been visiting relatives in nearby Bonfield, and intended to head to North Bay before returning to the house he shared with several friends in the Toronto area. Unfortunately, McMaster had other plans for him. After pumping five bullets into his unsuspecting victim, he robbed him of a paltry sum and dumped Girard's body in a wooded area outside North Bay. Continuing west across the province to Sprague, Manitoba, he used the same m.o. to murder and rob twenty-one-year-old Marc Darvogne, a tourist from Montrouge, France.

Half an hour past midnight on August 2, 1978, McMaster ran the Blazer through the orange plastic cones marking the border crossing into the United States. Startled awake, an immigration officer notified the local law enforcement, and Roseau County Deputy Sheriff Richard Magnuson was dispatched to intercept the vehicle. Border jumping at the Sprague–Roseau crossing occurred an average of twenty-five times a year, so Magnuson's task was considered a routine and relatively low-risk procedure.

Just under five kilometres north of Roseau on Highway 310, McMaster spotted Magnuson's cruiser in pursuit and pulled onto the shoulder. He hid the .22 behind a large road map and stepped out of the Blazer clutching it as if confused. The twenty-year-old Magnuson, who had only been on the force for two months, exited his vehicle and proceeded toward McMaster on foot. Before the rookie cop knew what was happening, ten shots ripped through the map and into his body. Perforated by bullets, Magnuson fell onto the road and began crawling back to the squad car to radio for help. Fortunately, the young policeman had already radioed in before pulling McMaster over, providing the Blazer's licence plate number.

When Deputy Jim Wright arrived, he found Magnuson by the door of the cruiser, drenched in blood and nearing death. Sheriff Paul Knochenmus and Deputy Curt Hauger soon joined them. Hauger informed the others that while racing to the crime scene he had spotted suspicious tail lights on a side road. Heading back to the area, Hauger caught sight of a red Chevrolet Blazer bearing the licence plate number that Deputy Magnuson had radioed in. He contacted his colleagues, and a road block was erected to prevent the vehicle's passage. As the Blazer approached, it swerved off-road into a ditch to circumvent the blockade. A member of the sheriff's department shot out the front tire, and the vehicle came to a halt. Accepting defeat, Gregory McMaster threw the sawed-off rifle and a gun belt he had stolen from Deputy Magnuson out of the open window. He was arrested and taken into custody, where he confessed his crimes to Sheriff Knochenmus, even drawing a map indicating where he had left the bodies of his Canadian victims. Despite receiving blood donations from most of the police force and members of the local community, Deputy Richard Magnuson eventually died at 4:30 p.m. He was supposed to wed his college sweetheart, Julie, in the autumn. Two days later, Louis Bertrand's decomposing body was discovered in a ditch forty-eight kilometres outside Drummondville.

Convicted of murdering Magnuson and sentenced to life imprisonment, Gregory McMaster did fifteen years hard time in Minnesota before being extradited to Canada in 1993. Shortly after arriving, he filed an unsuccessful lawsuit challenging the way his handcuffs were being applied. In 1997, he pled guilty to the second-degree murder of Marc Darvogne, and to manslaughter in the cases of Louis Bertrand and Marcel Girard, earning a "life" sentence in Canada with eligibility for parole in ten years. McMaster successfully sued Corrections Canada in 2007, earning $6,000 compensation because he had not been given his yearly running shoes and had been "forced" by a prison official to wear incorrectly sized footwear as a substitute. As a result, the 270-pound McMaster had slipped and injured his knee while pounding a heavy bag. Imprisoned, McMaster seems to have transformed his propensity for physical aggression into continued legal assaults on the correctional system.

Kay Feely

Jesse Imeson

*"What's to know? Shots were
fired. People died."*

Victims: 3 killed
Duration of rampage: July 18 to 31, 2007 (spree killing)
Locations: Windsor, Ontario; Mount Carmel, Ontario
Weapons: Ligature strangulation with belt; .22-calibre rifle

THE FULL JESSE

The Tap was one of Windsor, Ontario's few gay bars, boasting a stage where male dancers shed their clothes nightly, gyrating around a pole to DJ Carlos Rivera's pulsating beat. On the evening of Tuesday, July 17, 2007, Jesse Norman Imeson — a tall, dark, and handsome twenty-two-year-old — stepped into the establishment for the first time, accompanied by his friend Nick Cesljar. An alcoholic and a cocaine addict, Imeson was excited at the prospect of making big money as an exotic dancer. Though Nick had warned him against the idea, Imeson believed that he would earn more money stripping for a gay crowd because he thought gays were perverts. After twenty minutes, he convinced Nick to drive him to his sister's house to pick up a CD by the electronic music artist Moby, which Imeson wanted to dance to. Nick dropped him off at the club around 9:30 p.m. and went elsewhere.

Back inside The Tap, Imeson approached manager Eddie An to inquire about exotic dancing. Eddie provided him with an application form, which Imeson was unable to complete as he had forgotten his identification. Assuring An that he would return to complete it tomorrow, Imeson spent the next few hours hanging around the bar drinking.

He soon struck up a conversation with twenty-five-year-old El Salvador émigré Carlos Rivera — a bartender and DJ involved in auditioning dancers. A student of architecture at St. Clair College, Carlos had been hired earlier in the summer when Eddie An had purchased the establishment and changed the name from The Happy Tap. Most of the staff and clientele at The Tap regarded Rivera as a sweet and hardworking man who loved being involved in Windsor's gay scene. Though Imeson was not known to be homosexual, several customers would later claim to have observed him trying to pick up Rivera. At one point in the night, Imeson hopped on the stage for a little amateur pole-dancing. He did not strip, and his performance lasted mere minutes. Shortly before 1:00 a.m. on July 18, Nick Cesljar received a call from an unknown number. It was Jesse Imeson — he had borrowed somebody else's cellphone and wondered if Nick wanted to get some cocaine and party. He lied that he had made $80 stripping. Already at home in McGregor, Nick refused, and wished him a goodnight.

An hour later, Carlos Rivera helped close up, and headed out with Imeson to continue drinking at the home of a third man named Douglas. While they were there, Douglas snapped several photographs, including an image of Imeson with his arm around Rivera and tongue protruding suggestively toward his nipple. The party broke up at 6:00 a.m., and Imeson and Rivera headed to Imeson's boarding house on Erie Drive in Rivera's silver Honda Civic. Douglas had insisted that Imeson, the less intoxicated of the two, drive. What happened at Imeson's home is a matter of some controversy. Imeson claims that he awoke to find Rivera performing oral sex on him. Enraged, he grabbed a canvas belt and strangled him to death. Though possible, this is not the most probable account of the murder. Consider the evidence:

1. Imeson was seen "hitting on" Rivera by clients at The Tap.
2. A sexually suggestive photograph of the two was taken the same night at Douglas's house.
3. Imeson drove Rivera back to his place.

Perhaps most crucial was the discovery of Imeson's semen in Rivera's mouth. Though it is certainly possible that Rivera may have fellated the sleeping Imeson, it seems unlikely that he would have been able to bring Imeson to climax without waking him. More probable was that an unstable and sexually confused Imeson willingly allowed Rivera to pleasure him. After ejaculating, Imeson's Id subsided, and his Superego took over. Rather than feeling good about the experience, he realized that his masculine, heterosexual self-image had been compromised. Due to his personality disorder, he was unable to accept responsibility for his own choice to engage in a homosexual act, projected his anger and self-hatred onto Carlos Rivera, and strangled him.

Whatever the true explanation, when Imeson saw what he had done, he would have realized that not only had he killed a man in his own apartment, but he had also left DNA on his body, and a slew of eye witnesses who could put them together on the night of the murder. At 8:00 a.m., he called his cousin Samantha from Rivera's cellphone in tears. He arranged to pick her up later that morning, then called Brooke, his ex-girlfriend and the mother of his daughter, but got her voicemail:

> *Sorry about how things have to be. You'll hear about everything. I made a big mistake tonight and, uh, something I have to do but that's all right. And, ah, you'll understand. It's not how it sounds, the media makes things look one way, whatever. The matter is Brooke, I love you so much, take care of our baby.*[48]

Soon after, Jesse Imeson appeared at his cousin's house in Carlos Rivera's Honda Civic, and he drove her to the cemetery to talk. "I did something really bad," Imeson explained by his father's grave. "I killed a guy last night." He went on to feed Samantha his account of being sexually assaulted by Carlos Rivera, and claimed he had left the body in his room.

Bidding her goodbye, Imeson fled north in the Civic, stopping at a Walmart to purchase a CD and a pair of sunglasses. By the time he rolled into the resort town of Grand Bend that night, the manager of The Tap had already called Douglas to ask why Carlos Rivera hadn't arrived for his shift. Suspicious, Douglas contacted the police at 11:00 p.m. Meanwhile, Jesse Norman Imeson was using his good looks to his advantage.

SCRAPPER

Jesse Norman Imeson had always been a troubled child. But when, at the age of nine, he stumbled upon the body of his father Jeff, who had committed suicide, he lost his tenuous grip and went into free fall. Unwanted by his mother, Jesse was placed into foster care and shuffled between homes in Windsor and Leamington, before finally settling with family in Amherstburg, Ontario. Though a neighbour remembers him as a "good kid" who was always running over from his grandparents' to visit his cousins two doors away, students at the various schools he passed through recognized that Jesse had problems. Upon becoming a legal adult, he was removed from the foster system. He dropped out of General Amherst High School around grade eleven. Left to his own devices, Imeson alternated between short stints in roofing and construction, and petty crime, regularly abusing alcohol and cocaine. Imeson served time in Windsor Jail for drug offences and possession of stolen goods. One Corrections Canada worker referred to him as "career criminal as you're going to get."

Nevertheless, Imeson dreamed of becoming a police officer, enrolling in a law and security course at St. Clair College. Despite his problems, his friends considered him a likable guy: easy to get along with and generous. He also possessed above-average intelligence, with an IQ measured at 123. When he wasn't in school or prison, Imeson could be found at the casino or drinking draft beer and shooting pool at the Fort Malden Hotel. At times he was an angry drunk, and got into fist fights. "He could always handle himself," said lifelong friend Jim Bondy. "He's no super tough guy, but he ain't no pushover, either." Due to his propensity for brawling, Imeson was prohibited from entering a roadhouse near his grandparents' property. A fan of mixed martial arts, he often sported Tap Out–brand clothing and, to further this tough guy image, covered himself with tattoos, though his choices were fairly uncreative. He was a frequent client of Ideal Imagery in Windsor, where owner Jeff Vella permanently inked the "Imeson" surname in 2.5-centimetre letters over his belly. On other occasions he decorated Imeson's arms with Japanese symbols. However, Vella was irritated by his client's constant hyperactivity. During one appointment, Imeson requested that the tattoo artist ink an elaborate tribal design along his right arm. Vella started the procedure, but Imeson was unable to sit still for more than five minutes, and left with the work unfinished.

In November 2006, at the age of twenty-one, Jesse Imeson returned to Windsor Jail to serve a six-month stint for robbery and break and enter, and was placed on suicide watch. After parole, he spent a brief period at a homeless shelter in Windsor before moving into the boarding house on Erie Street. Around February 2007, he returned to Ideal Imagery and showed Vella a shoddily executed tribal tattoo from another shop, asking him to fix it. Vella agreed, but soon after he started, found that Imeson was similarly problematic.

"He would get up, go to the washroom, make a phone call, have a smoke, whatever…. It's more preferable to sit for at least an hour at a time," Vella told the *London Free Press*. "I was fed up. I was just like, 'If you are not going sit still, there are a lot of tattoo shops in the city.' I told him not to bother coming back."

There are several possible explanations for Imeson's restless behaviour. It may have been a sign of the irritability and irresponsibility commonly found in individuals with anti-social personality disorder. Certainly, one can draw parallels between the ages and early criminal careers of Imeson and **Robert Raymond Cook** (Chapter 4). More sinisterly, it could reflect a psychopathic proneness to boredom and poor behavioural control. A third explanation, which could also work in tandem with either of the previous two, is that Imeson was suffering from cocaine withdrawal. In June of that year, he had completed a forty-day Salvation Army drug rehabilitation program, but relapsed the day after.

Nick Cesljar, the man who had accompanied Imeson to The Tap on the night of the murder, had also witnessed the dark side of Imeson's personality. The two had met months earlier while Imeson had been working construction in a building where a friend of Nick's lived. They soon found out that they had a lot in common: partying, girls, and a love of the Ultimate Fighting Championship. Cesljar never recalled seeing Imeson sober, and remembered his volatile temper: "Every time we'd watch [Ultimate Fighting Championship] fights, afterwards we'd get rowdy, you know, some grappling matches. When he loses, man, he … freaks out. We're like Jesse, man, calm … down." This inability to accept defeat in a mature manner could indicate symptoms of narcissistic or anti-social personality disorders, as well as psychopathy. As did his repeated lies about serving in Afghanistan and being dishonourably discharged for possessing cocaine. "Everything that came out of his mouth, now I know, was a lie."

Cesljar also remembers Imeson expressing suicidal fantasies. On Saturday, July 14, they had attended a drug- and booze-fuelled party in McGregor. "He was saying that if he wasn't socializing with us, if he wasn't hanging out, he'd be out there thinking about committing suicide," Cesljar recounted. "All this crazy shit about his girlfriend, his daughter."

CRAZY LI'L CHICK

Grand Bend, Ontario, is a scenic beach community on the shores of Lake Huron, often referred to as "Florida north" by local business people and politicians. Most of the year this sleepy resort town hosts two thousand residents, but when Imeson rolled in during tourist season on Wednesday, July 18, 2007, the population may have been as high as fifty thousand. Parking the stolen Honda Civic, the tall, dark stranger headed toward the Rod and Gun Sports Lounge, armed with Carlos Rivera's credit cards and a thirst. He sat down for a few beers with a stranger, Bruce Gallman, and after half an hour, the two drinking buddies took the party next door to Gables bar. There, Imeson met teens Kaylee Barrett and her blonde cousin Lindsey Glavin, the latter describing herself on Facebook as "a crazy li'l chick" whose interests included "mostly just partying and chillin." Rather than remaining inconspicuous, Imeson ingratiated himself, bragging to his companions that he was the owner of the silver Honda Civic. He joked with the other punters and spun fantastical yarns about serving in Afghanistan. Considering he had strangled Carlos Rivera to death less than twenty-four hours ago, Imeson's easy gregariousness points again to a major personality disorder. When Gables closed, Lindsey drove Imeson and Barrett back to her family home at 69401 Airport Line in Exeter, where they spent the night. The next morning, Barrett left for work. Glavin and Imeson drove back to Grand Bend, where they passed the day relaxing on the beach before paying a visit to the local liquor store.

Meanwhile, at 9:00 p.m. back in Windsor, police investigators had located Carlos Rivera's strangled corpse lying supine on Imeson's bed, nude save for a golf shirt, and partially covered by a blanket. A canvas belt with metal rings was looped twice around his swollen neck, and his arms and legs spilled out from under the covers like a turtle. Rivera had also sustained an injury to the face. Immediately, Jesse Norman Imeson became the number one suspect in the slaying.

At 9:30 p.m. the following evening, Jesse and Lindsey entered Gar's Bar and Grill in Exeter. Imeson drank beer and Glavin rye. According to their server, Imeson "was a nice guy, a normal guy with manners," and he and Glavin "looked like a couple. I thought they were together a long time." Imeson spun a tall tale about serving in Afghanistan with the Canadian armed forces. They left at 11:30 p.m. and he stayed another night at the Glavin home.

Sometime the next day, on Friday, July 20, Lindsey's mother saw a television report warning of a dangerous fugitive on the loose. To her shock and horror, the screen flashed a photograph of the young man who had spent the last two nights under her roof. Imeson was promptly asked to leave, and Lindsey drove him out to Bronson Line — a country road — where he fled on foot. Reaching the Muller farm in Bluewater, Imeson broke into the dwelling and made off with a .22-calibre rifle, two hundred rounds of ammunition, and a green coat.

Common sense did not seem to run strong in the Glavin family, as neither Lindsey nor her mother called 911 to inform authorities about the whereabouts of Ontario's most wanted homicidal predator. Instead, the "crazy li'l chick" waited until the next morning to persuade her ex-boyfriend to call Crime Stoppers on her behalf.

On Monday, July 23, the bodies of seventy-two-year-old William Regier and his seventy-three-year-old wife, Helene, were discovered in their Mount Carmel home. At 10:00 p.m. on July 22, Imeson had attempted to kick down the door of the little farmhouse on Bronson Line, but had failed. Instead he broke a window and entered, leaving shoeprints from his size 12 Nikes on the floor. Brandishing his newly acquired rifle, Imeson herded the couple into the basement, where he tied them up with clothesline, telephone wire, and an extension cord. Once they were incapacitated, he fired the rifle seven times, striking

Helene Regier in the right shoulder, neck, chest, and chin, and Bill in the right temple and twice in the chest. Leaving the bodies in the basement, Imeson stole William's money and identification and loaded a suitcase with food, clothing, and knives. Hurried, he sped off east in the Regiers' silver 2006 GMC Sierra, forgetting the suitcase altogether.

Staff Sergeant William Donnelly of the OPP lamented that if the Glavins had called 911 immediately, he had "no doubt" that Imeson would have been caught, and the Regier double murder could likely have been prevented. Instead, Jesse Norman Imeson was allowed to graduate to the level of spree killer, slipping along the multifarious tentacles of Ontario's highway system like slime into a vast, dark ocean.

AND THE LAW WON

Fortunately, Imeson was leaving a trail of breadcrumbs wherever he ran. Aside from credit card purchases, Carlos Rivera's silver Honda Civic had already been found abandoned in Grand Bend on Friday, July 20, leading police to widen their manhunt to Lambton County. Soon all of South Huron was being scoured by ground and air. The break-in at the Muller residence on Babylon Line, in which the firearm had been stolen, was linked to Imeson by Sunday, along with the discovery of the Regiers' bodies the following day. A description of the Regiers' missing silver GMC Sierra was released to the public in an attempt to produce leads. By Wednesday, the fugitive and select details of his crimes appeared on the *America's Most Wanted* website. The next day, police as far away as Calgary, Alberta, and Whistler, B.C., had joined in the search. Imeson had contacts in both locations and had spoken of moving out west shortly before the murders took place. With Imeson on the lam for over a week, on Saturday, July 28, investigators announced that his appearance might have changed significantly. The dark-haired, clean-cut murderer whose face had been seared into the minds of Ontario residents could now very well be a bearded bleach-blond.

Around 7:00 p.m. on Tuesday, July 31, hundreds of kilometres east in Portage-du Fort, Quebec, Dale Lewis was watering his absentee neighbour Bob Simpson's plants, when he heard the blare of a television from inside the cottage. Alarmed, he peered through the blinds in the back window and saw a shadowy figure quickly skirt behind a supporting pillar. Wisely, Lewis hurried next door to Douglas Young's residence, and told him to dial 911. Before the authorities could arrive, Douglas spotted the intruder fleeing into the woods on foot. The SQ and OPP promptly arrived on the scene, and a manhunt ensued. At 9:00 p.m., a police dog led officers to Imeson's hiding place. Though clutching the same loaded .22 he had used to murder William and Helene Regier, when faced with armed opponents, Imeson threw down his weapon and surrendered. Like many of his UFC heroes, he had been caught in an inescapable stranglehold, and had submitted. Unlike the athletes he so admired, Imeson lacked the discipline to do anything exceptional with his time on this planet, turning to drugs and crime for a quick fix. Despite his manly veneer, he had been effectively "tapping out" his whole life.

Imeson was taken into custody and removed to Campbell's Bay provincial police detachment. The following day, complaining of stomach pain, he was escorted to Shawville hospital. While there, he remarked to a police officer that he would be facing a twenty- to twenty-five year sentence, and that his life was finished. However, he showed no remorse, even admitting to the officer, "The gay guy — if I had to do it again, I would do it." Later that evening, the shackled prisoner was transported by airplane back to Windsor and confined to a cell at the city police station. Imeson confessed to detectives that he had been hiding out in the Regiers' barn for days, entering the house through an unlocked garage side door to look for food and clothing. Once inside, he began packing these items into a stolen suitcase, when he was startled by William Regier, who he did not believe was home. When asked about what had happened next, Imeson replied, "What's to know? Shots were fired. People died." Considering that the Regiers' GMC Sierra was parked at their home, the victims had been bound before execution, and the window was broken, it is obvious that Imeson's account was just one more in the litany of lies colouring his sad existence.

Having left fingerprint, shoe-print, and DNA evidence, there was little chance that Jesse Norman Imeson would be found not guilty of the murders, so he opted for a plea bargain. On October 27, 2008, in a Goderich courtroom, Imeson pled guilty to the second-degree murders of Carlos Rivera and the Regiers. Denouncing Imeson's crimes as "savage," Justice Ronald Haines gave his condolences to the victims' families, before sentencing Imeson to life without the possibility of parole for twenty-five years — the maximum sentence possible under Canadian law. Though Imeson had occasionally seemed anxious during the proceedings, when assistant Crown Attorney Jennifer Holmes described him receiving oral sex from Rivera, he began to smirk and shift in his chair. As she went on to speak about him strangling Rivera with the belt, Imeson nodded his head and said, "That's right." Clearly he was proud of murdering Carlos Rivera. In the years since Imeson's killing spree, at least three gay bars in Windsor, including The Tap, have closed.

CHAPTER 6

THE EXTERMINATOR

Rare among spree killers, the Exterminator is an individual consumed by hatred, opting to eradicate members of a specific societal group or profession whom he deems unfit to live. In many ways, the Exterminator is the equivalent of Holmes and DeBurger's Missionary serial murderer (for a Canadian example, see my *Cold North Killers*), with the exception that once the Exterminator begins killing, he never cools off. Toronto repairman **Marcello Palma** was an Exterminator of the same prostitutes and transsexuals whose bodies he coveted. In probably the most controversial spree killing in recent history, **Stephen Marshall** of Cape Breton travelled around Maine using the state's online sex offender registry to locate victims. Was he an avenging angel, or a devil in disguise?

Kay Feely

Marcello Palma
The Victoria Day Shooter

"I popped her ... [Later] I did the other two."

Victims: 3 killed
Duration of rampage: May 21–22, 1996 (spree killing)
Location: Toronto, Ontario
Weapon: .357 revolver

NIGHT OF FEAR

Brenda Ludgate hadn't always been a prostitute standing in the rain. Before the drugs crept in she was the cherished daughter of a loving middle-class family. Now those memories brought only pain, but that could be solved — chemically. All she needed to do was turn a few tricks. At 11:10 p.m. on May 21, 1996, a red truck with a strange light on top pulled up to the curb where Brenda was working. This was her chance! Stepping toward the passenger-side door, she bent down to speak with the driver. The gunshot broke the night like thunder. In a nearby high-rise apartment, a woman doing her best to enjoy the stormy Victoria Day weekend with friends thought she heard arguing outside followed by a loud bang. She looked out the window just in time to see the red truck speeding away, leaving the twisted body of Brenda Ludgate staring back at her from a pool of blood. Arriving on the scene shortly after, Inspector James Ramer cursed his luck. A rainy crime scene was a homicide detective's worst nightmare. Already crucial evidence was being washed away from the body in a torrent of rain-diluted blood. It was going to be a long, wet night. He had no idea.

Nineteen-year-old transvestite Sean Keegan ran away from his home east of Toronto because he didn't fit in. Though he took advantage of the various shelters scattered about the city, he had few ways of making money and turned to prostitution to get by. Like Brenda Ludgate, he wasn't kicking off his high heels for a relaxing Victoria Day weekend either. When the red van with the curious light rolled to a stop beside him, he would have shared Brenda's sense of relief. A short time after, his lifeless body was discovered in a stairwell by two security guards. He had been shot through the head.

Meanwhile, back at the Ludgate crime scene, the eyewitness was unable to identify the vehicle's make or model. James Ramer was grasping at straws when he heard the news of the second killing on the radio. Dawn would bring a new revelation. As the morning light spread across the dank, dripping city, it revealed the body of thirty-one-year-old Thomas Wilkinson lying in a muddy laneway. A prostitute and transsexual, Wilkinson had also been shot in the head, dropping his umbrella at his side.

Despite the poor weather, police were able to collect bullets from some of the crime scenes. At the site of the Wilkinson slaying they also discovered a man's boot print of undisclosed size.

A PORTRAIT OF NORMALCY

Almost a week passed with no suspect emerging in the case. Autopsies conducted on the three murdered sex workers revealed they had all been shot at close range with a .357 revolver. With few other leads, investigators decided to concentrate on the strange truck spotted at the Ludgate crime scene. In an attempt to jog the eyewitness's memory, a hypnotist and police sketch artist were brought in to work with her. Although she could not recall the licence plate, they did produce a much clearer picture of the vehicle: a narrow-bodied red truck with a pink light vaguely reminiscent of a taxi cab's on top. Speaking with other prostitutes in the area, police learned that the truck had been sighted many times trawling the streets. Then on May 26, they finally got the break they were looking for. Police received a telephone call from a lawyer claiming to represent a man who had important information on the red truck. Eventually the man agreed to speak with the authorities, candidly revealing that just after midnight on May 22 his friend Marcello Palma called unexpectedly at his house. Soaked with rain and seemingly apprehensive, the thirty-year-old Palma asked if he could leave a bag containing a knife, handgun, and ammunition in his care. He agreed, but later, deciding he wanted nothing to do with it, left the bag and weapons with Palma's brother. As if that wasn't enough, the witness also revealed that Palma had made several alterations to his truck in the days following the murder. Perhaps most surprising was the revelation that their suspect was not only a successful business man, but happily married.

Convinced that Marcello Palma and "The Victoria Day Shooter" were one and the same, investigators descended on Palma's air conditioning business, where they believed he was hiding. Though his truck was parked outside, after two days of surveillance there was still no sign of him. It was as if the city had swallowed him whole. With few other options, on May 29 they issued a Canada-wide warrant for Marcello Palma's arrest. The next day they received a tip that Palma had been spotted in Montreal but had vanished soon after.

Obtaining search warrants for the suspect's home, workplace, and parents' residence, the police soon uncovered various firearms, including a snub-nosed .357 revolver which had been altered so that bullets couldn't be linked to the gun. A search of his truck revealed a slip of paper with the phone number of the building where Keegan's body had been discovered, along with drops of blood under the passenger seat. The front cab had recently been cleaned. Investigators also found the phone number of a transvestite sex worker who Palma had contacted sometime before. If there was a shadow of a doubt, it was fading fast.

As police continued to search across the country for the elusive gunman, on June 1 they received word that Palma's credit card had been used to check into an expensive Halifax hotel. They immediately contacted the authorities in Halifax, advising them that Palma was likely armed and dangerous. Three uniformed police officers arrived at the waterfront hotel and quietly began to clear guests from the other rooms on Palma's floor. A chambermaid claiming to have spoken with him revealed that he had seemed agitated. When the floor had been evacuated, the policemen burst into Palma's room only to discover it empty. As they waited inside for their suspect, they heard somebody pass close by the door. Soon after, the phone rang, but when they answered there was only the sound of heavy breathing before the caller hung up. A second call turned out to be the desk clerk. Palma had just been seen leaving the building, heading in the direction of the boardwalk. At 6:45 p.m., police began to comb the area. Eventually they spotted Palma sitting on the edge of the wharf, and took him into custody. Among his possessions they found ammunition and the key to a bed and breakfast across town. Inside this second room, Detective Phil McDonald located a .357 rifle hidden in the mattress — evidently in preparation for a final stand-off with the police. Palma had also been reading several books on psychological abnormalities, including Dr. Robert Hare's landmark *Without Conscience*. Two days later, he was transferred to Toronto to eventually stand trial.

DNA testing revealed that the blood in the truck belonged to Brenda Ludgate. Faced with overwhelming evidence, in April 1999 Palma pleaded "not guilty by reason of insanity." During the course of his trial he was arrogant, showing no remorse for having senselessly ended three lives. Taking the stand, Palma's wife and his mistress testified that he was something of a Jekyll and Hyde, frequently erupting in unprovoked rages and threatening suicide. At one point he had even pointed a gun at his wife's head. It was also revealed that five years before the murders, Palma had sought psychiatric help for a violent hatred of prostitutes and transsexuals. Though this "control freak" claimed to loathe them, he also frequented them regularly, a contradiction that could only be resolved with bloodshed. Palma was found guilty on three counts of murder and imprisoned for life in a maximum security penitentiary with the possibility of parole in twenty-five years. He claimed to have selected Victoria Day for his murder spree because he thought the gun shots would be mistaken for fireworks.

Elizabeth Roth-Gunter

Stephen Marshall

"I am sorry to admit that I will not likely ever choose to attempt to intervene in a violent situation to save any person because of my fear of the bad legal consequences."

Victims: 2 killed/committed suicide
Duration of rampage: Sunday April 16, 2006 (spree killing)
Location: Maine, U.S.
Weapons: .45-calibre pistol, .22-calibre pistol

FATHER AND SON REUNION

Stephen Marshall and his father Ralph had always been close. Having spent his early years in Cape Breton, Nova Scotia, when his parents' marriage crumbled Stephen uprooted with the old man to Culdesac: a tiny community of less than four hundred people in northern Idaho. There the two bonded over a mutual love of firearms and hunting, regularly attending gun shows together. Things seemed okay. Ralph Marshall served as executive director for the Clearwater Economic Development Association, and later became town mayor. Throughout his teens, Stephen was a quiet but reasonably popular student who enjoyed playing video games and making prank phone calls. On the surface, he appeared more or less normal and well-adjusted — save for one troubling incident. In April 2001, local boys Chris Reisdorph and Nathan Tyler started brawling in the Marshall family front yard after Chris sprayed Nathan with a water gun. Stephen, a good friend of Chris's older brother Joe, pointed a rifle at Nathan and was subsequently charged with aggravated assault by the Nez Perce County Sheriff's Department. He was fifteen years old and about to move … again.

After sitting for three years as Culdesac's mayor, plus a stint in Arizona, Ralph Marshall relocated to Maine, where he found employment with a local Native American band. Stephen returned to Canada. By the age of twenty he had a job washing dishes at the Canton Family Restaurant in North Sydney, Nova Scotia, where he was considered "nice, quiet," and "reliable." On Tuesday, April 11, 2006, Stephen showed up on time for his last shift before Easter weekend, when he planned to visit his father in Houlton, Maine. Nobody on the staff recalled seeing him acting peculiarly. They wished him "safe travels" and expected him to be back washing their dishes in a few days.

BLOODY SUNDAY

It was three degrees above freezing on the morning of Easter Sunday when a white pickup truck rolled into the town of Corinth, Maine. Just before 8:15 a.m. it parked outside the mobile home of twenty-four-year-old William Elliott and his family. A junkyard operator by trade, William had been convicted of statutory rape and jailed for four months in 2002. His name, photo, and address were logged among 2,200 others in Maine's online sex offender registry. That morning William was hanging around with his girlfriend, Terri, and father, Wayne, when there was a knock on the door.* He opened it to find himself confronted by a pimple-faced gunman. From her vantage point, Terri looked on in horror as the visitor emptied his pistol into her unsuspecting boyfriend, dropping him to the floor. He continued to fire long after William was dead before fleeing the scene. Darting toward the doorway, Terri saw his white pickup truck peel away and scribbled down the licence plate number.

It wasn't long before police connected the slaying with that of Joseph Gray, a fifty-seven-year-old child rapist who had been gunned down in his Minot apartment five hours earlier. Like William Elliott, his name and details appeared in the state sex offender database. Running the licence plate number through the computer, police discovered that the mysterious white pickup belonged to a Ralph Marshall of Houlton. They contacted Ralph and learned that his son Stephen had stolen the truck, a .22-calibre pistol, a .45-calibre pistol, and a rifle. Maine state police sent out an alert, declaring Stephen a "person of interest" who should be considered armed and dangerous. Ralph Marshall couldn't believe it. Just days before, the two had been laughing and eating ice cream cones. Now, his son had become the object of a police manhunt.

Stephen's white truck was discovered that day, abandoned outside a hockey arena in Bangor. When a worker pulled some corresponding bullets out of a toilet tank at a nearby bus depot, investigators surmised that Stephen had probably caught the Vermont Bus Lines coach to Boston. They informed the Massachusetts police, who intercepted the bus just outside of South Station.

Inside the vehicle, the doors opened and two transit officers stepped aboard. "Turn on the overhead lights," they commanded the driver. The bus lit up like a dance floor after last call, exposing the bewildered expressions of the holiday travellers. Before anyone knew what was happening, there was a loud bang, and blood splattered the passengers. Thirteen rows behind the driver, Stephen Marshall slumped forward in his seat — dead. He had blown off a portion of his skull with a .45-calibre handgun, most of the brain matter flying through the open window. Rushing to

---

* Terri's name is a pseudonym.

the scene, paramedics found a second .22-calibre pistol in his backpack along with a laptop, passport, and "some personal papers."

JUSTIFYING MURDER

Everybody knew that Stephen Marshall had committed suicide by gun-shot to the head. The autopsy they were interested in was psychological. What would lead this polite young man from Cape Breton to embark on his killing spree? Eager to find out, Maine state detectives descended on Nova Scotia to interview friends and family of the deceased. His apart-ment was thoroughly searched for some clue to his motivation, and his laptop dissected electronically by police technicians. Eventually, it was learned that Marshall had indeed logged onto Maine's sex offender reg-istry, viewing the profiles of thirty-four out of 2,200 convicted perverts. Among the names of those whose information he had accessed were Joseph Gray and William Elliott. Not only did the registry provide each man's name, but also his address and the specifics of his conviction.

Back in Idaho, Stephen's friend, twenty-year-old Joe Reisdorph, admitted to the press via telephone that whenever a rapist or child molester appeared on the news, Stephen and his friends would discuss how vile the perpetrator was. To use Reisdorph's own words, "We just said the people who were guilty of it were worthless. We all agreed it was heinous.... We thought sexual predators were worse than killers." They weren't the only ones — many Americans voiced their support for what Stephen Marshall had done. William Elliott's father, Wayne, saw things from a different perspective: "My son, my only son, was my best friend.... I couldn't understand who would hate him this much."

At the end of the day, Marshall knew even less about his victims than we know about Marshall. Was he an enraged sexual abuse survivor who enforced his own brand of justice against those who, at least on the computer, resembled his tormentors? Or was he simply a disturbed young man with a gun fixation, using his victims' sex offender status to dehumanize them, and justifying his overwhelming urge to kill? Could it be some combination of the two? Marshall's mother has repeatedly asked American police to divulge the contents of her son's laptop, but as of this writing, she has been consistently refused.

Though we have far less access to information than the authorities, we will now examine Marshall's personal history and psychology, in an attempt to gain an understanding of his actions. A good starting point is the killer's own writings. Source #1 is the content of a personal website Marshall created at the age of fourteen. Source #2 is an essay on guns and juvenile violence he was required to write as part of his probation for pointing the assault rifle at Nathan Tyler. Source #3 is a 2005 email reply to a long-lost buddy in Idaho, in which Marshall speaks rather candidly about his personal life and situation.

Source #1: Website Content[49]

Marshall provides a link to the "sweetist [*sic*] pics of weapons that you can find anywhere."

He also includes a list of "personal dislikes:

- minorities getting special treatment
- men who don't keep their women in line
- Asthma
- women in general
- the beautiful people
- my job
- cleaning
- school
- society
- the disgusting commercialization of our daily lives
- the economic system
- capitalism (But it'll do for now)
- rich people
- the United Nations
- a world government
- the feds
- the man and his rules
- civil oppression
- the 'Patriot Act' of 2001."

Source #2: Essay on "Guns and Their Influence on Juvenile Crime" mandated by Marshall's probation[50]

Note to the reader: In order not to disrupt the flow of Marshall's essay, I included footnotes wherever I saw fit to provide analysis.

Guns and Their Relation to Juvenile Crime

August 19, 2001

Introduction

When you hear the title of this paper, what comes to mind? "Guns and their relation to juvenile crime." What I think of is, of course, serious crime that I see on the news.[a] Liquor store robberies, gang related violence, drug dealing, ect [sic]. The types of youth involved in these activities have not been raised around firearms. They have never been through a safety course, and have almost no prior experience around guns. They live in the city where hunting and target shooting is not practiced. The fact is, an extremely small percentage [of] youths who have access to guns rob stores or do drugs.[b] They are kids raised on good values and have had their shooting and hunting heritage passed on from their parents. They go shooting with their friends and family and would never think of using a gun in a violent crime.[c] Such was my attitude until I was presented with a situation in which I made a hasty decision, and inadvertently committed a crime. I know that what I did was wrong, and Nathan said that it scared him.[d] I have since written an apology letter addressing my actions and the way they impacted him. I believe that Chris Reisdorph has since recovered from his assault, also.[e]

This paper will address some of the concerns of society on juvenile crimes involving guns. From the point of view of a concerned citizen, I will make suggestions on sentencing and how to solve this problem. I will obtain some useful information from the internet, and will list my sources on my resource page. This paper will mostly be about personal opinions. I will state my point of view on the different types of crime I research. Juvenile gun crime can [*sic*] is a significant problem, and I hope that my point of view will help solve it somehow.

Types of crime

As I said before, when I think of "gun crime" related to youths, I think of what I see on the news and on television. There are people shot down on the street for gang related activity, rare school shootings, drugs, and muggings.[f] School shootings, though, are all we ever hear about in the national news out of all these types of crime. In the specific crime that I committed, it was an emergency situation. My alternatives had to have been considered and action taken in a split second. Under such pressure, my judgment was faulty. One of the alternatives I had was to do nothing. The alternative I should have selected was to call 911 and wait for the sheriff to come. But I believe that any long delay could have resulted in grave harm to a 13 year old boy at the hands of a much bigger, stronger 16 year old.[g] In the future, if I am a witness to any violent situation my response will be to contact the proper authorities.

Victim Impact

Most violent gun related crimes usually end in death for the victim. If this victim is not in fact killed, the impact is usually severe. Paralysis and other disabilities can result from gun wounds. But the people who are shot are not the only victims. Their friends and family suffer, also. Take the so-called "Million Mom March" for example. These people were friends and family of youths killed by people using guns. They were obviously very hurt by what had happened to someone who they loved so much. It was their opinion that increased gun control was the answer. Though I disagree with this opinion, I can understand the way they feel. They are hurt and angry for their loved ones [*sic*] death, and some of their arguments about guns are respectable.[h]

Further to address psychological impact, I refer to my case. Nathan told police that he was scared and worried that he was going to be shot. His fear and "worry" are legitimate psychological impacts on him, and though I had no intention to do anything of the sort to him, I do feel remorse for making him feel that way.

Other emotional problems can arise from things like muggings and other street crime. Victims of these crimes often feel scared and even paranoid if and when they go out on the street again, some cannot even go out for weeks after a traumatic incident like this happens.

Sentencing

I do not believe in mandatory sentencing for gun related crime. Such as if I was automatically required to serve 90 days in jail and probation until I was 21 for "aggravated assault" or "assault," just because it involved a gun. I do not believe that that would have been fair, or necessary to correct my actions. Each case is unique, and must be treated that way by the judge. I do believe that since gun related juvenile crime is a problem, sentencing should be harsher than with other violent crime. But I think that the judge should use his judgment to fairly deal with each case. Further, I think that youths should be educated beyond what they learn in hunters ed. They should learn about inappropriate ways to use a firearm in an emergency, and they must know the laws. If I knew that what I was doing was illegal in trying to save Chris, I would never have done it that way.

Recommendations for Solving the Problem

Unlike many, I do not believe that gun control is the answer. When we make new laws, restrictions, regulations and gun bans, one must remember that only the honest citizen is the only one that follows these rules. I mean if I were a criminal I wouldn't really care, because

I would already be breaking the law by using the weapons inappropriately in a crime.[i] I believe that no convicted felon should own a gun.

Making snap legislation over rare youth shooting incidents is not the answer, either. Take, for example, the murder of six year old Kayla Rolland, the Michigan first grader shot by a classmate not long ago. Now keeping in mind how rare these incidents actually are, look at the case of Brianna Blackmond, a 23 month old Washington, D.C. girl who died from a blow to the head shortly after being returned to her mother from a foster home. But only Kayla's murder prompted President Clinton to call for trigger locks on all handguns. Brianna's death did not prompt him to call for tougher child protecting laws against abuse. Brianna's incident is more statistically typical of young children killed in this country, but the President virtually ignored it.

Your chances of being killed in a public school is just under 1 in 1 million. In the case of Columbine, the juveniles who committed this act acquired their guns 100% illegally. They were bought from a dealer whose actions were near as reprehensible as the two high shooting [*sic*] itself, and I believe he gives gun dealers a bad name and should be sentenced harshly.

And thus I come to my own opinions.[j] I believe that nothing can replace growing up around firearms since a child, and learning safety and responsibility through the parents.[k] I think that as long as we have poverty level neighborhoods, there will always be crime, even if we somehow take all the guns away. I however do not believe that guns make juveniles commit crimes. They may make an inexperienced kid feel powerful or something, but if the guns weren't there, a knife would replace it. As you know, Canada has a very stringent gun policy. Mandatory locked storage with ammo separate, almost no handguns, ect [*sic*]. I was talking to one of my Canadian friends not too long ago, and he says that he knows of people who pack around brass knuckles to school, and he even had a knife held to the back of his neck by a classmate to intimidate him.

Society is to blame, not an inanimate object like guns.[1] I think that constant media attention and perhaps television desensitize youth to this crime and irresponsibility with guns. These kind [*sic*] of actions are even admired in "rap" culture. The solution to this problem is not easy, nor can it be just one solution. I don't think that I can come up with a solution to juvenile gun crime. My main opinion still stands, though. I think that there is no substitute for good parenting.

In Closing

I am sorry to admit that I will not likely ever choose to attempt to intervene in a violent situation to save any person because of my fear of the bad legal consequences.[m]

Sources

www.nra.com; www.millionmommarch.com; www.stats.org
Direct Personal Experience

---

a. This is the first of many incidences in which Marshall seeks to distinguish himself from "real criminals." In his bizarre logic, threatening a teenager with a loaded assault rifle does not constitute a "serious crime."

b. However, Marshall seems to believe that kids who "do drugs" are more "serious" criminals than himself.

c. If this were true, Marshall, who obviously views himself as a kid raised on "good values," would not have conceived using the rifle to threaten Nathan Tyler in the first place. That he did undermines his entire argument.

d. Here Marshall is being coy. He pretends to have been oblivious to the fact that Nathan Tyler had been scared, when the entire purpose of pointing the weapon at him in the first place was to intimidate him.

e. It is a testament to Marshall's lack of remorse that he sees fit to continually remind the reader of Tyler's assault on Reisdorph. The reformative purpose of the essay was for Marshall to address the influence that guns had played in his own crime. He has already explained that he intervened to stop Tyler's assault on Reisdorph. We understand. Still, he reminds us again, even though there is no context to necessitate this.

f. So in Marshall's world view, the definition of a "serious crime" is one he sees on television?

Source #3: Email reply to Steve's friend Derek McFarland in Idaho[51]

From: Steve Marshall <iliketoburnthings88@yahoo.com>
Sent: Thursday, March 17, 2005 9:51 AM
To: Derek McFarland [email address blacked out to protect privacy]
Subject: Re: Hey Steve! What's up?

Weird, I just fired up the comp and I was thinkin how nuts it would be to hear from you guys. But I'm kinda psychic like that or something it seems. Anyways, I came up to Canada from Phoenix to join the militia, but the

---

g. Though we do not know the extent of Reisdorph's injuries, I, perhaps controversially, agree with Marshall's decision to intervene. People can be killed in fist fights, and it is unreasonable to rely solely on police protection, considering the time it takes for them to arrive on the scene. However, there were many less extreme courses of action available. For instance, Marshall might have continually shouted for help while trying to physically separate the two boys (unlike Reisdorph, he was around Tyler's age at the time). That Marshall's first reaction was to grab a gun perhaps reflects his physical insecurity (related to his asthma?) and unhealthy obsession with firearms.

h. Note that Marshall doesn't bother to include or comment on these specific views; rather, he shrugs them off as "respectable" and continues with his polemic.

i. Point taken. What Marshall fails to realize is that he *is* a criminal. This comes back to the issue of him attempting to distance himself from the "real criminals" he sees on television.

j. In reality, nearly the whole essay has comprised Marshall's opinions.

k. If this worked so well, then how is it that Marshall was oblivious (if we are to believe him) to the gun laws he violated?

l. Once again, Marshall displaces responsibility for his actions onto an entity other than himself. It is the fault of society as a whole that gun crimes occur, not individuals like himself who perpetrate them.

m. This final sentence is by far the most telling, if barely readable. Marshall concludes his essay by essentially saying that he is sorry he will no longer use a gun to break up fights because of the legal ramifications. The implication is that, if the laws were different, he would take the same course of action. If so, then his expressions of remorse for scaring Nathan Tyler are completely insincere. In fact, his whole essay is invalid, and would have better been replaced with, "I will not point guns at people anymore because I don't want to be punished by the criminal justice system." Narcissism, manipulation, and deception; all three of these traits and behaviours are evidenced to varying degrees in Stephen Marshall's half-hearted and snide attempt at a self-reflective essay.

asthma fucked me even though the guys said it wouldn't before I moved, they said because I was on perscriptions [*sic*] I couldn't join. Bastards. So I took a computer trade, got a few jobs, now I'm unemployed and looking. Need an apartment, stayin at a friends [*sic*] for a couple days cause I got the boots put to me here (again). Prolly [*sic*] go back to school, community college for a couple years then university, might do it in Maine where my dad is now, or Georgia where my half-brother lives. But in the mean time [*sic*] I smoke a bit here and there and this that and the other, you know how it is. Well I gotta get out of my ex-house before the stepdad comes home (bastard) and I have to beat him with bats and stuff, you know how it goes. Say hi to Harrison, and your mom.

Keep your pants on,

Steve

PSYCHOLOGICAL AUTOPSY

Having examined these three primary source materials (the fourteen-year-old Marshall's website content, his mandatory essay about juvenile gun crimes, and an email from the spring of 2005) along with his child-hood history, we can now develop a clearer understanding of Stephen Marshall's character. Three major themes are evident:

1) A Rootless, Unstable Existence

Despite his polite demeanour, Stephen Marshall's life totally lacked structure. Born on August 9, 1985, within twenty years he moved a total of eight times (on average every two and a half years) between two countries, one province, and three states. Certainly many children have lived transient lifestyles and not turned into rampage killers. However, we should note that after his eighth birthday, every time Stephen moved, he ended up living with a different guardian.

Table 7: Timeline of Stephen Marshall's Twenty-Year Life

Location	Age	Living With
1985: Fort Worth, Texas	Birth–3 years	Parents
1988: Cape Breton, Nova Scotia	3–7 years	Parents
1993: Arizona	7–13 years	Mother, sister, grandparents
1999: Culdesac, Idaho	13–16 years	Father
2002: Phoenix, Arizona	16–17 years	Half-sister and her family
2003: North Sydney, Nova Scotia	18–19 years	Mother and stepfather
2005: Sydney, Nova Scotia	19 years	Rooming house
2005: North Sydney, Nova Scotia	19–death	Roommates

Marshall lacked motivation or direction. His March 2005 email response notes his failure to accomplish his goal of joining the militia. Since then, he had tried his hand at computers to no avail, drifted from job to job, and found no permanent residence. Undoubtedly, his problems with his stepfather would only have complicated his relationship with his mother. Though Marshall wrote of returning to school, his plans come off as vague and noncommittal. All his life, Stephen Marshall was a lost soul — one who, unfortunately, loved guns.

2) A Fascination with Guns and Violence

In his single, rather brief email, Marshall expresses an admiration for violence on three occasions, even enshrining it in his email address: "I like to burn things 88." He speaks of trying to join the militia, and later jokes about beating his stepfather with a baseball bat. This behaviour was consistent through his adolescence. Five years earlier, he had inexplicably provided a link on his website to the "sweetist [*sic*] pics of weapons that you can find anywhere." His farcical "Guns and Their Relation to Juvenile Crime" mostly defended firearm ownership, and in it he insincerely professed remorse for having "frightened" Nathan Tyler by targeting him with an assault rifle.

3) Racism, Misogyny, and Anti-establishment Views

Though they did not factor directly into his murders, Marshall's racist, misogynist, and anti-establishment views appear to varying degrees in each of the three sources we examined. His racism is most apparent on his website, where he lists "minorities getting special treatment" as one of his personal dislikes. More subtly, in his essay, Marshall notes that gun violence is "admired in 'rap' culture." He is, of course, generally right; however, one could also argue that shooting people is equally revered in country and heavy metal music. Anyone remember what Johnny Cash did to that man in Reno? What was the name of Axl Rose's band? Yet Marshall completely overlooks these genres, focusing exclusively on music developed by urban blacks. Curiously, the number "88" at the end of Marshall's email address is a known white supremacist code for "Heil Hitler" (*H* being the eighth letter of the alphabet). We could dismiss its presence as coincidental, if it was not paired with a statement proclaiming a predilection for arson and used by a future murderer who attempted to join a militia.

Beyond the race issue, Marshall also claimed on his website to dislike "men who don't keep their women in line" and "women in general." Nowhere is there any mention of him ever having had a sexual or romantic relationship in his life. Whether this was the cause or result of his misogyny is another matter altogether.

Finally, Marshall writes of his disdain for "the beautiful people," "society," "the disgusting commercialization of our daily lives," "the economic system," "capitalism," "rich people," "the United Nations," "a world government," "the feds," "the man and his rules," "civil oppression," and "the 'Patriot Act' of 2001." For the sake of brevity, he could have just said "society" and left it at that. He criticizes President Bill Clinton for what he perceives as an anti-gun bias in his essay.

So taking Marshall's murders, directionless existence, fixation on violence, and racist/misogynist/anti-establishment views into consideration, what conclusion can we draw? I propose that this child, raised by a highly conservative father, and lacking any sense of self, strove to find meaning, albeit immaturely, in a militant totalitarian right-wing philosophy. This did not spark his killing spree; it was merely symptomatic. Marshall's sense of personal failure and confused identity fed his resentment and anger, which in turn affected his ability to achieve, creating an increasingly rapid loop of hatred. Feeling that his life had spiralled completely out of control, Marshall sought power in the only place he'd ever found it: guns. At some point in 2006, he seems to have forsaken hope, giving in to his twin urges to kill and, in turn, bring an end to his pointless existence. Yet simultaneously, he still wanted to be someone. By murdering sex offenders, Marshall satisfied his need for destruction and to establish an identity, becoming a "vigilante hero" in his own eyes and those of many Americans. But this was no Christ figure, self-sacrificing for the benefit of all humanity; rather, he was a confused and misanthropic young man who used his victims' criminal status as an excuse to commit murder. The psychological parallels with Marc Lépine are startling.

CHAPTER 7

THE SIGNATURE KILLER

Of all the categories of spree killer, the Signature type bears the closest resemblance to the public conception of a serial murderer. During his formative years, his sexuality becomes warped, leading him to develop abnormal fantasies and numerous paraphilias, which can range from the desire to rape (**Jonathan Yeo**), to cannibalism and necrophilia (**Dale Merle Nelson**).

Dale Merle Nelson

Kay Feely

Victims: 8 killed
Duration of rampage: September 4 to 5, 1970 (spree killing)
Locations: Creston and West Creston, British Columbia
Weapons: 7-mm Mauser rifle, fire extinguisher, carving knife

TONIGHT THE BOTTLE LET ME DOWN

There's an old saying that alcohol brings out the real you. If that's the case, then Dale Merle Nelson was no less than a monster. For years the curly haired blond lumberjack played the role of loving husband and father, inhabiting a small but cozy home along Corn Creek Road in British Columbia's Creston Valley. His wife Annette and his three children considered him to be a decent, hard-working man with one overriding flaw: a tendency for cruelty when he drank. At times he would become physically and verbally abusive, shaking the foundation of his family. There was clearly something sinister gnawing at his psyche: in early 1970 he attempted to take his own life, and spent the following two months at Riverview Psychiatric Hospital. Given the events of that September, perhaps it would have been better if he had succeeded.

It was 3:00 p.m. on a breezy Friday afternoon when Dale Nelson stepped into his local liquor store in Creston. Purchasing a 375-millilitre bottle of vodka and a six-pack, he relocated to the Kootenay Hotel tavern where he downed another eight to ten beers and gabbed about the impending hunting season, set to commence in less than ten hours. Incredibly, after drinking sixteen beers and a mickey of vodka, Nelson left the hotel with another six-pack in tow. Two friends offered to drive him across the Kootenay River to the tiny farming community of West Creston to pick up his rifle. Weeks before, he had lent the 7-millimetre bolt-action Mauser to his sister-in-law, Maureen McKay, who had complained of prowlers. Arriving at the home, he discovered that Maureen's thirty-year-old aunt Shirley Wasyk had also stopped in for a visit. Dale made small talk with the two women before bidding them farewell and returning to Creston with his gun.

At 7:00 p.m., he refuelled his light blue 1966 Chevy at Brennan's Garage, where he also purchased a box of ammunition. Driving three kilometres east to the tiny village of Erickson, he swung by an auto shop and had a drink with the proprietor, Armand Chauleur. Behind the building he practised shooting at targets with his beloved rifle — he was a crack shot, even when totally drunk. Dale's thirst for booze was paralleled only by his love of firepower, and by 8:00 p.m. he had bought a second box of 7-millimetre ammo from Swanson's Sporting Goods, along with a press and die he had pawned to them a month earlier. Then, returning to the Creston liquor store, he added a mickey of brandy and a bottle of wine to his arsenal. At the King George Hotel bar, he shared a few more beers with his drinking buddies John McKay and Rex Smith, who rented a room at the establishment. It was now 10:30 p.m., and the trio decided to move the party to Rex's, where Dale continued to pour alcohol onto the slumbering beast in his belly. At the stroke of midnight, it awoke. Though his vision was blurred by the booze, Dale's mental crosshairs slowly came into sharp focus. He took a swig of brandy. Hunting season had begun.

FAIR GAME

Shirley Wasyk sat upright in her bed. Somebody had pulled a car into her driveway. Unexpected visits at this hour were creepy enough, but with her husband, Alex, sleeping overnight at his logging camp, she would have been particularly nervous. Her fingers drew back the curtains to reveal Dale Merle Nelson, stumbling up her driveway with a rifle. He was visibly intoxicated — and that usually meant trouble. Donning a housecoat, Shirley quickly telephoned Maureen for advice. Thankfully her niece was entertaining a gentleman caller — her old school chum Frank Chauleur. He promised Shirley he would be right over. *Boom boom boom!* The house thundered as Dale Nelson knocked against the door with his leathery mitts. For the time being, Shirley realized she would have to deal with him herself. If she ignored him, he would get angry, and that could only make things worse. She opened the door to the ruddy-faced Nelson, invited him inside, and offered him a coffee. Before he could respond, she heard Frank Chauleur's car engine rumble into the driveway. Shirley met him at the door.

"Is your husband there?" Frank asked, catching sight of Dale lingering in the living room.

"No, Alex isn't home," Shirley replied. Frank would later admit that he got the impression he was intruding, and after a brief exchange, wished her good night and headed back to Maureen's. Whatever was going through Shirley Wasyk's mind at that moment, we will never know.

Unbeknownst to Shirley, her twelve-year-old daughter Debbie had also been startled awake, and was now huddled in her bedroom trying to make out the conversation. At some point, she heard Shirley cry, "No, Dale, don't!" Curious, Debbie crept into the dark kitchen and stopped short. A strange gurgling sound was emanating from the master bedroom, punctuated by heavy footsteps. Debbie hid in the narrow gap between the fridge and the wall just in time to see her seven-year-old sister Tracey being led into the kitchen by Nelson. But this wasn't the nice Uncle Dale who took her hunting; rather, in the dim light filtering in from outside, his countenance was terrifying.

"Find me a sharp knife!" his voice boomed. Shaking from head to toe, Tracey opened one of the kitchen drawers and dipped her hand inside. A twenty-five-centimetre steel blade glinted momentarily. Dale ushered Tracey out of the kitchen into the room where eight-year-old Sharlene Wasyk lay blissfully asleep. Seeing her chance, Debbie slipped off her sandals and sneaked quietly into her parents' bedroom, locking the door. Instead of being greeted with her mother's reassuring embrace, she recoiled in horror. Shirley Wasyk lay motionless on the bed, her hands tied behind her back. Blood drenched the linens, freckling the walls and ceiling. As Debbie struggled to free her mother from her bindings, she noticed a bloody fire extinguisher lying nearby. She turned back to the body. Shirley's head had been almost completely obliterated. Suddenly, a high-pitched shriek broke the silence. Instinctively, Debbie seized the fire extinguisher and began dragging it back toward her bedroom. After closing the door, with all her might she hefted the heavy metal object and pitched it through the window, shattering glass onto the ground outside. As Nelson's hands wrenched at her bedroom door, Debbie leaped into the autumn night and ran.

Having just settled back into their conversation, Maureen McKay and Frank Chauleur were startled to hear footsteps running across the porch followed by a frantic hammering at their door. Alarmed, Frank opened it to find Maureen's younger cousin Debbie, trembling in her night dress. The story she was about to tell would later set the scene for one of the most macabre tales in Canadian history.

HOUDINI

The last thing Constable Ernie Moker was expecting to hear when he answered the phone at the Creston RCMP detachment was that a woman's head had been bashed in with a fire extinguisher. However, when Maureen McKay fitfully explained that Dale Nelson had murdered her aunt and was now potentially doing the same to Tracey and

Sharlene Wasyk, Moker immediately sent Constable Gary McLaughlin to West Creston to investigate.

With the towering silhouettes of pines flitting by as he sped across the Kootenay River Bridge, McLaughlin was surprised to see another vehicle approaching at a similar speed. Was this Dale Nelson making his getaway? Getting closer, he saw that it was in fact a couple trying to flag him down. They identified themselves as Maureen McKay and Frank Chauleur, and explained that they were taking Debbie to the hospital. McLaughlin, who was unacquainted with the labyrinth of country roads, requested that, instead, Frank show him the way to the Wasyk home.

Within minutes they reached the foot of the driveway, where they spied Dale's blue Chevy. Knowing that the suspect was armed with a rifle, McLaughlin decided to play it safe, and radioed for backup. Constables Ernie Moker and Gus Slomba soon arrived, and the trio descended upon the property, instructing Frank to stay back. As they trudged apprehensively toward the house, a figure emerged from the blackness. It was Sharlene Wasyk — miraculously, she had been left alive and unscathed. Hoisting the eight-year-old into his arms, Moker motioned for Frank to drive toward them, and when he did, asked him to take the two sisters for medical treatment.

Inside the Wasyk residence, the officers found Shirley's body, bludgeoned repeatedly to death, in bed. As horrific as the scene was, they had been expecting it. No amount of foreknowledge, however, could have prepared them for what they found in Tracey's bedroom. The seven-year-old lay face up on her cot, her mouth sliced from ear to ear in a grotesque grin. The slippery coils of her innards protruded from a second slash running vertically down her chest to her genitals. An elk antler–handled carving knife had been placed beside her lifeless body. Moker and McLaughlin decided to vacate the premises immediately and head east to evacuate the Nelson family from their home. If there was one thing the Mounties could comprehend about this level of violence, it was that it could happen again.

Once Dale's wife and children were out of harm's reach, the three policemen returned to process the crime scene. As the cruiser's headlights swept over the driveway, the men felt their stomachs churn: Nelson's car was gone, and as they would soon discover, so was little Tracey's body.

FROM THE CRADLE TO THE GRAVE

"There's a man here with a gun!" Isabelle St. Amand cried into the phone. Before Corporal Harvey Finch could reply, she cut out. Shocked, Finch tried repeatedly to call back, but to no avail. It was 1:30 a.m. on September 5 and, determined to prevent another catastrophe from happening, Finch and fellow Creston RCMP officer Constable Dennis Schwartz jumped into a police cruiser and sped to the little residence on Corn Creek Road. It was home to forty-two-year-old Ray Phipps and his common-law wife, Isabelle St. Amand, along with their eighteen-month-old son, Roy, and Isabelle's children, Paul, ten; Bryan, seven; and Catherine, eight. Built in a clearing of trees, the tiny two-room cabin creaked forbiddingly in the wind. Taking a deep breath, Finch moved cautiously toward the front door while Schwartz kept him covered. They had arrived too late. The lifeless body of Raymond Phipps was sprawled in the doorway, a crimson trail streaming from a bullet wound through his forehead. Three metres away, Isabelle St. Amand lay, shot once execution-style through the back of the skull. In the bedroom, Finch found Paul and Bryan St. Amand murdered in their beds, large pieces of their heads blown away by 7-millimetre shards of death. Even baby Roy had not been spared, killed with a single shot. On the lower half of the bunk bed, where Catherine St. Amand normally slept, there was only an empty mattress bereft of any signs of violence. Droplets of blood fell like tears from above.

With two missing girls and twin massacres occurring within the space of two hours, the RCMP responded in full force. By daybreak, an additional forty officers had poured in from detachments in Vancouver, Castlegar, Cranbrook, and Nelson to assist their ten colleagues in Creston. Roadblocks were erected barring all exits from East Kootenay, and an APB was broadcast to the community cautioning that the fugitive Dale Merle Nelson was armed and considered "extremely dangerous."

Aided by an army helicopter, fifty armed foot patrollers began scouring the vicinity of the Phipps–St. Amand home. Despite the fog cloaking the pines, 275 metres to the west they happened upon some tire tracks trailing through a broken section of fence. Though the discovery came early, at 6:00 a.m., by afternoon the progress had stalled, and a decision to augment the search with tracking dogs and a spotter plane was made. It proved to be a decisive move — by 3:30 p.m. the pilot caught sight of a

1966 blue Chevrolet mired in a ditch just off a logging road east of Ezekiel. Surrounding the vehicle, the ground searchers slowly converged, weapons drawn. Rather than dodging bullets, they found the car deserted, its passenger seat and floor mats soaked in blood. Hair clung in dried, dark-red globules to the head of a hammer. It wasn't long before they found the source — or at least part of it. When a disembodied arm, separated at the shoulder, was found twelve metres from the car, investigators could not determine which of the missing girls it belonged to. It wasn't until the recovery of Tracey Wasyk's severed head, six metres away, that positive identification was made. Next, they recovered a leg, followed by the rest of the dismembered body, all within seven metres of the Chevy. Amazingly, Nelson had somehow managed to escalate the scale of his depravity. Worse yet, Cathy St. Amand was still unaccounted for.

Darkness soon descended upon the forest, and the decision was made to resume the manhunt at daybreak. Searching under such conditions would be fruitless and place the Mounties in danger of being ambushed by the crazed Nelson. The search continued at dawn. By 10:30 a.m., a pajama leg was fished out of Ezekiel Creek, in the area south of the access road to the forest. Nearby, the patrollers found a rope in one of the trees, surmising that Nelson had spent the previous night hidden there. By all appearances, somebody had been bound to the tree.

A further six hours of searching passed without result, and it wasn't until one of the policemen decided to check the Nelson house that a vital clue emerged. Somebody had recently entered and left the dwelling by cutting the plastic around the window. Corporal Alan Marcotte, a specialist in fingerprints from Cranbrook, was sent to examine the scene. Circling the home, he discovered a trail of footprints leading into the woods. He followed them for almost thirty metres before stumbling upon Dale Nelson — asleep against a log at the edge of a clearing with his arms folded across his chest and his rifle propped up against a tree nearby. Deciding it was best to let sleeping lunatics lie, Marcotte returned to the house and informed the head of operations, Superintendent Terrance Stewart. The clearing was soon surrounded by armed policemen.

"Dale Merle Nelson — this is the RCMP," they announced. "You are surrounded. Stand up, put your hands in the air, and walk toward the cabin. All units hold your fire." Nelson remained unresponsive. When two similar warnings were repeated to no avail, Constable Glenn Marsden and his dog, Count, were sent in to make an arrest. The snarling canine got Nelson's attention, but before he could reach for his gun, Count was upon him. The beast who had disguised himself for so long in human form had finally been taken down by an animal far more civilized than himself.

CRAZY

Following his apprehension, Nelson confirmed everyone's worst fears by shaking his head when asked if Cathy St. Amand was still alive. After sketching out a crude map of the area, and some deliberation, Nelson finally planted an X at the location of Cathy's body. An hour later, she was discovered lying semi-prone, naked except for a t-shirt. Like Tracey, she had been partially disemboweled. Her skull had been fractured, and there was a vicious stab wound to her back. The pathologist, Dr. Otto Brych, determined that she had been sodomized after death. But Dale Nelson's litany of ghoulish acts didn't stop there. Brych noted that beyond her dismemberment, Tracey Wasyk's vagina and heart had been removed and were still unaccounted for.

At Nelson's trial, which commenced on March 22, 1971, in a packed forty-eight-seat Cranbrook courtroom, it was learned that he had choked Tracey unconscious, then eviscerated her alive. Once her stomach had been opened, Nelson had plunged his face into the bloody wound, gobbling up undigested pieces of cereal. With this considered, the notion that Dale had later devoured the girl's heart and vagina seemed entirely plausible. Having battered their mother to death, Nelson had also forcibly performed oral sex on little Sharlene. When the RCMP cruisers had appeared at the Wasyk residence, he had fled into the bush, dragging the helpless eight-year-old with him. Fortunately, she had become snagged in the undergrowth and he had been forced to abandon her. Instead, once police had left the scene, he had absconded with her sister's corpse. If Sharlene's entanglement had not coincided with the timely arrival of the police, she would have undoubtedly suffered the same gristly fate.

Given the magnitude of his client's depravity, it is unsurprising that defence attorney Michael E. Moran argued that Nelson had been utterly insane and therefore not guilty of the murders during his forty-hour killing spree. Yet Crown prosecutor T.G. Bowen-Colthurst posited a different theory: Dale's repulsive acts were the result of extreme sexual perversion, behaviour that may appear crazy to normal people but did not meet the legal requirement of insanity. The jury chose to believe this explanation of events, and on April 1, 1971, found Nelson guilty of two counts of non-capital murder. He was sentenced to life imprisonment without the possibility of parole for ten years. In February 1999, Dale Merle Nelson died at Kent Institution in Agassiz, B.C., at the age of fifty-nine.

Kay Feely

Jonathan Yeo
Mr. Dirt

"Shit is a higher level of life than I am.... I am the great septic tank of life."

Victims: 2 killed/committed suicide
Duration of rampage: August 9 to 14, 1991 (spree killing)
Locations: Burlington, Ontario; Petitcodiac, New Brunswick
WEAPON: .22-calibre rifle

THE OTHER SON

He was a born reject — a rootless half-breed discarded by his mother and adopted by Mae and Raymond Yeo out of pity. At least that's how "Mr. Dirt" viewed himself. Of his earliest days Jonathan knew only that he was born in Hamilton on September 21, 1958. The identity of his birth parents remained an eternal mystery. The Yeos had initially taken him into their home when he was four weeks old, but had to return him at twelve months because Mae was diagnosed with cancer. Three months later, they changed their minds and took him back again. It is more than likely that this instability and lack of affection during his formative years had damaging effects on Jonathan's psyche, sowing the seeds of the killer who was to emerge later. Jonathan's self-esteem took another blow when he was finally old enough to play outside. The working-class youths of Hamilton made it quite clear what they thought of his mulatto skin, mocking him with racial jibes. Whenever he was in the company of his younger, white adoptive brother, James, the duo was dubbed "Salt and Pepper." Even at home, Mae reportedly called Jonathan "little chocolate boy" and "black baby." It was certainly clear which brother got preference in the Yeo household. James Yeo sadly recounts that when he received a brand new bicycle for Christmas, Jonathan got a used one, seeming happy to get anything at all. The boys' father Raymond, a painter at the Dofasco Steel mill, was withdrawn and emotionally unresponsive. He had little interest in rearing his sons. As the dominant parent, Mae beat the boys with a belt. Nevertheless, James's wife Laura accuses her of letting the children run amok and failing to instill values. She describes the boys' environment growing up as characterized by "backstabbing and lies."

The instability in Jonathan Yeo's life continued well into his school years. Growing up, he was forced to move to eight separate elementary schools and two high schools, ensuring he would never develop lasting friendships. No matter where he went he was constantly bullied, forcing him to sink inward, toward a ravenous fire growing in his heart. Jonathan fought constantly. In 1969, a particularly astute principal observed the boy's social introversion, and recognized that he seemed to suffer from a crisis of identity. No action was taken. Instead, the Yeo brothers continued to express their individual frustrations, slashing tires or burning down abandoned buildings.

As the two reached high school they began to part ways. Where James was social, continuing to attract the attention of local law enforcement, troubled Jonathan withdrew into the sanctity of his room. Academically he was a disaster, failing grades nine and eleven. Of average intelligence and technically skilled, his grades reflected his lack of self-esteem. Any attempts to break out of his bubble met with embarrassing failure, sometimes violence. Though he excelled in cadets, where he first learned to handle a rifle, he had a reputation for exploding into sudden fits of anger.

Later in life, when employed at Dofasco, he would earn the nickname Zulu Warrior for using an iron bar to close a valve in a sulphur tank. On other occasions they referred to him as Nuts, though nobody dared to say either insult to his face. His foreman remarked that Jonathan would "fly into a rage" if his equipment malfunctioned or if he made a mistake.

In 1978, Jonathan Yeo met his future wife, Sheila, through the militia. At first the heavy-set corporal didn't take to Jonathan — although he was good-looking, she found his isolationism childish. As they spent more time together, she discovered that he had a good sense of humour and could actually be quite a gentleman. They began dating, and two and a half years later were married on December 27, 1980, settling into a home on the shores of Lake Erie. As a highly socialized, educated woman, Sheila provided structure and a sense of control in Jonathan's personal life. There were already signs that he was beginning to slip. During his courtship he had grown obsessed with James's ex-girlfriend Sandra, assaulting her in November 1979. Sheila was apparently unaware of his transgressions. Jonathan's occasional use of marijuana, cocaine, and LSD was something she had resigned herself to, along with his extensive pornography collection. This last habit he had apparently picked up from his adopted father — when Sheila visited the Yeo house she was shocked by the number of pornographic magazines in plain view. One thing she absolutely would not stand for was drinking, and Jonathan seems to have honoured her wishes for a time.

Jonathan's attitude toward women was ambivalent to say the least. The public face he presented was that of an old-fashioned moralist who believed that sex was fundamentally bad and that women should be housebound and dedicated to meeting their husbands' needs. Matriarchs shouldn't want to make love, since fornication was the province of whores. At the same time he experienced an overwhelming need for female acceptance, flying into a rage whenever a woman rejected him. In reality he was probably trying to keep his mind off sex, because for Jonathan Yeo lust was inextricably linked with rage and frustration.

In 1984 Sheila became pregnant. Breaking down in front of his brother James and James's wife, Jonathan stated that he didn't want a child and that Sheila had tricked him into it. Two weeks after the birth of his daughter, Jonathan began to vent his frustrations on other women.

A HISTORY OF AGGRESSION

Janet was a career-focused single woman living in Hamilton when she met the Yeos through her ten-pin bowling league. Her interest in Sheila's husband never extended past sharing a beer after hitting the lanes. Unfortunately, he had different feelings. Sometime in 1983, Jonathan appeared on her doorstep, explaining that he was passing by and needed to use her phone. Puzzled as to how he had learned the address of her downstairs apartment, Janet nevertheless let him inside. Though there was nothing unusual about Jonathan's behaviour, from that moment on he frequently dropped by to share her coffee and conversation. Then things started to get weird. One day out of the blue, he informed her he had broken up with Sheila and asked her if she wanted to go on a date. Janet declined, explaining that she didn't get involved with married men. Or so she thought. Arriving home after visiting a friend one night, she found Jonathan standing in the lobby of her building.

"Where have you been?" his voice boomed. Terrified, Janet informed him that it was none of his business.

"Aren't you going to invite me in for a coffee?"

"It's too late," she said firmly. "I'm going to bed."

"Fine. We'll go together."

"No!"

But it was too late — Janet had already unlocked the door. Jonathan forced himself inside.

"All right, you can have one coffee but then you're out of here," she said, trembling.

While she prepared the coffee, he crept up from behind and began to kiss her. Whirling around, Janet thrust her knee as hard as she could into his groin. To her horror, instead of buckling, Jonathan seized a knife from the kitchen table and pressed it to her throat.

"You'll be sorry." His dark eyes flared like embers.

Hearing footsteps upstairs, Janet warned him that she was going to scream and it would only be seconds before her neighbour came to check on her. This seemed to get Jonathan's attention. Saying nothing, he placed the knife down on the counter and slipped out the door.

Sadly, Janet's ordeal was just beginning. Days after, Jonathan telephoned her to apologize for his behaviour. She accepted his apology but added that she never wanted to see him again and hung up. This did nothing to deter him; in fact, he called her so many times over the following days that Janet was forced to change to an unlisted number. On another occasion, she arrived home to find him chatting in the lobby with her neighbour Jim and told him to leave immediately. When he departed, she explained to Jim that he was stalking her. Jim told her to call him if he gave her any more problems.

One spring morning in 1984, after working the night shift, Janet awoke to go to the bathroom. As she rose, the closet door opened and Jonathan Yeo stepped out into the darkness. Screaming, she reached for her bathrobe, but he seized it away from her.

"You won't be needing that!" Janet raced to the front door and had just unfastened the deadbolt when he grabbed her arm. She continued to scream, though she realized he had probably taken measures to ensure Jim was at work. Jonathan explained that he wasn't going to hurt her, and told her to keep quiet. Then, for reasons unknown, he left without saying a word. Shaking with fear, Janet telephoned her father immediately. In turn, he contacted the police but learned they were powerless to do anything unless Jonathan physically hurt her.

Things finally came to a head on May 29, when Jonathan telephoned explaining that he was dropping by the apartment to speak with her. Janet told him that if he did she would call the police.

"If you do, I'll break through your window and kill you!" he threatened.

That night, Janet awoke to a sound outside her apartment door.

"Who is it?" she cried.

"It's me," Jonathan Yeo's voice answered.

"I'm going to phone the police."

"Yeah, you always say that," he said, hammering his fists against the door.

By the time the police cruiser arrived five minutes later, Jonathan was gone. The responding officer ran his name through the computer, but as somebody had neglected to take fingerprints for the 1979 offence, no criminal record showed up. Brushing the potential rape off as a domestic dispute, the officer told Janet she had forty-eight hours to lay charges. To his credit, he kept the police cruiser parked outside her home for the remainder of the night.

Not long after, Janet married, and when Jonathan discovered she had a man in her life she never heard from him again. Instead he focused his depraved attentions on his mother-in-law. At 5:30 p.m. on March 27, 1987, Sheila's mother, Nancy, arrived home to discover the lights were not working in her Hamilton apartment. When she left to check the power in the rest of the building, Jonathan emerged suddenly from a nearby fire door, dishevelled and stinking of booze. Though Nancy was surprised to see her son-in-law, the two had a wonderful relationship and she had no qualms about inviting him inside. He explained that earlier in the day he had entered her apartment and turned off her lights at the fuse panel. When Nancy asked him why he would do such a thing, he claimed to have hurt somebody in a bar brawl and had gone to hide in her apartment. The story made little sense. Nancy noticed that he was carrying around a bottle of rye. The next thing she knew, he was strangling her. Confused by his sudden aggression, Nancy rasped through her constricted larynx that he was hurting her and would do the same to Sheila and the children unless he stopped. This seemed to make Jonathan snap out of his trance, and he released her immediately. Turning away, he burst into tears, sobbing that he didn't want to hurt her. Then, without warning, he ran full speed into a glass balcony door, shattering it and cutting himself badly. As he retreated to the bathroom to clean his wounds, Nancy alerted the police that her son-in-law was suicidal, and Jonathan was taken to nearby St. Joseph's Hospital for a psychiatric examination. She decided not to mention the attack, as she did not believe he intended to murder her. Had the hospital psychiatrists been made aware of his attempts to strangle her, their subsequent diagnosis of Jonathan might have led to some kind of positive intervention.

Jonathan agreed to seek psychiatric help at St. Catharines General Hospital, and during his therapy sessions he revealed that he was driven to an overwhelming rage by minor annoyances such as something dropping on the floor or a change in the topic of a conversation. As disturbing as this was, his doctors found no evidence of psychosis, meaning he could not be committed to an institution or cured with medication. Instead this wholly irresponsible man was given total control over his own participation in a lengthy treatment program. Unsurprisingly, this approach failed, with Jonathan dismissing the matter as a result of drinking.

On August 14, 1987, Jonathan attacked Sheila's best friend Lindsey at her lakeside home in Grimsby, Ontario. After struggling with her knife-wielding assailant, Lindsey managed to flee the house. Twenty minutes later she returned with the police to find Jonathan sitting in the middle of the living-room floor playing with her children's toys. She screamed and ran out, allowing him a chance to escape. The police caught up to him splashing around frantically in the nearby lake.

"I need help," he surrendered. "My mind has gone. I'm all rambling. I put a knife to my friend."

As he had before, Jonathan was taken to St. Catharines General Hospital to be assessed. The police deemed him a danger to others and himself, and concluded that he needed immediate psychiatric intervention. Unfortunately, the fact that their patient hadn't been charged led hospital staff to treat his case as a minor domestic dispute. Two days after the attack, Sheila Yeo phoned Lindsey threatening to inform the police that she was a drug dealer if she pressed charges. Faced with Sheila's threats and confident that Jonathan was safely detained at a mental hospital, Lindsey chose not to follow through. Two weeks later she ran into the Yeos at a David Bowie concert, and her illusions of safety were shattered. Didn't anybody care that this man had conned his way into her house and held a knife to her throat?

The next woman to fall prey to Jonathan Yeo's misogynist impulses was Sheila's twenty-three-year-old cousin Yvonne. At 7:00 a.m. on August 30, 1990, he knocked on the door of her apartment and explained that he had come to install some fans that Yvonne and her mother had purchased. Unaware of Jonathan's history of aggression, she let him in. He was carrying a large army-style bag that she assumed contained tools. Jonathan produced a length of rope and began eagerly showing her the various knots he could tie while Yvonne feigned interest. At one point he tricked her into letting him bind her hands together. It was a terrible mistake. Instead of honouring her requests to untie her, he began to laugh sinisterly, and dragged her helpless into the bedroom. Throwing her on top of the mattress, he bound her arms and legs to the bed posts, tore off her clothes, and raped her.

It was some time before Yvonne worked up the strength to tell anyone about what had occurred. Rather than confiding in her excitable mother, she chose her Aunt Nancy, Jonathan's mother-in-law, who took her immediately to the Sexual Assault Centre. There she learned she had twenty-four hours to decide whether or not to press charges. If she did agree to, she would be subject to an internal examination and would likely have to testify against Jonathan at his trial — her privacy violated again by prying defence attorneys. Even if Jonathan was convicted, there was still a chance he would walk free. Faced with an insensitive and inefficient justice system, Yvonne ultimately chose not to press charges, and the family resolved to seek professional help. By now they had repeated the story so many times that the words were meaningless.

The final warning came on the night of April 7, 1991. Alison Prescott,* a thirty-year-old social worker, was walking up the Wentworth Street stairway near her home when she came across a man jogging on the steps. Alison had just moved into a low-rent basement apartment, and had temporarily put garbage bags over the windows until she could afford curtains. Minutes after she entered her apartment, she answered an unexpected knock on the door. Behind the thin chain stood the man from the steps. Flashing a bloody arm at her, he spun a harrowing tale of being attacked by a gang of youths who were still looking for him. Suspicious, but not wanting the man to get hurt, Alison decided to let him inside. She showed him to the phone and helped him clean his wound. He told her that he was a widower and a worker at Dofasco who lived on a pig farm outside the city. A counsellor by trade, Alison sensed that the man calling himself Chris Johnson needed somebody to talk to, and poured him a glass of wine. After chatting for an hour or more, she declared that it was her bedtime and offered to phone for a taxi. He refused politely, and left. But several minutes later, as Alison was clearing the glasses from the table, there came another knock on her door. She opened it to see Chris Johnson and, assuming he had changed his mind about the cab, turned to dial the telephone. When she looked back she was shocked to see him standing in the doorway, aiming a rifle at her head.

"Go to the bathroom," he ordered menacingly. There was no trace of the meek widower left in his tone.

"I don't understand, Chris. What are you doing?"

---

* A pseudonym.

"Go to the bathroom," he repeated, motioning with the rifle. "I don't want anybody to see what I'm going to do to you." Fixed in the rifle's sights, she had little choice but to comply. Jonathan followed her into the bathroom where, placing the firearm on the floor, he told her he was upset and needed a hug. Feeling a strange mixture of confusion and relief, she accommodated him. Over the next hour, Alison employed her skills as a social worker in a sustained attempt to prevent him from going any further. It was as if his mind contained two personalities: the moral Jonathan who apologized and tried to assure her he would never hurt her, and the cold-hearted, authoritarian aggressor who seemed completely detached from reality. At one point, the moral Jonathan even poured cold water onto his genitals in an attempt to prevent himself from becoming erect. Unfortunately, when the bad Jonathan noticed the garbage bags taped over the bedroom windows, he led Alison into the room and proceeded to sexually assault her over several hours. Whenever rape seemed imminent, the good Jonathan suddenly intervened, tearing himself away from her with mumbling apologies. This happened so many times that, even though he was clearly attempting to minimize her pain, Alison was placed in a state of perpetual psychological torture.

Finally, he admitted to her that he was faced with a conundrum: if he left her alive she could charge him with forcible confinement. Alison was now involved in a negotiation for her life, one that she came very close to losing. At one point, Jonathan even aimed the rifle at her and told her he was going to kill her. In the end, Alison won the battle of wits, convincing him to leave. Ninety minutes later she called the police. Constable Kenneth Wilson arrived at the apartment around 7:40 a.m. and proceeded to re-victimize her, calling into question her composed manner and the time it took for her to call. Despite the officer's insensitivity, Alison forged ahead with the charges, and in mid-May Jonathan was arrested for sexual assault. At a pre-trial hearing, he was released on $3,000 bail, prohibited from drinking or using drugs, and slapped with a 10:00 p.m. curfew.

SO MANY HORRORS

The case would never make it to trial. On Friday, August 9, 1991, Jonathan left the house without kissing his children goodbye and went to the doctor to demand more antidepressant medication. That afternoon he appeared in court, where the judge remanded his trial to a later date. Not long after, Sheila Yeo unlocked the medicine cupboard to find Jonathan's cache of pills missing. She immediately became concerned — her husband should have been home by now. Had he decided to end his life? Frightened, she contacted the police, who told her he was probably "out celebrating with his buddies." But Jonathan Yeo didn't have any friends — never had, never would. He only had his hatred and a gun.

In fact, at that moment he was sitting in his Toyota hatchback at the Niagara Falls border, telling a U.S. customs officer of his plans to drive to Key West. Something about Jonathan's agitated manner prompted the officer to search his vehicle. Inside he uncovered an ancient-looking .22-calibre rifle and two packets of ammunition. Though Canadian law required a licence for possession of the firearm, the officer reasoned from the antiquated state of the rifle that it may have predated the licensing act. Jonathan responded to his concerns by offering to leave the rifle at the border. Yet the more questions the officer asked, the more suspicious he became. Not only had Jonathan been convicted for growing marijuana, but he was also out on bail, facing charges of sexual assault with a weapon, unlawful confinement, and uttering death threats. Upon searching Jonathan's person, he discovered a hand-written letter that appeared to be a suicide note.

What the hell am I, not human anyway. Just a cheap imitation, a phony, nothing but a piece of shit. I don't deserve to be alive in this world, in fact not any world. I have helped sire four beautiful children that I cannot believe could be mine. I don't feel I deserve to be their father. My life is nothing but a dream, reality is not real because it is too cruel to be true. What kind of life is this, nothing but horror. Living is not worth it, neither is death. So what the hell are we here for. It must be to see how much shit we can take. I take so much, but can't get rid of it, there's so many horrors to live through. I believe we are all flies on a piece of shit, only good enough to break down more decay. Shit is a higher level

of life than I am. I am the ground that shit lies on, only
to be broken down by the flies that we are. I am the great
ceptic [*sic*] tank of life.
Mr. Dirt
(Jonathan Yeo)[52]

After he read the note, it was clear to the officer that Jonathan was
not only attempting to break bail, but was suicidal. This was not the kind
of man they wanted roaming around the United States. Immigration
Officer Hugh O'Hear telephoned the Grimsby police. They seemed
unconcerned; after all, there had been no stipulation made against
Jonathan owning a firearm and he hadn't missed curfew — yet. Still,
O'Hear knew that this was a dangerous man, and contacted Canadian
customs official Alexander Welsh, informing him of the rifle and suicide
note. As Welsh listened, he became deeply concerned about the safety
of the eleven other customs workers on duty that night. He waited until
Jonathan's car started back, and approached it cautiously, asking him for
proof of citizenship. Believing they had no reason to seize the weapon, at
7:30 p.m. the customs officers sent Mr. Dirt on his way. Instead of defus-
ing this human bomb, Alexander Welsh merely tossed it into the night
and waited for the sound of an explosion.

NINA AND KAREN

Even at nineteen years of age, it was clear to everyone who knew her
that Nina de Villiers was a driven woman. Born in Capetown, her lib-
eral-leaning family had fled the civil upheaval of 1970s South Africa to
a country where they believed they would be safe from random acts of
violence. This early exposure to social injustice led the gifted student to
undertake a variety of causes, from organizing a blood drive for the Red
Cross to fundraising for African schools.

On the evening of Friday, August 9, 1991, Nina arrived at Burlington's
Cedar Springs Racquet Club only to discover that she had mistaken the
starting time of her round-robin tournament and missed it. Brimming
with energy, and with a half hour to kill before her father arrived, Nina
decided to burn off her frustrations by jogging along a nearby service

road. Dusk was settling on the city of Burlington, and she could hear the chirping of crickets from the nearby grass. In this safe upper-middle-class area, it was not unusual for club members to take a quick run around the block. To disappear suddenly into the warm summer night, however, was something nobody was prepared for. Half an hour later, Rocco de Villiers finished his racquetball game and settled down to wait for Nina at the club coffee shop. When she failed to arrive, he spoke with the attendant at the front desk and learned that she had left her car keys in their care. This troubled him — Nina was never one to stand somebody up. Concerned, Rocco nevertheless acknowledged that his daughter was a full-grown adult, and returned home to await news from her. It never came.

By dawn, friends, family members, and staff began to search the area around the club. At 9:00 a.m. a fitness instructor found Nina's rainbow headband in the shade of a nearby willow tree. Now the authorities were willing to take the missing person case seriously. When Sheila Yeo learned the news that Nina's disappearance coincided with her husband's, she telephoned the Niagara police immediately and informed them of Jonathan's past.

Three days later, in Petitcodiac, New Brunswick, twenty-eight-year-old Karen Marquis finished work at the Moncton rail yards and chatted briefly with her husband, Neil, who was just beginning his afternoon shift, before heading home to watch some videos. Just after midnight, Neil pulled into the couple's driveway to find Karen's car parked in his spot. Upon entering the house he noticed that coffee had been spilled on the kitchen floor, and he called for his wife. No response. Neil headed downstairs, where he expected to find Karen curled up with her movies. Both the VCR and television were turned on, but there were no signs of her. It wasn't until he searched the rest of the house and stumbled over something in the upstairs hallway that he discovered the shocking truth. Concealed beneath a pile of blankets lay the body of Karen Marquis — shot at close range through the head.

It didn't take long for police to find the killer's mode of entry — a broken downstairs window bearing two clear fingerprints. Within two hours they were matched to Jonathan Yeo, and a warrant for his arrest was issued across Canada. A forensic swabbing of Karen's body revealed traces of semen in her vagina and rectum. Among the items missing from the house were the two romantic comedy movies that Karen had rented, her wallet and keys, and *Playboy* magazines from an upstairs cupboard.

On August 13, Jonathan was sighted a number of times 130 kilometres west of Hamilton in London, Ontario. That afternoon he had unsuccessfully attempted to cash a cheque for $50 at a local bank. Later, he was seen at a bowling alley talking to the machines in the adjoining arcade before leaving at around 10:00 p.m. Sometime after, a twenty-five-year-old woman escaped his clutches and identified him as her would-be abductor. With Jonathan's return to the area confirmed, Hamilton-Wentworth police contacted Alison Prescott, advising her to stay clear of her apartment.

The next afternoon, Jonathan's brown Toyota was spotted driving on Hamilton Mountain. With two cruisers on his tail, the police dragnet began to close. Realizing that, if caught, he would be spending the rest of his life in prison, Jonathan decided enough was enough. Struggling to steer as he placed the barrel of the rifle into his mouth, he took one last breath and pulled the trigger. Eight hours later, he was pronounced dead.

Two days after Jonathan's suicide, the naked, decomposed body of Nina de Villiers was found floating in a creek between Napanee and Kingston, Ontario. She had suffered a gunshot wound to the back of the head. Despite the nude state of the body, the coroner found no evidence of sexual assault. Back in Burlington, investigators had located spots of blood under a willow tree near the racquet club, and surmised that Nina had been shot there execution-style. Judging by the dearth of blood and injuries to the back of the skull and spine, her death had probably been instantaneous. If the killer had not raped or robbed his victim, then the motivation for the attack was presumably anger. Bloodstains located by forensics investigators on the back seat of his car indicated where Jonathan had stowed Nina's corpse after the shooting. An eyewitness claimed to have seen the crazed Dofasco worker pulling out of the racquet club between 9:30 and 10:00 p.m., giving him a chilling stare as he passed. The dumpsite, exiting Highway 401 onto Highway 133, was 286 kilometres east of where Nina had been murdered. Likely Jonathan had spotted the secluded bridge from the highway and pulled off to secret Nina's body underneath it.

CAVEAT

Following an inquest into the Jonathan Yeo murders, Nina's mother, Priscilla de Villiers, drafted a petition to the federal government demanding that violent crimes be taken more seriously, and that laws regarding bail and parole be changed in accordance. No longer should justices of the peace be allowed to conduct bail hearings; instead, the hearings should be subject to the consideration of a judge. Furthermore, the rights of violent offenders should not take precedence over the safety of society at large. Priscilla spoke out in favour of the petition at church organizations, service clubs, and women's groups. Everywhere she went, she found her fellow Canadians in staunch agreement with her proposals. Among them was Karen Marquis's mother-in-law, Jean, who travelled by train from city to city collecting signatures. The end result was not only a petition containing hundreds of thousands of names, but the forming of CAVEAT (Canadians Against Violence Everywhere Advocating for its Termination), a non-profit corporation dedicated to constructive justice system reform. For more information, see *www.caveat.org*.

PART D

MASS MURDERERS

Table 8: Holmes and Holmes's Typology of Mass Murderers*

Type	Motivation	Anticipated Gain	Geographic/Spatial Mobility
Family Annihilator	Intrinsic	Psychological	Typically a long-term resident of the area
Ideological Killer	Intrinsic	Material and psychological	Moves across country to find new members or escape notoriety
Disciple	Extrinsic	Expressive or psychological	Typically geographically transient, following the movements of leader

* This table is an amalgamation of traits and characteristics outlined for the various mass murder categories found in Holmes and Holmes's *Mass Murder in the United States*.

Type	Motivation	Anticipated Gain	Geographic/Spatial Mobility
Disgruntled Employee	Intrinsic	Expressive or psychological	Typically geographically stable
Disgruntled Citizen	Intrinsic	Psychological or expressive	Tends to be geographically stable, though there are some exceptions
Set and Run	Intrinsic	Typically expressive, in a few instances the gain may be material[53]	Typically nomadic, travelling from place to place to kill.[54]
Psychotic	Intrinsic	Expressive or psychological	Tends to be geographically stable

Type	Victim Selectivity	Victim Relationship	Victim Traits
Family Annihilator	Non-random/family members	Family members	Physical traits not important
Ideological	Victims are members of the leader's group or cult. Usually entire group is murdered	Known members of the leader's group or cult	Physical traits not important
Disciple	Victims selected by leader	Typically strangers	Physical traits not important
Disgruntled Employee	Usually random/former, current, or fellow employees	Strangers, although many were fellow workers	Physical traits not important
Disgruntled Citizen	Random	Usually total strangers	Physical traits not important
Set and Run	Random. Killer is usually away from the crime scene at the time	Victims of killer are strangers	Physical traits not important
Psychotic	Random	Victims are strangers	Physical traits not important

CHAPTER 8

THE FAMILY ANNIHILATOR

Statistically, the majority of homicides in Canada occur between acquaintances (approximately 0.5 per 100,000 people) or family members (approximately 0.4 per 100,000 people).[55] Simply put, despite the sensationalism surrounding serial murderers, you are more likely to die at the hands of somebody you know than any sex maniac or unscrupulous gangster. The first category of mass murderer we examine reflects this unsettling trend. As we have seen in the **Cook, Swift Runner, Easby**, and **Sovereign** slayings, the Family Annihilator is by far the most common mass killer, though their motivations vary from profit (Cook) to psychosis (Swift Runner) to anger (Sovereign). Whereas in other chapters I have been forced to rely on American or British cases to provide brief preliminary examples of types of rampage murderers, there is such a grim legacy of domestic mass murders in Canada that in this instance, we need not look outside our own borders.

In the mid-nineteenth century, Quebec resident Mathilde Laventure succumbed to madness and murdered her seven children, who ranged in age from thirteen years down to four months. The thirty-three-year-old mother then committed suicide and, atypically for a Catholic, was buried on consecrated ground, having been deemed insane.

Alberta politician John Etter Clark went similarly nuts in the summer of 1956, borrowing a .22-calibre rifle from his uncle. He then fatally shot his wife, Margaret; four children; a farm hand; and a visitor. After fleeing 550 metres from the crime scene, Clark put a bullet through his own skull, bringing the final death toll to eight.

Swearing vengeance against the wife, who had divorced him, on April 6, 1996, Mark Vijay Chahal entered her family's home in Kamloops during preparations for her sister's wedding. Wielding dual pistols, he massacred nine members of the family, including his estranged wife, before committing suicide in a hotel room.

Vancouver policeman **Leonard Hogue**'s motives are particularly fascinating: slaughtering his entire family seemingly in order to spare them the details of his crimes.

Other Family Annihilator mass murderers in this book: Thomas Easby, Henry Sovereign, Robert Raymond Cook

Kay Feely

Leonard Hogue

Victims: 7 killed/committed suicide
Duration of rampage: April 19 or 20, 1965 (mass murder)
Location: Coquitlam, British Columbia
Weapon: .357 Magnum revolver

MONEY FOR NOTHING

On August 8, 1963, a team of armed robbers stopped a Royal Mail train near Bridego bridge in Ledburn, England. Contained within its steel walls was a cache of used banknotes scheduled for destruction. In the space of fifteen minutes, the hijackers boarded the train and made off with 2.6 million pounds. Amazingly, during the robbery, most of the employees remained blissfully unaware that anything unusual was happening. Though twelve of the fifteen gang members were eventually convicted, the heist would go down as one of the most brilliant and brazen in British history.

We may never know if Constable Leonard Hogue and his accomplices were inspired by the Great Train Robbery of '63, but it is hard to imagine they were unaware of it. On Thursday, February 11, 1965, three men walked up to the Canadian Pacific Railway Warehouse at 44 Pender Street in Vancouver. Noting that one of the strangers was dressed in a CPR policeman's uniform, the attendant allowed them to enter. Once inside, they pulled a gun on a clerk and demanded access to boxes of used banknotes scheduled for incineration at Ottawa's Royal Mint. Encountering no resistance, the trio managed to haul three three-hundred-pound fibreglass boxes to their getaway vehicle — a station wagon — before speeding away. Their plan had seemingly come off without a hitch. Unfortunately, they had no idea that the currency had been mutilated specifically to prevent such abuse, and was completely worthless. One thing seems reasonably certain, though: when Leonard Hogue first laid his eyes on the bills, each one punctured with three half-inch holes, he would have been devastated. Not only had the thirty-four-year-old constable put his reputation and freedom at stake, he had done so for nought.

Things got worse in April, when two of Hogue's accomplices, Joseph Percival and James McDougall, were arrested in Edmonton for violent robbery and possessing $12,000 in stolen currency.[56] Percival had been a former Vancouver policeman. Rumours began circulating of an internal investigation into the force, and Hogue learned that he was under particular scrutiny. The pressure was unbearable. Bit by bit, he sensed his whole world closing in on him. Soon the truth would be revealed: his six children would learn that their policeman father was actually a criminal in disguise. They would abandon him, and he would be locked up. Maybe they'd send him to the federal correctional work camp in Agassiz where his brother Lawrence was serving four years for theft. Between the constant paranoia and intense feelings of guilt, Leonard Hogue's mind began to slowly unravel.

A FAMILY AFFAIR

At 5:30 p.m. on Monday, April 19, Hogue rented a blue 1965 Meteor Montcalm station wagon from a Vancouver U-Drive. It has never been determined how the Coquitlam resident managed to arrive in the big city — that same morning he had totalled his Volkswagen on the Port Mann Freeway. What is known is that at some point during the evening he purchased a .357-calibre Magnum revolver from a CPR policeman before the two wound up drinking at a Vancouver hotel. Upon returning to his $25,000 home in Coquitlam's sleepy Harbour Chines subdivision, Hogue shot his wife and six children. Once he was certain that they were dead, he turned the gun upon himself.

The following day, service station owner Ray Ellis found a blue station wagon on his lot at 1695 Como Lake Road in Coquitlam. Initially he assumed that somebody had left it for repairs, but when nobody contacted him by Wednesday, he telephoned the police. Meanwhile, Leonard Hogue's absence from work had not gone unnoticed, and fearing that he had flown the coop, Chief Booth sent an officer to the Hogue residence to check things out. It was a dank, cloudy day, and the white suburban home with the green shutters was still wet with the morning rain. After knocking on the door and receiving no reply, the investigating officer stooped down to peer through the basement window and recoiled. At the foot of a blood-spattered chesterfield lay the body of a young girl. What they thought had been a simple case of truancy had suddenly become homicide.

Within no time, detectives entered the premises to discover a bloodbath. Leonard's wife, Vera, lay murdered in her bed, shot through the head while sleeping. Likely, she was the first to die. Her spouse and executioner had opted to end his life beside her — Leonard's partially clad body was sprawled across the bedroom floor with the revolver nearby. Roused by the shots, their thirteen-year-old son Larry had made an attempt to flee his top bunk, only to be gunned down by his father. Raymond, eight, and Clifford, six, had raced downstairs to the main floor with Leonard in hot pursuit. One boy ran for the bathroom as Leonard fired at him, missing, before a second bullet exploded through his head in a shower of blood. Possibly reasoning that he could not outrun his father, the other boy attempted to hide in a closet, and was killed in the doorway. The Hogue daughters, twelve-year-old Noreen and four-year-old Darlene, made it as far as the basement before their lives were similarly deleted with two callous clicks of the trigger. To quote Inspector Ian Macgregor,

> I have seen death many times on this job. I have seen men dead, women dead, children dead, but I've never seen death like this. Nothing as tragic as this. It would have been one thing if they would have all been killed at once, like a machine gun. But here you had kids running away, trying to hide, with one trying to get into the closet. Further on top of all this, Hogue had to stop and reload. He must have been insane.[57]

Leonard's final victim hadn't even attempted to flee his bed. Like his mother and siblings, three-year-old Richard Hogue had died from a gunshot to the skull. Only the family dog had been spared. Amidst the blood splatters, brains, and bullet holes, investigators made a curious find: six Easter baskets on the kitchen counter, one for each of the children. How could a man spoil his sons and daughters on Sunday, only to cruelly stalk and execute them in their own home on Monday? Was this a father's selfish attempt to ensure his family would never leave him, or a twisted and irrational act of mercy?

Though Hogue's suicide ensures we will never know the answers to these questions, one mystery could be solved: his involvement in the CPR warehouse robbery. Alerted to the presence of the abandoned station wagon at Ray Ellis's gas station, detectives quickly traced it to Hogue, and began searching its contents. In the rear deck they discovered traces of clay and hemp fibres, probably from a rope used to bind the containers of junk cash. There were markings where something heavy had been dragged from the vehicle. A crowbar sat in the front seat, near a box of .357-calibre ammo.

It wasn't until mid-June that the marked money was finally recovered: $1,185,165 of worthless paper in a rented Victoria garage that had been sealed with a custom padlock. The custodians remembered speaking to a "rough-looking" man in his mid-forties who had wanted to rent a unit. A day later, they remembered a second "fair-haired man," and witnessed two different individuals unloading crates from a rental truck into the garage.

On Wednesday, April 28, 250 mourners attended a funeral service for all eight members of the Hogue family, including Leonard. Neighbours had viewed the Hogues as a tight-knit church-going brood. Many of Leonard's fellow policemen expressed shock that he could be capable of such an atrocity. "He was the last guy to worry about anything," one officer stated. "If anything happened he laughed it off."

CHAPTER 9

THE DISCIPLE AND THE IDEOLOGICAL KILLER

As it is impossible to comprehend Disciple mass murderers without examining their Ideological counterparts, this chapter will explore both types of slayers. Generally, they fulfill complementary roles in a homicidal cult, with the Ideological mass murderer indoctrinating and gaining psychological control over the Disciple. The Ideological murderer frequently orders the murders of dissident cult members, convincing the Disciple to do the dirty work, though this is not always the case.

Arguably the deadliest of these cults was the People's Temple, founded in 1955 by American preacher Jim Jones (Ideological). Between 1974 and 1978, Jones convinced nine hundred of his flock to uproot to Guyana to inhabit a utopian religious commune dubbed Jonestown. Hearing rumours that several members of the organization had been physically prevented from leaving the commune, California congressman Leo Ryan flew out personally to investigate. When Ryan learned that Jones was indeed holding defectors captive, Jones commanded his Disciples to gun down the congressman and his entourage on the Port Kaituma airstrip. Knowing that these murders ensured the American government's retaliation, Jones declared that the end was nigh. On November 18, 1978, he convinced hundreds of his followers to commit "revolutionary" suicide by drinking grape Flavor-Aid laced with cyanide. Those who resisted were either physically forced to, or were shot.

Many among his congregation were so brainwashed that they actually administered the poison to their own children. In total, over nine hundred people perished in the jungle that day, including Jim Jones, who died from a self-inflicted gunshot wound.

On rare occasions, the Ideological mass murderer opts to shed blood himself. When self-proclaimed prophet Jeffrey Lundgren discovered that devoted follower Dennis Avery had squirrelled some money away in a bank account rather than donate it to their Mormon splinter cult, Lundgren informed his flock that it was time to "prune the grapevine." He convinced Disciple Ron Luff to individually lure the five members of the Avery family into a barn, where Lundgren shot them to death one after another.

Canada is no stranger to cult activity, though the only example to perpetrate a massacre is the Swiss-based Order of the Solar Temple. Led by Ideological mass killers **Joseph Di Mambro** and **Luc Jouret**, in 1994 they successfully commanded Disciple **Joel Egger** to butcher a family of three in the tourist community of Morin-Heights, Quebec, and later, an untold number of others in Switzerland.

Joel Egger
Order of the Solar Temple

Victims: 3 murdered in Canada, more overseas/committed suicide
Duration of rampage: October 4, 1994 (mass murder)
Location: Morin-Heights, Quebec
Weapons: Knife, wooden stake

A FIERY ASCENT

Morin-Heights, Quebec: a quaint tourist community nestled in the Laurentian Mountains. Until 1994, this town of 3,500 was known primarily for its picturesque ski slopes. A nearby recording studio boasted world-class clientele, including the Bee Gees, David Bowie, Rush, and The Police. On the morning of October 4, flashing lights and blaring horns broke the frosty silence, as fire engines rushed to battle an inferno raging at a local condominium. The owner of the building was sixty-nine-year-old Frenchman Joseph Di Mambro — the spiritual leader of an international religious sect known as the Order of the Solar Temple. Inside the dank ash and dripping beams of the burnt structure, respondents happened upon the blackened remains of two figures in the upstairs bedroom. Immediately, they suspected the bodies belonged to Di Mambro and his business partner and "prophet," forty-seven-year-old Luc Jouret. Downstairs, the bloody corpses of a man and woman were discovered in a closet. Rather than perishing in the fire, the male had been knifed fifty times in the back, while the female had suffered similar mortal wounds to her breasts and throat. The body of a murdered infant was found crammed behind a water heater, a plastic bag covering his head. In a truly bizarre, almost ritualistic, act, a wooden stake had been driven through him six times, as if he were a supernatural entity whose life force was impervious to conventional weapons. The child had been literally bled white.

Between the autopsies and investigation, the identities of the Morin-Heights victims were soon determined, though the results were entirely unexpected. The bodies found upstairs did not belong to either Luc Jouret or Joseph Di Mambro; they were those of Swiss couple Gerry and Collette Genoud — both devoted members of the Solar Temple. Unlike the stabbing victims, the Genouds appeared to have committed suicide by fire, placing time bombs about the room and hanging gasoline-filled garbage bags from doorknobs before drugging themselves. The murdered were identified as thirty-five-year-old Swiss Tony Dutoit; his English wife Nicky Robinson-Dutoit, thirty; and their eighteen-month-old son Christopher-Emmanuel. Autopsy results indicated they had been dead for a period of three days before the fire. Despite these revelations, many questions still remained unresolved. Who had killed the Dutoits, and why? What had prompted the Genouds to end their own lives in such an excruciating fashion? The answers were encrypted in the Order of the Solar Temple, and to decipher them, the investigators would have to stare into its blinding sun and, somehow, see clearly.

ANTICHRIST

Once upon a time, Tony and Nicky Dutoit had been committed members of the Order of the Solar Temple, with ties to the organizational leadership. An adept seamstress, Nicky had tailored many of the robes worn during the religious ceremonies, and held a special place as governess to Di Mambro's daughter Emmanuelle. Revered as a "cosmic child" and "avatar," Emmanuelle was referred to as "he," and disallowed physical contact with anyone outside "his" immediate family. Tony Dutoit's role was even more crucial than Nicky's: he engineered the elaborate holograms, laser projections, and sound effects which mystified onlookers took for apparitions in Di Mambro's subterranean chamber in Cheiry, Switzerland. Amazingly, though Tony was a knowing accomplice in this elaborate magical fraud, in 1991 he had a sudden crisis of conscience when rumours surfaced regarding the origin of the Order's financial resources: money laundering, gun smuggling, and confidence scams. Jaded, the Dutoits left the cult, demanded a refund of money they had invested in it, and began to confess the illusory nature of the "miracles" to other members of the group.

The Dutoits were already treading on dangerous ground, but they would soon make a decision that would seal their fate once and for all. After Nicky miscarried a baby, Joseph Di Mambro had forbidden her to ever have a child. But spurious religious declarations were no match for natural instincts, and in defiance of his orders, the Dutoits relocated to Quebec in 1993, where Nicky gave birth to a son, Christopher-Emmanuel. Di Mambro was furious; not only had they exposed his trickery and rebuked his commands, now they had even gone so far as to steal his daughter's name. Unable to tolerate this flagrant undermining of his authority, Di Mambro decided that the Dutoits should be "symbolically executed." There was no better man for the job than Joel Egger — a muscular thirty-four-year-old fanatic devoted to the Order of the Solar Temple. On September 29, 1994, Egger left Zurich on Swissair flight 138 and arrived at Mirabel airport in Montreal. From there, he drove forty-five minutes north to the condominium in Morin-Heights, where he was met by Emmanuelle's mother, Dominique Bellaton, along with fellow cultists Gerry and Collette Genoud.

The following day, the Dutoit family arrived at the residence to visit their old friend Dominique. Egger lured Tony into the basement, where he struck the unsuspecting man on the back of the skull with a baseball bat. When Tony toppled to the floor, Egger flew into a savage frenzy, slashing the poor man's throat and plunging the knife fifty times into his back. Carrying the dripping blade upstairs, he then turned his vengeance on Nicky, stabbing her repeatedly in the neck and torso. Once they were dead, Egger drove a wooden stake through Christopher-Emmanuel's heart as the infant sat strapped in his car seat. With their grisly task complete, Dominique relayed instructions to the Genouds before she and Egger departed for Zurich. Convinced that they were heading for a heavenly planet orbiting Sirius, on October 4 the Genouds torched the building, burning themselves alive in a drug-induced haze. Sadly, this was not the last or the worst murder/suicide to be attributed to the Order of the Solar Temple. As the following section will reveal, Egger and Bellaton would eventually follow the Genouds' fiery ascent to Sirius.

Kay Feely

Kay Feely

Joseph Di Mambro and Luc Jouret
Order of the Solar Temple

"Do you realize that we are the only people on the planet to see these things? Even great saints never saw such signs!" — Joseph Di Mambro

"Liberation is not where people think it is. Death can represent an essential stage of life." — Luc Jouret

Victims: Approximately 75 people have died as a result of the OTS/ committed suicide
Duration of rampage: October 4 to 5, 1994 (multiple mass murders)
Locations: Morin-Heights, Quebec/Cheiry, Switzerland, Grange-sur-Salvan, Switzerland
Weapons: Guns, fire

TWIN TORCHES

Six thousand kilometres across the Atlantic, a second mysterious fire broke out in the mountains of Cheiry, Switzerland. Smoke was spotted around 1:00 a.m. on October 5, 1994, billowing from Albert Giacobino's farmhouse on the outskirts of the village. Firemen rushing to combat the blaze soon happened upon the seventy-three-year-old Giacobino lying on his bed with a plastic bag covering his head. Their initial theories of suicide soon dissipated with the discovery of a bullet hole in his skull. When the flames were finally extinguished, investigators descended onto the Giacobino property to try and make sense of what had happened. Inside, they discovered a number of incendiary devices which had failed to ignite, leaving several of the outbuildings still intact. One of these contained what appeared to be a ceremonial meeting hall — reminiscent of something you would expect to find at a Masonic lodge. Personal items, obviously belonging to various people, were scattered about the room. It was as if their owners had disappeared into the smoke.

Viewing the exterior of the building, it became apparent to investigators that it was significantly larger inside than accounted for by the meeting room. Suspecting the presence of a secret chamber, they began searching inside, soon discovering a sliding wall that led to a narrow corridor filled with more undetonated incendiary devices. Heading cautiously down the hallway, they entered another room. What they found within was so absurd that it was terrifying, and so harrowing that it bordered on ridiculous. Eighteen lifeless bodies, each clad in a black, white, or gold ceremonial cape, lay in a circular formation around a triangular altar, their feet pointing inward, like rays emanating from the sun. Plastic garbage bags obscured their grim visages. The chamber itself was completely red. Though the ritualism and organization of the scene suggested a group suicide, the abundance of blood seemed to indicate that many had been murdered. To the investigators' amazement, they uncovered a second secret chamber, containing three additional bodies. The room was octagonal and lined wall to wall with mirrors, reflecting the bizarre tableau from eight different angles. All in all, there were twenty-two dead. Subsequent autopsies would later reveal traces of tranquilizers and hypnotic drugs in each of the bodies. Twenty of the deceased had been shot multiple times in the face at close range with hollow-point bullets, literally obliterating their features. Fifty-two shots had been fired in total. One of the residents of the Giacobino farm had been Joel Egger, though at that time his connection to the Morin-Heights massacre was unknown.

Before the secret chambers were even discovered, at 3:00 a.m. that same morning fire engulfed neighbouring chalets in the ski resort town of Granges-sur-Salvan, 160 kilometres south of Cheiry. Fire crews raced to the inferno to find the doors had been nailed shut from the outside, and were forced to break them down. The same peculiar scene awaited them: a total of twenty-five corpses dressed in ceremonial garb, many shot in the head, with the remnants of incendiary devices scattered among the buildings. The fire had been much more effective this time, blackening the bodies beyond recognition, even reducing some of the dead to one-metre cinders. Three of the victims had been teenagers and another four were children. They ranged in age from four to fifteen years old, and unlike their elders, were not dressed in silk capes. When Joel Egger's car was found parked outside the chalets, the deaths were immediately connected to those in Cheiry. Although the majority of those killed had been French and Swiss, a number of the victims were Canadian citizens.

Later, dental records would confirm that Joseph Di Mambro, Luc Jouret, Joel Egger, and Dominique Bellaton were among the dead at Granges-sur-Salvan. It is believed that after returning from Canada, Egger and Bellaton proceeded immediately to the Giacobino home to perpetrate the murders and facilitate the suicides there, before carrying on to Granges-sur-Salvan, where they "ascended to Sirius" with their ideological leaders Di Mambro and Jouret. It is fascinating to think that even though Di Mambro and Jouret intentionally swindled their flock, using technology to deceive them into believing that they were witnessing miracles, they too had committed ritual suicide. Who were these megalomaniacs who repeatedly orchestrated religious deception, but, bafflingly, bought into their own bogus belief system?

THE SNAKE AND THE SPIDER

Attempting to decipher the esoteric and infinitely complex doctrine of the Order of the Solar Temple (OTS) would not only consume the rest of this book, it would still ultimately make very little sense. Those who wish to delve deeper into this theological cesspit are advised to consult *The Order of the Solar Temple: Order of Death*, a well-written and detailed examination of the group's beliefs organized in several essays and edited by James R. Lewis. Suffice it to say, the OTS's core beliefs were rooted in ancient Egyptian mysticism, Rosicrucianism, and legends involving the Knights Templar, but also incorporated elements of New Age spirituality, white supremacy, Christianity, and that ever-productive and stabilizing religious obsession with imminent Armageddon. Though the OTS's elaborate mythology and rituals were drawn and bastardized from numerous sources, the man responsible for rendering these disparate ingredients into a single digestible hot dog was Joseph Di Mambro.

Born on August 19, 1924, in southern France, Di Mambro grew to become a watchmaker and jeweller, like fellow mass murderers Généreux Ruest and **Albert Guay.** Always fascinated with fringe religious movements, he joined a group calling itself the Rosicrucians, which he remained a member of for thirteen years. Upon leaving, he drew several followers away from the order and into the Centre for the Preparation of the New Age, a faith he had invented in 1973 and built a temple for on the French-Swiss border. He wielded absolute spiritual authority over his followers by claiming to be the reincarnation of political and religious figures from the Egyptian god Osiris to Moses. Similarly, he imbued the lives of his followers with meaning by telling them that they were the reincarnation of various historical figures. Unsurprisingly, none of his flock had ever been a mundane peasant — Di Mambro actually informed one member that they had been a Roman soldier who was present at Christ's execution. Like many religious leaders, Di Mambro used his status to con his disciples out of vast sums of money, under the auspices of using it to help their community. As most were wealthy upper-middle-class citizens, Di Mambro eventually netted a small fortune, and in 1984, was able to purchase a mansion in Geneva. He also enjoyed wielding control over their sex lives, deciding who was permitted to have children and who was forbidden. Over time, his group rituals evolved from simplistic to elaborate ceremonies involving symbolic objects such as capes, crosses, and swords, all orchestrated to maintain cohesion. In 1978, the "Cosmic Master" Di Mambro identified an elite core of followers whom he called the Foundation of the Golden Way, eventually transforming into the Order of the Solar Temple in 1984. Though disallowed from this exclusive inner circle, members of associated fringe movements willingly gave financial contributions and carried out the OTS's ceremonies.

In the early eighties, Di Mambro invited a charismatic young Belgian homeopath named Luc Jouret to deliver a lecture to his congregation. Like Di Mambro, Jouret was heavily involved in esoteric religious orders, particularly the International Order of Chivalry Solar Tradition, headed by neo-Nazi Julien Origas. Born on October 18, 1947, in the Belgian Congo, Luc Jouret moved to Belgium with his parents to escape the violence and instability ushered in by African nationalist movements seeking to throw off the colonial yoke. He studied at the Free University of Brussels in the Department of Medicine, graduating with an MD in 1974. During this period, he had become interested in communism, and unknown to him, came under close scrutiny by the Belgian government. Confiding in a friend that he wanted to "infiltrate the army with communist ideas," Jouret joined the paratroopers in 1976 and participated in a rescue mission of Belgian citizens who were being held hostage in the Belgian Congo. Dissatisfied with his classic medical education, Jouret turned to homeopathy, and studied informally in France. Over the next few years he would journey to the Philippines and allegedly China, India, and Peru to learn the secrets of non-traditional healers. By the early eighties, he had set up a homeopathic practice in Annemasse, France, and eventually garnered so much acclaim that he was also servicing clients from Switzerland and Canada, two countries where he would set up practice. He also began to lecture and give conferences on ecology and naturopathy, starting a business called Atlanta to manage his talks.

Di Mambro and Jouret quickly recognized their common ground, and began to collaborate in a number of contexts, joining forces in 1984 to forge the Order of the Solar Temple. With his good looks and deft manipulative abilities, Jouret took on the role of recruiter and prophet — the face of the organization. Di Mambro preferred to stay behind the scenes, secretly coordinating projects and weaving international webs of intrigue. By 1989, the group had reached between 420 and 600 members, mostly in Francophone areas such as Quebec, France, Switzerland, and the former French colonies of the Caribbean. Di Mambro and Jouret had amassed $93 million through selling their disciples' assets and dabbling in organized crime.

Of course, all good things must to come to an end. As they grew older, Di Mambro's children began to rebel against their role as cosmic children, either refusing to perpetuate the charade any longer, or in the case of his son Elie, denouncing his father as a fraud to members of the Order. Tony Dutoit's admissions that he had fabricated miracles through the use of technology only exacerbated their doubts, and many of Di

Mambro's own congregation began demanding refunds on the money they had invested. Though immediately charming, Jouret had soon irritated OTS members with his controlling demeanour. As a result, he was replaced as Grand Master of the Quebec chapter, causing Di Mambro to lose faith in his golden boy. Furthermore, Di Mambro was plagued by health problems: kidney failure, diabetes, and incontinence, not to mention the fact that he was under investigation for money laundering. The final straw came when the Dutoits not only defied his orders never to conceive a child, but named it Christopher-Emmanuel — the antichrist to Di Mambro's own cosmic child Emmanuelle.

It is perhaps of little surprise that, with their Solar Temple crumbling around them like in an Indiana Jones movie, Di Mambro and Jouret opted to usher in the doomsday they had prophesied was coming for so long. On October 5, 1994, their world did cease to exist; everyone else carried on watching the *X-Files* and listening to grunge music. However, the bloody legacy of the Order of the Solar Temple did not end with Di Mambro and Jouret's deaths.

ECHOES OF THE SUPERNOVA

In December 1995, more flames licked the Alpine snows. Thirteen members of the OTS had disappeared on December 16, only to have their gas-soaked corpses found smouldering in a forest known as "The Well of Hell" near Grenoble, France. Among them were three of their children, aged nineteen months to six years. Fourteen of the sixteen dead were arranged in the signature circular pattern. All had taken or been administered the drugs Myolastan and Digoxin, some had taken their own lives, while a significant number showed signs that they went unwillingly to their deaths. A sampling of suicide notes expressed their desire to ascend to a "higher spiritual plane," and worryingly, warned of another impending mass suicide.

After more than a year of carefully monitoring the remaining members of the OTS, police all over the French-speaking world had let down their guard when tragedy struck the village of Saint-Casimir, Quebec. On March 20, 1997 — the date of the spring equinox — five adults and three teenagers had assembled at a local home and rigged gasoline bombs to reduce themselves and the dwelling to ash. When the device failed to detonate, the three teenagers escaped to the shed, leaving the remaining five initiates to ingest tranquilizers, lie down en masse in the shape of a cross, and burn themselves alive. The contents of their suicide notes contained the same deluded ideology as the "Well of Hell" members' notes. A final attempt at mass suicide/murder was thwarted in 1998, when it was learned that a German psychologist had convinced twenty-nine members to ride the inferno from the Canary Islands to Sirius. In the fourteen years since, no further suicide attempts have been made by members of the Order of the Solar Temple, though it isn't like they haven't taken us by surprise before.

CHAPTER 10

THE DISGRUNTLED EMPLOYEE

The Disgruntled Employee is a mass murderer who targets current or former co-workers, transforming the workplace into his own personal hunting ground. Like **Valery Fabrikant** and Oklahoma postal worker Patrick Sherrill, he might turn to violence upon learning that his position is under threat. Having been warned that due to unsatisfactory work he faced possible termination, Sherrill drove into the post office the following morning dressed in uniform, and proceeded to shoot fourteen "sitting ducks" dead with a .22-calibre pistol.

After stalking and threatening fellow ESL Incorporated employee Laura Black for two years, California computer technician Richard Farley was fired by the company in 1986. With little to lose, the obsessive Farley escalated his harassment. Black successfully filed for a temporary restraining order, with a hearing to make it "permanent" scheduled for February 17, 1988. On the day before the court date, Farley burst into the ESL building with a shotgun and several pistols, murdering seven people and wounding Laura Black along with three other employees. He eventually surrendered to police, but continued to write Black letters from prison. Farley's primary motive was not to exact vengeance on his employer for firing him, but to exert absolute control over Black's thoughts for the rest of her life. In fact, until his rampage, he hadn't intended to physically harm her. In one letter preceding the massacre, Farley wrote, "If I killed you, you won't be able to regret what you did.... In between the two extremes of doing nothing and having the police or someone kill me, there's a whole range of options, each getting worse and worse."

In many ways, OC Transpo shooter **Pierre Lebrun** was the opposite of **Valery Fabrikant**. Where Fabrikant used bully tactics to ensure his advancement in the workforce, Lebrun was a victim of bullying. His case demonstrates that, though on the surface two offenders may display remarkable commonalities, when placed under a microscope, our broad typologies can often appear tenuous, at best.

Other Disgruntled Employee mass murderers in this book: Valery Fabrikant

Kay Feely

Pierre Lebrun
The OC Transpo Shooter

"It's judgment day!"

Victims: 4 killed/1 wounded/committed suicide
Duration of rampage: April 6, 1999 (mass murder)
Location: Ottawa, Ontario
Weapon: Remington 760 .30-06 hunting rifle

PIERRE STUTTERS

In a society that bombards us with ads designed to play on our insecurities, it's unsurprising that many men and women go through life dissatisfied and, whether consciously or subconsciously, feeling like failures. One way of coping is to look for somebody vulnerable to humiliate publicly, giving the aggressor the false impression of strength.

Unfortunately, several workers at Ottawa's OC Transpo garage chose to cope with the mundanity of their day-to-day existence by ribbing Pierre Lebrun, a quiet forty-year-old bachelor who stuttered. To people who took the time to know him, like high school friend Michel Pelletier, Lebrun "really was an excellent guy." Those who mocked his speech impediment had no interest in finding out.

Despite his large and powerful physique, Pierre Lebrun struggled with mental health issues. In the summer of 1997, one of the mechanics took the taunting too far, and Lebrun struck him. Lebrun was subsequently fired for the incident, but the union intervened on his behalf, claiming that 1) the dismissal was unwarranted; 2) management had neglected to thoroughly investigate the issue; and 3) they had terminated an employee with known disabilities. According to long-time bus driver Jim Smith, the climate of the workplace was already tense. Workers had been complaining about labour conditions at the garage for years to no avail. Lebrun kept his position, returning after a mandatory sick leave to assess his health. However, the other workers shunned him, and he was transferred to the main garage, where he ended up working alone, counting parts as an auditing clerk. Outwardly, things seemed to be improving, but in January 1999, under the advisement of his physician, Lebrun quit his job and went in search of work out west. A condition of his reinstatement had been that he participate in an anger management program. Upon completing the course, one of the questions on Lebrun's self-evaluation form was, "Did you reach the goals set for yourself?" His answer was, "No."

PIERRE SPEAKS

At 2:30 p.m. on April 6, 1999, Lebrun returned to the OC Transpo garage. The stuttering outcast calmly parked his car and walked toward the bus garage carrying a Remington 760 .30-06. As he entered the parts area, he spotted long-time employees Joseph Casagrande and Rick Guertin, and fired at them from the hip. The bullet struck a metal drum and ricocheted, showering them with shrapnel.

"It's judgment day!" Lebrun shouted.

In his confused state, Casagrande thought the gunman was playing a joke, and began walking toward him until somebody screamed, "Run!"

"He had blank eyes. This sunken look," Casagrande would later relay. "I just started running through the [parts] rack area." Fortunately, the Remington 760 .30-06 is a pump-action rifle, necessitating that Lebrun eject the spent cartridge after every shot. This allowed the panic-stricken workers time to run to safety. Casagrande and Guertin escaped with three other employees, breaking down an exit door. Startled by the ruckus, fifty-six-year-old Brian Guay arrived to investigate, and was greeted by a fatal shot through the chest. Harry Schoenmakers was next to die when a bullet pierced through three sheet metal dividers, striking him in the head. At some point, Lebrun entered the stores office, pumping a slug into fifty-two-year-old Clare Davidson's back. Witnessing the carnage, David Lemay exclaimed, "He's nuts!"

"What did you say?" Lebrun fired the rifle at him. Lemay never had a chance to clarify.

During the rampage, one particularly quick-thinking employee took command of the public address system and announced, "There's a guy with a gun! Call 911!" Upon hearing the message, workers began to flee the facility. Others hid in closets as the clamour of fire alarms rang out a symphony of chaos for hours. Above the cacophony, Lebrun's voice boomed: "OC Transpo, your warranty is up." The man who had once been laughed at had commandeered the P.A. and was speaking clearly and confidently. Meanwhile, an employee had telephoned the police and informed them of the situation, providing details of Lebrun's every movement. By then most of the workers had fled the building, and though Lebrun had a further thirty-six rounds, he lacked targets. Igniting a small fire, he climbed the stairs to a loft, hoping to get a better vantage point. Finding there were no more victims left to claim, Lebrun angrily shot out some computer terminals. As police tactical units began moving through the scene, the forty-year-old outcast blew off his own head, bringing a lifetime of misery and mockery to an end. The avid hunter had displayed uncanny marksmanship, killing four men in just five shots. However, his choice of firearm had hindered his ability to exact the devastation he so desired. In the end, this mistake had been a final stutter in Lebrun's parting statement to the world.

QUESTIONS AND ANSWERS

Far from being over, the tragedy continued to rage. Workers at the transit depot were so distraught that a trauma team was brought in to counsel them. Several went on disability. Survivor guilt was endemic, especially among employees who recalled that Lebrun had pointed his gun at them, but for some reason had spared their lives. Two months later, employee Ray MacDonald became the sixth person to die. According to his suicide note, MacDonald and Lebrun had conversed about shooting their managers in the months before he quit. He had not realized how serious his colleague actually was.

> I have been unable to sleep well since the shooting at OC.... The gunman, Pierre, had talked with me to great length about it and where to be for a better shot at some managers. As it turned out, he shot himself at this location in the loft. I feel guilty as hell for not telling anyone. Who was I to know if he would do it or not?[58]

In the days immediately following the massacre, there was an outpouring of support from the local community, as passengers offered flowers, cards, and condolences to the hardy drivers of the OC Transpo. On January 18, a service for the four murder victims was held at the Corel Centre, with five thousand in attendance. Candles were lit in honour of the fallen, and Prime Minister Jean Chrétien and other officials placed memorial wreaths.

Police, survivors, and family members of the victims sought an explanation for the tragedy. It was learned that Lebrun had purchased his rifle legally seven years earlier, and that current gun legislation could not have prohibited it. He had been diagnosed with depression, anxiety, paranoia, and insomnia, but due to the confidentiality of medical records, could not have been identified as a potential threat. Until the massacre, Mr. Lebrun had no criminal history of violence.

Tracing the killer's footsteps, authorities learned than he had driven back from Las Vegas, arriving at his parents' house in Ottawa on April 6. Putting pen to paper, he had written a note apologizing to his mother and father for what he was about to do:

> I fear for my life because of these retards from the union
> who are following me.... I am being followed, spied
> upon, humiliated from Vancouver, Kamloops, Kelowna
> and even Las Vegas. They will never leave me alone. I
> can't go on living like this. They have destroyed my life, I
> will destroy their life.... I never wanted it to come to this
> but it was probably my destiny.[59]

In the letter, Lebrun accused seven of his former co-workers of causing him pain, warning that they would pay for their ridicule. Strangely, none of the people on his list were slain during his rampage, and it is even reported that three of them had actually tried to help him through his problems.

One of the dominant themes expressed in the many statements and speeches following the massacre was the notion that the event was somehow beyond comprehension. At a memorial service for the victims, held on April 18, 1999, Lebrun's supervisor Richard White said, "I don't know if we will ever understand what happened. Time heals, people have always told me that. I hope to hell it does." In 2000, David Halloran spoke similarly to his co-workers regarding the anniversary of the murders, "One year later we find it difficult to understand [why] life can make such a difficult turn." When news of the deaths first reached him, Prime Minister Jean Chrétien stated,

> All Canadians were stunned to learn about this sense-
> less and horrible act. The reason for what happened will
> always defy our understanding. All that we know is that
> lives have been taken, families have been shattered and
> a peaceful workplace has been deeply shaken.[60]

Mr. Chrétien's condolences, along with the other speeches, were obviously well-intentioned expressions of emotional solidarity. However, the attitude that the OC Transpo massacre "will always defy our understanding" is a dangerous one. If we throw up our hands in frustration every time a mass murder occurs, how can we adequately adjust our society and legislation to prevent future tragedies?

In truth, there is ample evidence to draw conclusions as to why the mild-mannered Pierre Lebrun became a rampaging maniac. His "going postal" is among one of the easier cases to explain in *Rampage*. To quote union president Paul Macdonnell, "In every work site, some kidding goes on. Regarding Mr. Lebrun's stuttering, we investigated it over two years ago; we talked with his co-workers. I believe Mr. Lebrun's illness greatly exaggerated what he believed people were doing to him."

There is an acceptable framework in which teasing can occur, and conversely, an area where such behaviour is psychologically harmful to the recipient. Anyone with even a shred of empathy should be able to recognize that focusing public attention on a speech impediment goes beyond the realm of "kidding" into outright meanness. By semantically transforming cruelty to "kidding," Macdonnell minimized the attack on Lebrun's disability happening at OC Transpo. Life is harrowing enough for somebody suffering from a socially humiliating impediment without having it rubbed in his or her face on a regular basis.

Does this excuse Pierre Lebrun's actions? No, but the teasing certainly contributed significantly to the mental illness that provoked them. According to Lebrun's family doctor, John Joanisse, his patient struggled to deal with anxiety, depression, insomnia, and paranoia. He was not a psychotic. Judging by the disorganized thoughts in Lebrun's suicide note, it seems that paranoia was the main cause of his murders. Those with paranoia are more sensitive to personal slights, bear lifetime grudges, and can even perceive insult where none has occurred. This explains much of Lebrun's psychology. Paranoia originates in an early history of trauma or persecution. After repeated emotional or physical attacks or both, an individual begins expecting to be targeted. As a result, he or she develops a deeply suspicious attitude, which hinders social skills and begets more negative interaction. Eventually, someone with paranoia will start to conceive notions that others are speaking ill of, or conspiring against, him or her, when this is not the case. A very simplistic but understandable model proceeds as follows: **trauma — pain — fear — defensive attitude — unfounded suspicions**. The sustained emotional attack which triggers paranoia may begin domestically with abusive or overbearing parents, or through bullying in school or extracurricular youth activities. The teasing of Pierre Lebrun likely began at a young age, when he was either mocked for his stammer or harassed to such a degree that he developed a stammer, which provoked more criticism and humiliation, worsening his impediment. The childhood teasing made Lebrun more emotionally vulnerable to teasing as an adult. Eventually, he became overwhelmed with feelings of exclusion and persecution. It takes a special person to cope with constant antagonism. Did being ridiculed at OC Transpo cause Pierre Lebrun's severe paranoia? No — the cumulative effects of a lifetime of "kidding" did.

If we are going to judge Pierre Lebrun, something must be said about his funeral. Seventy-five people packed Vanier funeral home to remember a man who, despite his personal difficulties, they loved and respected. His mother kneeled by his closed coffin and wept. Many who spoke on his behalf expressed that they felt a good man had been driven too far. Michel Pelletier, a friend from Lebrun's hometown of Kapuskasing, recalled how they would play tennis every summer. "I can't begin to explain what he did, but I can say he isn't getting the respect he deserves." Also on hand were four of his co-workers from OC Transpo, who refused to write off Lebrun as a monster. "He was a good guy," one female employee lamented. "It wasn't fair the way he was treated by everyone.... They pushed him over the edge."

CHAPTER 11

THE DISGRUNTLED CITIZEN

The Disgruntled Citizen is usually what the average Joe envisions when he or she hears the term "mass murderer." Rather than selecting specific victims, he directs his rage at society as a whole, storming unexpectedly into a public space, armed and ready to kill. Predictably, he is the most feared permutation of mass murderer, because anyone and everyone can find themselves in his crosshairs.

On September 5, 1949, Howard Unruh shot thirteen dead in the streets of Camden, New Jersey. A paranoiac, Unruh had compiled a list of perceived slights perpetuated against him by his neighbours, planning his bloody vengeance through target practice.

For over fifteen years, former merchant marine George Hennard held the record for America's worst firearm massacre. Driving his pickup truck through the front window of Luby's cafe in Killeen, Texas, Hennard screamed, "This is what Bell County has done to me!" before gunning down random customers with a Glock-17 semi-automatic pistol. Twenty-two would die, while another eighteen were injured. Hennard ended his October 16, 1991, rampage via gunshot to his own head.

Thus far Canada has been largely spared from this deranged subcategory of mass killer. One of the closest examples we have is **Denis Lortie**, who on May 8, 1984, entered the Quebec National Assembly intent on executing representatives of the Parti Québécois government, along with anyone else who got in his way. Ultimately, despite the stated political motive behind his crimes, he would only claim the lives of the latter.

Kay Feely

Denis Lortie

"I'll kill everyone — everyone in my way."

Victims: 3 killed/13 wounded
Duration of rampage: May 8, 1984 (mass murder)
Location: Quebec City, Quebec
Weapons: Two C-1 sub-machine guns; 9-mm Inglis pistol

THE LANGUAGE OF VIOLENCE

At 9:30 on the morning of May 8, 1984, a bearded man in a beret and army fatigues stepped out of the rain and into the offices of a Quebec City radio station. Until eighteen years ago, the now-defunct CJRP had broadcast live from suburban Sillery, specializing in oldies, talk, and news radio. In his hand the commando carried a sealed envelope addressed to André Arthur, an outspoken Francophone radio host. When the man asked to see Arthur in person, reporter Maritchu d'Ab-badie-d'Arrast informed him that the host was currently "on the air." The stranger and d'Arrast spoke privately outside, where he introduced himself as "Mr. D." and handed her the package, with instructions not to open it until 10:30 a.m. D'Arrast agreed, all the while eyeing the hunting knife strapped to his trouser leg.

Once "Mr. D." had sped away, the staff tore into the envelope like hyenas on a sickly gazelle. Inside, they found an audio cassette labelled, "The Life of a Person." Sliding it into the tape player, they listened as a disembodied voice blared, "I'm a person who knows myself very well, but you don't know me. What I want is not for me, but for the future of the French language ... the government now in power is going to be destroyed, including [Premier] René Lévesque ... [for] doing much wrong to the Francophones of Quebec and Canada." The madness continued in bursts of terrifyingly incoherent thought, interrupted only by equally indiscernible patches of dialogue:

"Between 10 and 11 o'clock the party won't exist anymore. I'll kill everyone in my path at the National Assembly.

"I want to destroy the Parti Québécois.

"The Parti Québécois wants to have only one language in Quebec. For what reason? They want to confine us to Quebec. They tell people not to go live elsewhere.

"I've travelled a lot in Canada, and I've noticed that people of the other language find us French Canadians stupid.

"Maybe I will hurt a lot of people, but what do you expect? To achieve something good, you have to destroy.

"I could have attacked something more important, like the Liberal Party in Ottawa. This is a very important point for me because my language is in Quebec and I don't want anything or anyone to destroy it.

"But one thing I can tell you: I only have one life to live.

"Politics is a real circus. I'm going to destroy them before they do more harm.

"The PQ is worse than the communist party. They want to make Quebec independent, but they won't succeed. I will destroy them. No one will be able to stop me — not the police, not the army."

Convinced that tragedy was imminent, the staff at CJRP contacted the police within fifteen minutes. It was already too late. A man matching Mr. D.'s description had entered the Quebec National Assembly armed with a sub-machine gun. Shots had been fired, and people were hurt. There was no going back now.

THE KILLER CORPORAL

"Mr. D." was, in fact, twenty-five-year-old Corporal Denis Lortie — a Québécois supply technician at CFS Carp in Ontario, thirty kilometres west of Ottawa. Born in 1959, he had been raised in the provincial capital of Quebec City. Lortie's father was a tyrant, allegedly abusing his children and committing incest with his own daughter. As an adult, Denis Lortie joined the army, and was stationed in Halifax. There he met fellow Francophone Lise Levesque, whom he married in 1980. He sired a son in 1982 and a daughter in 1983.

Eventually Lortie was reassigned to CFS Carp, to which he commuted daily from his home on the Uplands base, located in a small farming community near Ottawa airport. Also known as "The Diefenbunker," CFS Carp had been constructed as a nuclear shelter during the Cold War, and could house up to five hundred politicians. On the surface, Lortie seemed to be a regular family man, occasionally going for a beer at the Crazy Horse Lounge with his fellow soldiers. Neighbours on the base recalled that during a blizzard in the winter of 1984, he had helped them free their cars from knee-high snow.

Despite his air of normalcy, on the inside Lortie was losing control. With the birth of his young daughter, he became increasingly worried that he would become sexually abusive like his father. He was also insecure regarding his grasp of the English language, and felt that it was hindering him socially and professionally. Instead of addressing these issues, Lortie's thoughts turned to violence. For a time he considered murdering his wife and two children before committing suicide, but eventually he directed his anger at Quebec's ruling political party, the sovereignist Parti Québécois. On May 7, 1984, Corporal Lortie told his superiors that he needed time off to arrange a divorce. Stealing two C-1 sub-machine guns and a 9-millimetre Inglis pistol from CFS Carp, he rented a Buick Skyhawk and drove northeast across the provincial line to Quebec City. There, he took a tour of the National Assembly before checking into a room at a Laurier Boulevard motel to await his destiny.

The next morning, after delivering his manifesto at CJRP, Lortie drove to the city's treasured Citadelle, which straddles the historic Plains of Abraham. One of the oldest structures in Canada, its first walls were erected in the seventeenth century by Louis de Buade. Whether Lortie targeted it for its cultural significance or simply because it housed the Royal Twenty-Second Regiment of the Canadian Armed Forces is unknown. Regardless, at 9:30 a.m. he stepped out of his car and, for thirty seconds, unloaded a barrage of sub-machine gunfire at the windows, while frightened tourists took shelter behind a cement wall. Soon after, Lortie parked his car outside the National Assembly, Quebec's provincial legislature, and stormed in through a side door on Grande-Allée Boulevard, draped in bullets and brandishing his weapon.

"Where are the legislators?" he screamed in French, unleashing bursts from the C-1. "I am going to kill them!" If Lortie had used his watch rather than André Arthur's radio show to time his 10:00 a.m. entrance, he would have had no shortage of PQ politicians to assassinate. However, Arthur had wrapped up twenty minutes early that day, prompting Lortie to accidentally enter at 9:45 a.m. Rather than firing on legislators, the killer corporal's bullets flew at assembly workers and tourists. Jacynthe Richard, a receptionist, was the first to be hit, suffering serious injuries. Lortie strode out of the hallway and into the main lobby, where civil servants hurried past a gang of schoolchildren on a field trip from Ste. Foy. Again, the C-1 roared its mechanical message of hate, killing fifty-four-year-old messenger Camille Lepage as he came down the staircase. The hall was filled with children's screams, their teachers ordering them to lie on the floor, as Lortie stormed by.

Five minutes into his rampage, he began marching up the National Assembly's central staircase, shouting, "I've got a gang to kill on the second and third floor." Splinters and casings filled the air as he unloaded his rage on inanimate objects. Many more people were wounded. Making his way toward the "Salon Bleu" Assembly chamber, Lortie inadvertently passed the building's restaurant, where several important political leaders were dining. Among them were Electoral Reform Minister Marc-André Bédard and Finance Minister Jacques Parizeau. The latter, who would go on to lead the Parti Québécois through Quebec's 1995 sovereignty referendum, would have suited Lortie's victimology perfectly. Instead, the killer corporal entered the Assembly chamber, where preparations were underway for a presentation of the chief electoral officer's estimated 1984/85 budget. The workers looked up in horror as Lortie unloaded his sub-machine gun, fatally wounding sixty-one-year-old Assembly page

George Boyer and fifty-seven-year-old aide Roger Lefrançois. Several others sustained non-lethal injuries. If he had arrived ten minutes later, the legislature committee would have been present.

"I came to kill," Lortie announced. "I'll kill everyone — everyone in my way. I should have come at 2:00 p.m." Enraged, he loosed a plethora of bullets, striking National Assembly cameraman Rejean Dionne in the right arm as he dove to the floor. Frustrated but feckless, Lortie seated himself in the Speaker's chair, lording over the assembly like a mad king.[61] By this time, police SWAT teams had cordoned off the National Assembly and were beginning to evacuate people from the lower levels. There was no escape for Denis Lortie now, other than death. The question remained: how many more innocent people would he drag to the grave with him?

A CANADIAN HERO

Denis Lortie had arrived at the National Assembly on May 8, 1984, armed with a lethally accurate sub-machine gun, but undermined by a scattered mind. He would meet his match in the form of sixty-three-year-old Sergeant-at-Arms René Jalbert — a veteran of the Second World War and the Korean War whose cool, collected intellect would prove far more formidable. Jalbert arrived for work at the National Assembly at 9:30 a.m. and made his way to the Salon Bleu to ensure that the pages had prepared the room for the 10:00 a.m. meeting. Stepping out of the elevator on the second floor, he immediately heard a burst of machine-gun fire. Rather than attempting to escape, the unflappable Jalbert entered the Assembly chamber to find Lortie sitting upon the Speaker's throne. Enraged at his interruption, Lortie sprayed the room with bullets. Jalbert remained calm. Noting that Lortie was dressed in army garb, Jalbert introduced himself as a fellow soldier, and offered Lortie a cigarette. When Lortie accepted it, Jalbert asked him if he could show the gunman his military identification. Once again, Lortie acquiesced.

"Seeing as I showed you my identification card, could you show me your identification card too, so that I would know who I am talking to?" Jalbert continued. Lortie handed Jalbert his ID. Slowly and methodically, the sergeant-at-arms built a rapport with the gunman, and suggested that they relocate to his office.

"Listen! I want to negotiate with you, I really want to have a talk with you and help you, but we're going to do it in my office," Jalbert insisted. "In the meantime, before we go, you must promise me that the pages that are still in the chamber will be allowed to leave."

"Yes," Lortie replied.

"Do you promise?"

Lortie pointed his gun at the ceiling, indicating that he would not open fire.

"All those who are in the chamber, leave right now!" Jalbert implored them. Three of the hostages hurried toward the exit. As Rejean Dionne passed by, Lortie said, "I'm sorry for wounding you, but that's life!" A lone policeman remained in the chamber with a walkie-talkie, communicating the details of the situation to the officers outside the building.

"Why are you doing this?" Jalbert asked Lortie.

"I want to make everyone aware," Lortie barked back. "I want to make the federal government, the provincial government, and everyone aware. That's all."

"You want to make them aware, but why?" Jalbert probed. "What do you want to tell them?"

"Oh!" the gunman sighed. "It's too long, too difficult, we won't talk about it; talk to me about something else." By now, it was apparent that Lortie's hatred was deflating like an old balloon. Jalbert offered again to take the conversation downstairs to his office where they could "find a solution" to Lortie's "problem." The weary Lortie agreed, and after a total of twenty-four minutes of negotiation, the two left the Salon Bleu together. Eventually they entered the office, where Jalbert introduced him to his secretary. In typical Quebecois tradition, Lortie bent down and kissed her cheek.

"You are a gentleman, Corporal," remarked the sergeant-at-arms. "You treated that woman very nicely." Once Lortie and Jalbert were alone inside his office, Jalbert asked him to place the C-1 on his desk, which Lortie did. A man of his word, Jalbert conversed with Lortie at length, helping him to understand the predicament he was in. Over the next few hours Lortie admitted to firing at the windows of the Citadelle, but when questioned about his motivation, would only reply repeatedly that his *"esprit"* had done it. Around noon, the gunman complained that he was hungry, and Jalbert had a security guard bring him a tomato sandwich. Interestingly, whenever Jalbert asked him about his family, Lortie replied that he didn't want to talk about his "personal affairs" — a request which the sergeant-at-arms eventually honoured. On this topic, one cannot help but draw parallels with **Marc Lépine** (Chapter 1) and **Robert Poulin** (Chapter 2). Unlike the other two rampage killers, however, Lortie twice expressed deep regret for his actions, his eyes welling with tears.

"Listen, cry, that will make you feel better," Jalbert encouraged the weeping corporal. "Don't hold it back, cry as much as you want. The two of us are alone and I won't tell a soul."* When Lortie had finished, a great calm seemed to come over him. Jalbert decided to seize upon the opportunity.

"Listen! If you want, I'll phone Valcartier, the military authorities. I've got a friend there; maybe he can find a solution to your problem. Will you let me phone?" His madness abating, Lortie seemed to be looking for a way out without losing face, and was amenable to the idea of surrendering to the military police. Jalbert called Colonel Armand Roy and explained the situation. Roy promised to send along the officers within forty-five minutes.

"It's Colonel Armand Roy on the phone," Jalbert turned to Lortie. "Do you want to talk to him to make sure I'm really speaking with a soldier at Valcartier?" Lortie drew a 9-millimetre revolver from his pocket, loaded it, and pointed it at Jalbert to guard against an ambush. He took hold of the receiver, spoke with Colonel Roy, and agreed to his proposal. When Lortie turned back to Jalbert, the sergeant-at-arms noted the safety catch was still off the pistol, and successfully convinced him to place the weapon on the table beside the C-1. In a further show of good faith, Lortie opened his shirt to permit Jalbert to search him for explosive devices. There were none.

At 2:22 p.m., Denis Lortie walked out of the National Assembly and into police custody, a cigarette dangling from his sheepish smile. His rampage had resulted in three deaths and thirteen injuries. René Jalbert was presented with the Cross of Valour, Canada's highest civilian award for bravery, on November 9, 1984. He claimed to have never once been afraid for his life, and he shrugged off his courageous acts, saying, "Every sergeant-at-arms across Canada would have done the same thing."

---

* Considering Jalbert subsequently informed the entire world of Lortie's breakdown, it's only fair to point out that he was not *always* a man of his word.

After three trials, on May 11, 1987, Denis Lortie was found guilty on three counts of second-degree murder and sentenced to life imprisonment with a ten-year minimum before eligibility for parole. Having undergone years of psychiatric treatment, he was released on full parole in 1996. Sixteen years later, the fifty-three-year-old has not reoffended. Lortie has stated that he was "disconnected from reality" at the time of the murders, and that as a result of his counselling, he now has "the tools" that he didn't have before. He has since remarried, holds down a steady job, and has purchased a home. In 2007, Denis Lortie began a process of reconciliation with an unnamed family member of one of his victims.

CHAPTER 12

THE SET AND RUN KILLER

When an incendiary device is planted in a deliberate attempt at mass murder, as **Alexander Keith Jr.** did in Bremerhaven, the results can shake the world to its very foundation. To this day, the worst mass murder in Canadian history remains the bombing of Air India flight 182 by Sikh extremists, resulting in the deaths of 329 people. Despite strong indications of a terrorist network's involvement, only bombmaker Inderjit Singh Reyat has ever been convicted in connection with the attack.

Inderjit Singh Reyat: the only man to be convicted in connection with the Air India Bombing, Canada's deadliest mass murder.

Kay Feely

Enraged by the U.S. government's siege of the Branch Davidian compound in Waco, on April 19, 1995, Timothy McVeigh retaliated by blowing up the Alfred P. Murrah Federal Building in Oklahoma City, extinguishing 168 lives in one of the deadliest acts of domestic terrorism in American history.

Forty-four people met their demise when an explosive device detonated on United Airlines flight 629 over Longmont, Colorado, on November 1, 1955. The perpetrator, John Gilbert Graham, had likely been inspired to commit his cold-blooded insurance scam by **J. Albert Guay** — a narcissist who holds the diabolical distinction of being the first airplane bomber in Canadian history. Also included in this chapter is set-and-run killer **Louis Chiasson**, who serves as an example of how stupidity and a pack of matches can be far more lethal than malice and a machine gun.

Other Set and Run mass murderers in this book: Alexander Keith Jr.

author's files

Albert Guay

"Well, at least I die famous."

Victims: 23 killed
Duration of rampage: September 9, 1949 (mass murder)
Locations: Bomb planted in Quebec City, detonated in Sault-au-Cochon, Quebec
Weapon: Time bomb

ALL THAT GLITTERS...

The youngest of five siblings, Joseph Albert Guay, born in 1917, had always been spoiled rotten by his mother. Whether it be candy or a new bicycle — whatever the baby of the family wanted, he got. Unsurprisingly, Albert grew up with a ferocious sense of entitlement, yet he was hardly born with a silver spoon. The Guay family hailed from Quebec City's Lower Town — a rough working-class slum at the bottom of "the hill." Overhead, historic battlements loomed like the impenetrable social barriers to the affluence he craved. Fellow Lower Towner and author Roger Lemelin would later describe the residents as "the mud of society." Yet young Albert was determined to go down in history, and was often heard proclaiming, "You will hear more about me someday. I will make something of myself!" Where many boys in the post-war era dreamed of being soldiers or hockey players, Albert fantasized he was a powerful military commander, able to send large groups of obedient troops to their deaths to further his personal glory through conquest.

Perhaps it was this desire to hurt without the risk of being harmed himself which, upon the onset of the Second World War, spurred him to take a $40 per week position at Canadian Arsenals Limited in St. Malo. While his fellow Canadians fought bravely across the shores and fields of France, Albert operated a grinding machine in the armouries, and augmented his income by peddling watches. Instead of heroism, Albert strove to impress by creating a film-star façade, dressing stylishly and cruising around town in his shiny Mercury. He inhabited an inner world of fantasy, playing the role of the dashing leading man in his ultimately unspectacular existence. Every action was choreographed — he never drank or swore, and was known to spring from his car as it rolled to a stop for dramatic effect. A favourite topic of discussion was his various get-rich-quick schemes: ingenious plans which he was certain would come off without a hitch. It is a sad (if predictable) testament to reality that his superficial charm worked, with female co-workers swooning over him.

In 1942, he finally picked the starlet to his star — Rita Morel, a buxom young munitions-plant worker with Mediterranean features. At first their marriage was like a Hollywood romance, with the dapper Albert sweeping his new bride into a passionate kiss in the middle of the street. She bore him a baby daughter in 1945. That same year, the St. Malo armoury closed with the last shots of the Second World War, and their marriage soon devolved into an ongoing argument. Albert set up shop selling jewellery, eventually with branches in Baie-Comeau and Sept-Îles. He masked his incompetence at appraisal by hiring a watch repairman named Généreux Ruest, who had been crippled by tuberculosis. Ruest would assess the value of an item once the customer had left it in Albert's care. Still, there were many occasions when Albert was duped by travelling salesmen who could spot a charlatan a mile away. The proverb "never con a conman" obviously does not hold true, for Albert was a confidence trickster to his core, walking to Mass every Sunday with a prayer book under his arm — a paragon of piety. Simultaneously, the oft-hustled hustler had finally discovered a way of making money in the jewellery business: insurance scams. "Robberies" and fires routinely plagued his stores, earning him thousands of dollars in compensation for insured items.

Guay's greed was paralleled by his lust, and his eyes began to wander. In 1947, he met seventeen-year-old waitress Marie-Ange Robitaille at a dance. Though she knew he was a married man, Marie-Ange was charmed by the flashy businessman, and the two began a steamy affair. Employing the suave pseudonym "Roger Angers," Albert introduced himself to her parents, and announced his plans to marry their daughter, for whom he had purchased an engagement ring. Apparently Albert was as lousy a philanderer as he was a businessman. Rita soon clued into his infidelities, and decided to pay the Robitailles a visit. When she showed them her wedding photographs, the jig was up. Rather than ending the affair, an infuriated Albert found Marie-Ange space in a rooming house owned by Marguerite Pitre, a former fellow munitions-plant worker nicknamed "The Raven" for her dark clothing, and Généreux Ruest's sister. Albert had loaned the dark-haired, corpulent woman money to purchase the building, and she promised to watch over Marie-Ange closely. When his lover protested, he relocated her to a room in the Lower Town, denying her access to a key so she could rarely leave. Since moving away from her parents, Marie-Ange had become aware that she and Albert had no future together. He didn't love her; instead he sought to possess her in the same jealous manner he had once done his wife, Rita. She absconded and boarded an overnight train to Montreal, determined to escape his grasp. As she waited for her bed to be made, Albert entered and calmly picked up her luggage. The terrified girl followed him back to the Lower Town in quiet compliance. Once back in her room, he struck her across the face and stole her shoes. Marie-Ange eventually fled his clutches, and returned to waitressing.

On the evening of June 24, Albert approached her on her way to work. He was armed with a revolver, and claimed to be depressed. When she told him that committing suicide was "a lazy way out," he responded, "Maybe both of us will be lazy." After following her to the restaurant, Albert ambushed her in the basement, prompting management to phone the police. He was arrested and charged with carrying an unlicensed pistol. Still, spoiled little Albert would not give up his toy, and after more stalking and serpentine persuasion, Marie-Ange finally agreed to settle with him in Montreal. Together they travelled to the big city, where Albert spent a small fortune buying her gifts. Ultimately, it was not enough. If he would not marry her, then she would leave him. At the time, provincial divorce legislation did not exist in Quebec. Only the passage of a private parliamentary act could end the Guays' marriage; that, and the death of a spouse. As the multiple fires in his jewellery shop proved, when Albert Guay was around, accidents tended to happen.

AIRPLANE AUTOPSY

On the morning of September 9, 1949, Rita Guay reluctantly boarded Canadian Pacific Airlines flight 108 at Quebec City airport. She didn't want to fly all the way to Baie-Comeau to collect jewellery for Albert, but as always, he had browbeaten her into compliance. At 10:25 a.m., the wheels of the little DC-3 lifted into the air, spiriting Rita away into the azure sky.

Approximately fifteen minutes later, Patrick Simard spotted the plane flying overhead as he was fishing for eels seventy kilometres northeast of Quebec City in Sault-au-Cochon. There was a sudden bang, and he looked on in astonishment as the aircraft began careening left toward Cap Tourmente's peak, a trail of smoke streaming behind it. Flight 108 smashed into the hillside, severing its wings upon impact. Simard hurried through the bushes to the crash site, and reached it an hour later. To his amazement, he found the plane jutting nose-first from the earth. Luggage and corpses were strewn haphazardly about the area. Though

author's files

The wreckage of flight 108 in the hills of Sault-au-Cochon, Quebec.

the smell of gas hung heavy on the air, miraculously there had been no fire. Simard scoured the wreckage for survivors, but found only husks of flesh and bone where life had once raged. He ran for help and came across some railway workers, who delivered the news to St. Joachim. From there it was relayed to Quebec City. Within hours, investigators from Canadian Pacific Airlines descended on the crash site like cops on a crime scene. They needed to know why the plane had malfunctioned and how many lives had been claimed. Upon observing the damage to the left front luggage compartment, the investigators immediately concluded that the DC-3 had been brought down by an explosive device. Fire extinguishers and storage batteries were discovered intact, ruling out any other possibility. As three of the passengers had been high-level executives at Kennecott Copper Corporation, some theorized that this was the work of a professional assassin. In all, twenty-three people had died — nineteen passengers, including four children, plus four crew members. The absence of fire left the corpses mostly intact and made them easily identifiable. Among them was Rita Guay.

On September 12, the Royal Canadian Mounted Police took charge of the investigation, aided by the Sûreté du Québec and the Quebec City Police Force. They soon learned that cargo had been loaded into the left front luggage compartment in Montreal, only to be fully emptied when the plane reached Quebec City, then loaded once more with cargo heading for Baie-Comeau — standard procedure. Wisely, the detectives examined the list of the passengers along with any life insurance policies taken out on them. Initially, nothing stood out as suspicious, but with financial gain the most obvious motive, they vowed to watch the family members of the deceased closely.

In the meantime, they questioned the Quebec City freight clerk who had been working on the morning of the explosion. Willie Lamonde did not remember anything out of the ordinary, other than loading some freight items. Scouring the airline's records for the names of senders and intended recipients, they learned that one Madame Delphis Bouchard had intended to ship a twenty-eight-pound crate to Monsieur Alfred Plouffe of 180 Laval Street, Baie-Comeau. When the detectives learned that both Bouchard and Plouffe were fictitious, they began to suspect that a woman going by the alias of Delphis Bouchard had entrusted a crate containing an explosive device into the care of Willie Lamonde. The freight clerk had subsequently packed it into the DC-3's luggage compartment. Lamonde was asked if he recalled a Madame Bouchard, and replied that he remembered an overweight woman arriving at the airport in a taxi. She had convinced the cabbie to haul the crate over to the weigh scale, then paid Willie the $2.72 shipping cost. Certain they were onto something, the investigators soon located the taxi driver, Paul Pelletier of the Yellow Cab Corporation. He described Madame Bouchard as an obese middle-aged woman, with dark hair accentuated by her black clothing. He had picked her up from Palais Railroad Station, driven her to the airport, and, after carrying the parcel for her, dropped her off behind the Château Frontenac hotel, where she began heading toward Lower Town. Around this time, the police formally announced in the *Star* newspaper that they were searching for the black-clad woman. The noose was slowly tightening around Albert Guay, and it wouldn't be long before he was swinging from the gallows.

CROCODILE TEARS

Despite winning the 1949 Best Actor award for his role in *All the King's Men*, Broderick Crawford could never have matched Albert Guay's portrayal of a bereaved husband. Rita's funeral was a magniloquent affair — her casket adorned with a cross of lilies reading, "From Your Dearest Husband."

"You know how much I loved her," Guay sniffled to Roger Lemelin in the packed funeral parlour. "But the important thing is she did not suffer. You don't think she suffered, do you?" Feigning fortitude, Guay shakily advised another widower to "be brave, Monsieur Chapados. Do as I do: put your trust in God. I have lost my young wife." Later, while standing with his daughter at Rita's grave, he sobbed, "Look, dear, Mama is leaving us forever." By the end of the ceremony, Guay appeared so emotionally overwrought that he needed assistance to get to his taxi.

Little did he know that he had already come under police suspicion. As Guay had not only paid fifty cents for $10,000 in flight insurance, which was routine at the time, but had also insured Rita specifically for another $5,000, they decided to examine his past. They learned that Guay had been fined $25 months earlier for waving a revolver in a restaurant due to some personal spat with a waitress. When they questioned the sultry young Marie-Ange, she not only confirmed knowing Guay, but also identified the black-clad woman as The Raven, Marguerite Pitre of 49 Monseigneur Gauvreau Street. The investigators clandestinely stationed taxi driver Paul Pelletier outside her home to identify her once she left. But Albert Guay got to her first. Arriving at the Pitre residence on September 20 with a copy of a *Star* article, he assured her that arrest was imminent.

"You had better do away with yourself," he handed her some sleeping pills. "And leave a note saying you were the one who blew up the plane." Terrified, Pitre washed down the yellow tablets, only to awaken later feeling painfully ill. Groggy, she telephoned for a taxi to take her to the hospital. As she plodded out of her front door, Paul Pelletier made a positive identification. Police soon arrived at Pitre's bed at Infant Jesus Hospital to charge her with attempted suicide. After her release on September 23, 1949, they began to question her aggressively. Pitre denied having taken a taxi to the airport on September 9 — at least until the investigators produced Paul Pelletier to contradict her. When her puffy eyes fell upon the cab driver, Pitre broke down, confessing to her involvement in the bombing. She explained that she owed Albert Guay $600 which he had promised to forgive if she could procure him some dynamite from her connections in the construction industry. He claimed that it was to be used for clearing tree stumps from a friend's property. Eventually she obtained ten pounds of dynamite and nineteen blasting caps.

With Pitre's testimony as evidence, the police arrested Albert Guay mere hours later. Once in custody, he confessed to everything except the killings. His trial commenced on February 23, 1950. The killer con man seemed bored by the proceedings, except for a theatrical display of weeping when a pathologist testified that every bone in Rita's body had been broken. Only when the object of his obsession, Marie-Ange Robitaille, took the stand did Guay lean forward in rapt attention. Dressed in a grey coachman's hat and dark coat, the pallid beauty recounted their affair to the whole courtroom. She told of how after the plane crash, Madame Pitre had invited her over to 49 Monseigneur Gauvreau Street. She arrived to find a smiling Albert waiting for her. He had attempted to win her back, pointing out that with Rita now dead, nobody could stand between them. A stronger woman now, Marie-Ange had reiterated that their romance was nevertheless over. At one point, the examining attorney asked her if she still loved the defendant.

"No." The pronouncement fired from her heavy, dark lipstick like a bullet. "I don't have feelings for him anymore." One particularly interesting witness for the prosecution emerged to testify that Guay had offered him a paltry $500 to poison Rita. Unlike the beads of water that had fallen so emptily from Albert Guay's eyes, tears streamed from Judge Sevigny's face as he showed the jury a photograph of Rita's mangled corpse, imploring them to fulfill God's law. In the end, they deliberated only seventeen minutes before finding the defendant guilty of murder. "Your crime is infamous. It has no name," Sevigny declared, sentencing Guay to death by hanging.

THE RAVEN: NEVERMORE

While awaiting his execution in Bordeaux Prison, Albert Guay alleged that Marguerite Pitre and her brother Généreux Ruest, the crippled clockmaker, had been knowingly involved in his conspiracy to blow up flight 108. He claimed to have guaranteed them money from Rita's insurance policy in order to secure their co-operation. In June 1950, both Ruest and Pitre were arrested and charged with murder based on evidence from Guay's own mouth. Defenders of the co-accused posit that Guay had falsely implicated them in his plot so that he would be called to testify at their trials, delaying his date with the hangman.

Investigators found a blackened segment of corrugated cardboard in Ruest's workshop, and sent it to a laboratory in Montreal for forensic analysis. Judging by the black deposits on the material, it was determined that blasting caps had been detonated in the workshop, with cardboard used to shield the explosion. The same black patterns were found inside the wreckage of the DC-3's left luggage compartment. Ruest admitted that he had built a time bomb mechanism for Albert using an alarm clock, and that they had performed tests with it in his workshop; however, he had been informed that the purpose of the device was to remove tree stumps. After the explosion, Ruest claimed to have been afraid to divulge his suspicions of Guay's involvement to the authorities because he assumed they wouldn't believe his version of the events.

During Ruest's 1950 trial, Albert Guay appeared on the witness stand to testify against his former employee. Doing little to help their cause, Marguerite Pitre was charged with uttering death threats to witnesses, and had to be forcibly removed from the courtroom. The most damning piece of evidence against Ruest came when a munitions worker testified that the crippled watchmaker had asked his advice on how to detonate twenty sticks of dynamite — hardly a blast fit for a tree stump. In December 1950, Ruest too was convicted of murder and sentenced to die.

If Albert Guay thought he could stall his execution by appearing in court, he was wrong. On January 12, 1951, he was taken from his cell to an anteroom at Bordeaux Prison. Though he allegedly said to prison officials, "Well, at least I die famous," his insouciant facade soon crumbled as he mounted the gallows, trembling so much that he had to be held up by two guards. When the trap opened, he died quickly.

Alas, this was not to be the case with Généreux Ruest. Confined to a wheelchair, the little clockmaker was carted onto the same gallows on July 25, 1952. The executioner, who lacked experience hanging a man in a seated position, miscalculated the length of the rope, and botched the procedure. It took twenty-one agonizing minutes for Ruest to strangle to death, an inexcusable act of torture, regardless of his level of complicity.

In the interim between the executions of her creditor and her brother, Marguerite Pitre stood trial on March 6, 1951. She claimed that at 7:30 a.m. on September 9, 1949, Guay had convinced her brother to collect a hefty box and deposit it in a locker at Palais Railway Station. Pitre had retrieved it an hour later, believing it contained a statue, and transported it to the airport where it was placed in the DC-3's luggage compartment. However, the testimony of a hardware store clerk from the Lower Town, who claimed to have sold her twenty sticks of dynamite, turned the jury against her. Sentenced to die for her role in the murders, on January 9, 1953, The Raven became the last woman to be executed in Canadian history. Unlike Albert Guay, she reportedly went to her death with poise and dignity.

Louis Chiasson

*"I didn't want to burn
my old people."*

Victims: 40 killed/many injured
Duration of rampage: December 2, 1969 (mass homicide)
Location: Notre-Dame-du-Lac, Quebec
Weapon: Fire

SMOKE ON THE WATER

Long before its 2010 merger with Cabano, Quebec, to form the city of Témiscouata-sur-le-Lac, there was Notre-Dame-du-Lac: a pleasant lakeside parish located roughly twenty-five kilometres west of the New Brunswick border. In the early morning hours of December 1968, the community of 2,200 stood poised to celebrate its one-hundredth anniversary. Some people even hung little flags in the street. By 6:00 a.m. the birthday candles had been lit — smoke appeared from the windows of a local retirement home. Marjorie Bergeron remembers being roused by the sound of voices crying, "My God, they're trapped! Good God, do something!" Within minutes, the town fire brigade rushed to Repos du Vieillard to find the decrepit wooden building engulfed in flames. So intense was the heat that Fire Chief Joseph Gagnon was forced to park his car downhill, hundreds of feet from the scene. As the screams of burning patients filled the winter darkness, Gagnon sensed it was already too late to avert catastrophe; but, if they could pull together, with a little luck, they could prevent more deaths from happening. Around the same time, Mayor Rene Berube awoke to the sound of frantic hammering on his door. Learning of the situation, he rushed out immediately in search of volunteers to assist the firemen.

To add to the complications, nobody had any idea as to the names, the identities, or even the number of residents at Repos du Vieillard. It was as if the very building had succumbed to Alzheimer's, its only record books cremated within. Estimates fell somewhere between seventy-one and seventy-eight inhabitants. Fortunat Blanchet, a local priest, grimly recalled the presence of at least seventeen bedridden geriatrics who were physically incapable of escaping.

Before volunteers from nearby Cabano and Riviére-du-Loup arrived to help combat the blaze, ash-faced survivors were already pouring into the street, spreading tales of panic and woe. Seventy-six-year-old Augustin Blanchard recalled an old woman who had decided to head back to the third storey to rescue her savings. She now lay among the estimated fifty dead. Blanchard himself had narrowly escaped death by scaling down a fire escape. Rudolph Beaulieu, sixty-eight, and A.J. Dupont, seventy-three, claimed to have been awoken by the ringing of an alarm bell, which they had initially dismissed as a wake-up call to kitchen staff. Looking outside, they saw black plumes of smoke and orange flames billowing from the main building. Beaulieu and Dupont headed down the fire escape with a few other evacuees, all clad in pajamas and many barefoot. The prudish succumbed to the inferno, walls caving in around them as they struggled feebly into their clothes.

One sixty-four-year-old survivor was particularly eager to talk to the press: Louis Chiasson. A handyman and resident at the home, Chiasson had climbed out of a third-storey window and down a ladder to safety. Earlier, at around 6:00 a.m., he recalled creeping to the first floor bathroom, only to discover the laundry room in flames.[62] After sounding the fire alarm, he ran from room to room, attempting to convince others to flee the building. "[I] tried to get an old man to come with me; he wouldn't go," Chiasson informed reporters. "I went to the third floor and told some girls to get out of the building, but they wouldn't move." After encountering a group of men, Chiasson proclaimed:

> I told them the whole building was on fire and they were too scared to move. They just stood there and looked at me.... All the people were very old and sick. That's what the home was for. A lot of them couldn't help themselves. There was nothing else to do but stay.... Some of the people who could walk were coming out of their rooms, but no one knew where to go.... I told an elderly couple to get out. She is at Notre Dame Hospital now, but he was crippled and burned in the fire.... It happened so fast everybody was stunned ... and then the smoke choked them and they couldn't see or breathe.... A lot of the people were very sick and the smoke seemed to make them stop thinking.[63]

Meanwhile, the mayor, firefighters, and volunteers continued to drag distraught survivors from the ruins. Gallons of water from Lake Témiscouata were pumped relentlessly into the inferno. By late morning it had been extinguished, leaving only a bed of ash and coal smouldering by the Trans-Canada Highway.

SIFTING THROUGH THE ASHES

With a final count of thirty-nine confirmed dead and one individual still missing, the tragedy at Repos du Vieillard would go down as one of the worst fires in Quebec history. Predictably, a host of politicians came out of the woodwork in an attempt to use the calamity to their advantage. Opposition leader René Lévesque of the Parti Quebecois was outraged, declaring the Repos du Vieillard incident "scandalous and bordering on criminal." Lévesque claimed to have witnessed this "unbelievable fire trap" first hand when he stopped by to campaign in 1966 for the upcoming election. At the time, Lévesque had been Family and Welfare minister, and allegedly told his secretary to inform local department officers to condemn the building. However, Mayor Berube explained that a year and a half before the fire, the Notre-Dame-du-Lac council, with support from National Union member Montcalm Simard, had demanded that the dry wooden building be replaced. Surprisingly, they had received a letter from the department of Family and Social Welfare explaining that this was unnecessary, as Repos du Vieillard met all of the requirements. Department official Paul Archambault explained that the building's exits, fire extinguishers, and fire escapes had all conformed to standards. The flames had simply spread so fast that these precautions were redundant.

Of all the questions, the most important still remained unanswered: how had the fire started? A nun residing nearby, Sister Helena, corroborated Louis Chiasson's account that it had begun in the vicinity of the laundry room. One of the dominant theories was that a boiler or other machine had exploded. Suddenly, on January 15, 1970, the Sûreté du Quebec made a surprise announcement: Louis Chiasson had confessed to igniting the blaze, and was now charged with non-capital murder. What dark force had led this sixty-four-year-old native of Miscou Island, New Brunswick, to burn forty innocent pensioners alive?

FIRESTARTER

The first clue as to Chiasson's motives was unveiled at a coroner's inquest in January 1970, when, after a seventy-five minute interrogation, the haggard handyman shakily admitted, "I only wanted to set a small fire so that I could put it out and so that everyone would realize how useful I was around the home.... I love old people.... I've been unable to sleep soundly ever since the fire.... I didn't want to burn my old people." At his subsequent trial, three prison inmates corroborated his story, testifying that Chiasson had explained that he had used paper matches to ignite the blaze as he wanted to "look useful."

Although it may appear that Chiasson was lying to make himself seem less monstrous, this was probably not the case. In 1980, Anthony Olen Rider, a researcher into arson-related crimes, identified several "types" of firestarters. Among them was the Would-Be Hero, later described by Holmes and Holmes as an arsonist who "rushes into his fire scene, saves a life, etc., and is the apparent hero because of his swift and decisive action."[64] In other words, an attention-starved loser wishes to boost his public image by competently fixing a crisis of his own design. Considering Chiasson's volubility to the media after escaping the fire, along with his testimony at the coroner's inquest, this explanation is actually the most plausible. Unfortunately, Chiasson was not even competent enough to control his own inferno. In his attempts to become a "useful hero," he actually exposed himself as an inept and rather pathetic villain.

Charged with the murder of Albert Lebel — the only pensioner among forty dead who could be positively identified, in January 1971, Chiasson was deemed fit to stand trial at a psychiatric examination in Quebec City. The proceedings commenced on Monday, January 11. During the trial, Chiasson changed his story, claiming his innocence and that his confession was elicited under intense pressure from the police. "I will not plead guilty to the charge until I die," Chiasson declared. Many thought that would not be long. Word had leaked out that the accused had been experiencing heart problems, and Defence Attorney Denis Rioux expressed concerns that his client might not last the trial. He did, and on January 15, a twelve-man jury in Court of Queen's Bench found Louis Chiasson guilty of the non-capital murder of Albert Lebel. Judge Fournier sentenced him to life imprisonment.

The shamed convict languished in his cell at Archambault Institution in Ste. Anne des Plaines for nearly two years before his heart finally failed him on November 21, 1971. His death came four days after the fatal attack on fellow inmate Leopold Dion ("The Monster of Pont-Rouge," profiled in my first book *Cold North Killers: Canadian Serial Murder*). A journalistic flub by a *Montreal Star* reporter led to misinformation that Chiasson had propositioned a psychotic inmate who had responded by almost decapitating him. The error, probably confused with Norman Champagne's murder of Leopold Dion, was soon corrected.

However, Dion and Chiasson, two of Quebec's worst multiple killers, remained inextricably entwined in death. Their joint funeral service was held at 2:00 p.m. on November 24 in Montreal. Chiasson's only brother, Martin, a lobster fisherman, drove over 1,125 kilometres from his home on Miscou Island, New Brunswick, to view his brother's body. However, upon arriving, he found the casket closed. An official explained to Martin that Louis's coffin could not be opened because they would then have to do the same to Dion's, and "The Monster of Pont Rouge," whose girlfriend had arrived to say her farewells, was too severely beaten for that to be permitted. Martin Chiasson later divulged his suspicions to the media:

> Well he die last week. I went up to Montreal to see him and could not see him. I don't understand the reason how they never show him to me. They say he die from heart attack and there was another guy buried in the same grave, and they say Dion was in the same penitentiary as Louis. I found that funny.... Those two men was buried the same day and they say that Dion fight with another man. Maybe its Louis and Dion fight to death.[65]

Rumours aside, Chiasson had been admitted to Montreal's Queen Mary Hospital three weeks prior to his death. Though he and Dion were both buried at St. Vincent de Paul Cemetery, prison official Yves Deschénes was admant: "They are not in the same grave.... Definitely not."

CHAPTER 13

THE PSYCHOTIC

As we have seen in the **Guay**, **Fabrikant**, **Cook**, and **Roszko** cases, the idea that a mass murderer *must* be crazy is a layman's superstition; all four men were lucid, calculating, and downright evil. However, there does seem to be a greater prevalence of insanity in rampage murderers than in serial killers. Unlike the personality disorders we explored in Chapter 4, "the term *psychotic* refers to delusions, any prominent hallucinations, disorganized speech, or disorganized or catatonic behaviour."[66]

While riding a New York City commuter train, Colin Ferguson, a thirty-five-year-old unemployed African-American, suddenly opened fire on his fellow passengers with a 9-millimetre pistol, killing six and wounding nineteen. Ferguson insisted on his right to act as his own attorney, rejecting both the opportunity for psychiatric assessment and the insanity plea. Instead, he built his case around a group of conspirators who had been working against him since he arrived in America at the age of twenty-four. In his opening statement, the delusional Ferguson explained that a Caucasian man had stolen the loaded weapon from his bag while he lay sleeping, and had committed the murders. This was also the same individual who had wrestled him to the ground — a claim proven by the fact that the man had seized his firearm. Continuing, Ferguson argued that acting president Bill Clinton should be forced to testify, and the only reason Ferguson had been charged ninety-three times was because it was 1993. If the year was 1925, he would only have twenty-five charges against him. Throughout the trial, Ferguson consistently referred to himself as "my client," and claimed to have spoken with a mysterious defence witness named Raul Diaz who had allegedly seen an Asian man insert a microchip into the sleeping Ferguson's skull. Completely contradicting his earlier theory of a white gunman, Ferguson then insisted that the Asian man had activated him to commit the murders using a remote control. Unsurprisingly, no Raul Diaz ever emerged to corroborate this claim. Found guilty, Ferguson may very well be an example of a Psychotic mass murderer.

More recently, schizophrenic Jared Loughner developed an overwhelming hatred of Arizona congresswoman Gabrielle Giffords when, at a 2007 political function, she failed to adequately answer his question, "What is government if words have no meaning?" By the end of 2010, Loughner had dropped out of college and purchased a 9-millimetre Glock pistol. At 4:12 a.m. on January 8, 2011, Loughner posted a bizarre farewell on his MySpace page:

> Goodbye friends. Please don't be mad at me. The literacy rate is below 5%. I haven't talked to one person who is literate. I want to make it out alive. The longest war in the history of the United States. Goodbye. I'm saddened with the current currency and job employment. I had a bully at school. Thank you. P.S. Plead the fifth!

Less than six hours later, Loughner shot nineteen attendees at one of Gifford's constituent meetings in Tucson. Six died, while thirteen were wounded, including Congresswoman Giffords, who was left in critical condition.

Like Loughner, **Victor Hoffman** represents a Canadian mass murderer driven to kill by schizophrenia.

Other Psychotic mass murderers in this book: Wolodymyr Danylewycz

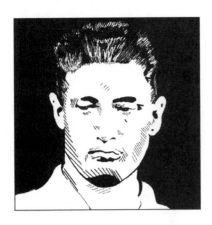

Victor Hoffman
The Shell Lake Murderer

Victims: 9 killed
Duration of rampage: August 15, 1967 (mass murder)
Location: Near Shell Lake, Saskatchewan
Weapon: .22 Remington rifle

BLOOD HARVEST

The morning of August 15, 1967, was a hot one. Six and a half kilometres west of Shell Lake, Saskatchewan, Wildrew Lang's truck puttered along the dusty path connecting his farm to the 1.6-kilometre half-section of land that belonged to his neighbours, the Petersons. Wildrew and Jim Peterson had a long, hard day of work ahead of them — they planned to transfer fifty bushels of wheat from feed bins to his truck, then drive it to the grain elevator in Shell Lake. The Peterson's seventeen-year-old daughter Jean was a promising athlete, and Jim had decided to use the money to pay for her track and field camp in Dundurn, a small community south of Saskatoon. Not one to dawdle, Wildrew pulled his truck up to his neighbour's makeshift granary, and got to work. When Jim failed to appear by 9:00 a.m., Wildrew trudged over to the house to investigate. The homestead felt like a ghost town — there was no playful clamour from the eight Peterson children, and when the family dog, Skippy, came to greet him, his normally friendly disposition seemed muted. Upon reaching the front door, Wildrew's guard went up faster than a burning hayfield. The lifeless body of Jim Peterson lay just inside the entrance, covered only by shorts and coagulating blood. Wildrew raced over to the Peterson's 1957 station wagon, turned the keys in the ignition, and floored it all the way to Shell Lake. After a few minutes, he reached the town, and telephoned the Spiritwood RCMP.

Corporal Barry Richards was the first respondent on the scene. Stepping past Jim's bullet-ridden remains, he found eleven-year-old Dorothy dead on the living room cot, and proceeded to the adjoining bedroom. Beneath their blood stained Rolling Stones and *Bonanza* posters, thirteen-year-old Mary, five-year-old William, and two-year-old Colin lay shot to death on their mattress. Miraculously, four-year-old Phyllis Peterson remained physically unharmed. Wedged between seventeen-year-old sister Jean and Pearl, nine, the child was burying her face in the bed, as if trying to escape the horror by forcing herself into a dream. She maintained her stunned silence as Richards lifted her from the bloody linens and drove her to the safety of her neighbours' farmhouse. The shaken corporal stopped by Shell Lake to request backup, then returned to the Peterson home, where he was joined by a Dr. Michaud from Spiritwood. Around the rear of the home, they discovered the bodies of Jim's wife, Evelyn Peterson, and her baby son, Larry, under an open window, bringing the total slain to nine. Powder burns on the victims' flesh indicated that each had been shot through the head at close range.

Backup soon arrived from the Battleford RCMP, and the arduous task of processing the crime scene commenced. Among the clues were two bloody footprints on the linoleum floor, bearing a diamond on the sole and a *V* shape on the heel, along with several used .22-calibre cartridges. Both were promising leads. In the meantime, a seemingly motiveless killer remained on the loose, and local families feared they might be next to fall prey to his deadly urges. The *Regina Leader-Post* would later dub the evening of August 15 the "Night of Fear," as concerned citizens slept with their lights on and firearms at their sides.

Faced with immense pressure to bring the Shell Lake Murderer to justice, the RCMP began an aggressive, pro-active investigation strategy. Seventy-five police dogs searched the area surrounding the Peterson farmhouse for evidence, while eight Mounties crawled through the grass from dawn to dusk. Roadblocks were erected, and locals encouraged to report any suspicious vehicles to the authorities. It wasn't long before the RCMP's forensic laboratory in Regina determined the footwear to be one of 1,800 pairs of Taiwanese-made rubber boots, distributed by a company in Prince Albert, Saskatchewan. Ballistics experts examined the cartridges and narrowed the number of potential gun models down to three. There was speculation that, given the scope of the massacre, there had actually been two killers involved. Some expressed disbelief that one person could execute nine people without any of them escaping. Lead investigators Inspector Brian Sawyer and Staff-Sergeant Ronald Sondergaard disagreed. They speculated that the Shell Lake Murderer was a local man with a history of mental illness. The Petersons were honest, hardworking folk with no real enemies. Robbery did not appear to be a motive, nor was there evidence to suggest sexual assault. To Sawyer and Sondergaard, madness seemed the only sane conclusion.

It would turn out to be a remarkable feat of offender profiling. On August 17, a farmer walked into the Shellbrook RCMP detachment and proclaimed, "My neighbour's son just got out of the mental hospital and he likes guns and is a good hunter." The man in question was Victor Ernest Hoffman: a twenty-one-year-old former patient at a North Battleford asylum, who had been released into his parents' care three weeks prior to the murders. Acting on the tip, Corporal Charles Nolan and five officers drove out to the Hoffman residence in the nearby village of Leask to interview the suspect. They spotted a pair of red-trimmed, red-soled black rubber boots on the stoop — identical to the ones worn by the Shell Lake murderer. Nolan asked Victor's father if the family had a .22 rifle, and he confirmed that they indeed had a Remington. When the farmer retrieved the weapon from the back seat of his grey 1950 Chrysler Plymouth, the officers noted that it was actually a composite: a Remington barrel fixed to a Winchester stock. Nolan had the items sent to forensics, and within twenty-four hours the lab technicians confirmed what he already suspected: Victor Ernest Hoffman and the Shell Lake Murderer were one and the same.

Hoffman was arrested on August 19 while mowing his field. A search of the bushes within three kilometres of the property yielded two empty wallets, both belonging to the Peterson family. That same day, 1,500 onlookers gathered at God's Acre cemetery in Shell Lake to watch as nine murdered members of the Peterson family were lowered into a mass grave. Meanwhile, Victor Hoffman cracked after a mere fifteen minutes of interrogation, confessing to all nine murders:

"Okay, I killed them. I tried to change the rifling on it [the Remington]. I should have burned the house, then you would not have found those cartridges. I didn't want to shoot anymore. The one I left didn't see me ... after it got just about daylight, I saw this house on the left side of the road. I just drove in there and started shooting."[67]

"Have you ever wanted to do anything like this before?" the police interviewer asked.

"No, just those few minutes there; it just popped into my mind, just like that, do you think I could get rid of it? No, sir; I just went and done it anyway."

"Is there anything else you want to tell us, Victor?"

"Just that I know I'm sick in the head; but I can never kill again, I know that."

For many residents of the Shell Lake area, it was enough to know that the killer was safely behind bars. Their only desires were to continue working the land and raising livestock in peace. But for the various police investigators, attorneys, judges, jury members, and psychiatrists working the case, it was crucial to establish a closer understanding of the man who had engulfed their respective worlds. Who was Victor Ernest Hoffman, and what had driven him to nearly exterminate two generations of the Peterson family?

THE DEVIL MADE ME DO IT

Growing up the fifth of seven children in a farming village seventy kilometres north of Saskatoon, Victor Ernest Hoffman had always been a strange, introverted boy. The Hoffmans were a devout Lutheran brood, claiming German descent on Robert's side and Ukrainian on Stella's. Like most other families in the area, they practised mixed farming, cultivating cattle and hay. Despite their determined work ethic, Sundays in the Hoffman household were strictly holy days, and Victor and his siblings attended the local church frequently. This religiosity would later shape the character of his mental illness.

In the eyes of his family, Victor was a "normal" if somewhat shy child, with nothing irregular in his development. By nine months he was walking, and his first words followed shortly after. He was responsible, worked hard around the farm, and was adept at problem solving. When asked in the years following the Shell Lake massacre about his son's childhood, Robert Hoffman replied:

> He was just as smart as the rest of the boys. He used to work here and fix bicycles for our neighbour's boys and what they couldn't do, he could. But the police and the detectives, they had it written that ever since childhood he was on the mental side. He was not … It [Victor's sanity] went just like that! [snaps his fingers] There were about three weeks when I knew there was something badly wrong, he got worse and worse, and finally we took him to Prince Albert. It was the first time we had taken him to a doctor for mental illness.[68]

Contrary to his father's claims, Victor admitted that around the time he started primary school at the age of six, he began receiving visits from a hallucinatory devil. The creature stood roughly six feet six inches tall, with jet black skin, porcine features, and a long tail. Victor also witnessed angels fighting with the devil, and felt like God and Lucifer were vying for his soul. Often, he would awake in the middle of the night to the sound of drums pounding faster and faster. During the daylight hours, these auditory hallucinations manifested as a continuous tapping, as if Morse code were being transmitted to him from the abyss. Victor also reported instances where clammy disembodied hands drifted through the air to seize his neck and torso. The fact that this not-unintelligent child failed both grades three and nine indicates that psychosis was affecting his concentration profoundly from an early age. In an interview with F.H. Kahan following the murders, Victor described sitting down to eat breakfast one morning when he heard the devil's voice beckoning from outside. Following the calls, he came face to face with the ebony beast, standing naked in the yard. The devil promised Victor riches beyond his wildest dreams if he bowed before him. Suspicious, Victor resisted at first, before finally dropping to one knee. He reasoned that by doing so, he might become half as wealthy and retain his soul. When financial success did not follow, he attributed this to his refusal to submit fully to Satan's requests.

By the age of ten, it seems clear that the "devil" was winning. Victor began to feel the urge to murder strangers. He kept these compulsions a secret, hunting game instead of humans, and clubbing cats and dogs as an outlet for his aggression. According to his own estimates, he slaughtered hundreds of "nice little tanned squirrels." Killing made him feel good, "like it makes any sportsman happy."[69] He once beat a young boy mercilessly, but was never caught.

On rare occasions, angels would appear, admonishing him to stop hurting animals, and informing him not to make plans because "only God could." Victor recalled witnessing the devil savage his guardian angel, and even found himself wielding a sword against a smaller female seraph. In a particularly bizarre twist, he remembered asking the angels not to tell his parents about his rebellion, but upon returning home, was harshly punished by his parents. Considering neither Robert nor Stella ever mentioned speaking with any celestial tattle-talers, we can only surmise that Victor's recollection of the incident was dramatically skewed by his mental illness.

Aside from his occasional truancy, Victor caused few problems for his teachers in high school; the police were another matter. Between 1961 and 1964, he broke into a Leask store twice to pilfer firearms. Following each burglary, the tapping sound in his head began, lasting for weeks. When his neighbour discovered stolen ammunition on the second occasion, the seventeen-year-old Hoffman was handed a two-year suspended sentence, and spent twenty-four hours in jail.

Exiting his teens, Victor's psychological problems deepened. He began to faint and have "fits." The devil appeared more often now, hounding him to sell his soul or suffer a million deaths. Alternatively, he received messages from God and his angels pledging to whisk him away to heaven if he slayed his ebony Mephistopheles. At age eighteen, Victor caught the devil, but its overpowering stench forced him to free the creature. A year later, he tried to shoot it out of the air like a clay pigeon, but to no avail. Finally, he ensnared the beast in a net, robbing it of its magical powers, but Victor's guardian angel betrayed him. Rather than opening the pearly gates, the treacherous seraph restored the devil's magic, and used its judo skills to wrestle Victor to the ground. The devil then absconded with one of Hoffman's prized shiny stones. Poor Victor — as if fighting celestial beings wasn't difficult enough, they were now conspiring against him and training in advanced Japanese throwing techniques. Given these circumstances, is it any wonder he was driven to murder?

By the age of twenty-one, Victor Ernest Hoffman was a babbling recluse. Holed up in the family farmhouse with his parents and brother, Allan, he was increasingly given to emotional outbursts, ranging from senseless laughter to explosions of rage. On the morning of May 27, 1967, he walked into a hayfield and began firing his .303 rifle wildly into the air. When his mother ran to stop him, he proclaimed, "I shot the devil!" Thankfully, Stella convinced him to hand her the weapon, which she placed in her room. Victor drove off, and while he was out, the Hoffmans hid their firearms. He returned that afternoon and asked to speak with his pastor. Pastor Post arrived shortly after, and the two had a conversation in private. The one sentence Stella Hoffman could make out was Victor confiding, "I'd like to kill Mom." Concerned, the next day Robert and Stella had Victor committed to the Saskatchewan Mental Hospital, where he was found to be "schizoid ... in the state of acute schizophrenic reaction."[70] On the advice of the examining psychiatrist, Hoffman voluntarily signed himself in for an extended period. During his stay, he informed the doctors of the pig-faced demon who had appeared to him on no less than twenty occasions, and explained that he had been trying to shoot the entity with his rifle. Hoffman showed signs of both mental and physical illness (having recently been exposed to a chemical farming product), and declared himself unfit to work. With regards to the latter, he couldn't have been more correct. Over the next month and a half, he was observed talking and laughing to himself, masturbating daily, and suffering from insomnia. Though he generally complied during psychiatric examinations, Hoffman displayed a flat affect, responding only with vague, emotionless answers. He stated that the devil had punished him by replacing his brain with that of a girl named Denise, causing him to question whether he was male or half female. The loathed Denise now sought to steal his body for her own, spurring Hoffman's wish to become an "eternity death."***

When the doctors explained that the angels and the devil were simply hallucinations, Hoffman argued that he had been able to touch them;

---

* Yes, this does not make any sense.

in fact, he had even ripped the blouse off a female angel. Diagnosed with chronic schizophrenia resulting in "severe social handicaps," he was pre-scribed anti-psychotic medication, therapy, and twelve sessions of elec-tro-shock therapy. The results of the ECTs are listed in Table 9.

Table 9: Pre-Massacre Electroshock Therapy Results for Victor Ernest Hoffman

E.C.T. #	Result
2	"Marked improvement ... more pleasant and less withdrawn ... still delusional and preoccupied with sex. He felt happy because he had stopped masturbating."
5	"More co-operative and sociable, and stated that his ideas of seeing the Devil and talking to him were probably just his imagination. But he said that he still had magic powers and wished that he were more human instead."
9	"Not much change was noted, but his father, who visited him, claimed he was his usual self."
12	"Although he appeared doubtful about all the happenings with the Devil and angels, he still believed at times that the black Devil was with him. He said that if he were discharged he would try again to catch and destroy him."

Though it is obvious that Victor was still living in a dangerous world of make-believe, a psychiatrist eventually telephoned Robert Hoffman and informed him that his son was "schizophrenic but not 'too bad,'" and that possibly in "a year or two [he'd] be just as good as ever."[71] On July 26, 1967, Victor was released into the custody of his parents, who were given the charge of tracking his medication. Victor was obstinate, claiming that the tranquilizers gave him a sore back, and spent most of his time sleeping. Deep down, he knew that something terrible was going to happen. Before he had been discharged from the hospital, Victor claimed a young patient had predicted he was going to murder someone with three weeks of his release. He reasoned that, like himself, the boy must have experienced visions of future events. Victor Hoffman certainly remained preoccupied with violence — imagining himself murdering his family and former schoolmates. The tipping point finally came on August 8, when he stopped taking his medication. Within three days, Victor found himself slouched over his tractor, gazing listlessly over the blond hayfields into a world of delusion. He deliberated killing his brother, but when he expressed his desires to his friends, they remarked that he wasn't "the type" to commit murder. Victor was having trouble sleeping now, and by August 12, was considering homicide as a means to strengthen his bonds with the devil.

In the twenty-four hours leading up to the Shell Lake Massacre, Victor had spent the day summer-fallowing the fields on his tractor. He had fallen asleep on the sofa at around 9:30 p.m. on August 14, and was sent to bed two hours later by his parents. Waking at 3:00 a.m., he found himself unable to get back to sleep, and went to work in the garage. After an hour or so, he tired of the labour, and began pacing. Suddenly, he was overcome by a strange sensation in the right side of his skull: a feeling of immense pleasure coupled with a strong compulsion to kill. Packing his .22 rifle into the back of his truck, Victor gassed up his Plymouth, and hit the road. As he chased stars across the Saskatchewan night, he saw a hawk swoop down to land on a pole, and considered shooting it. Instead, he drove past farmhouse after farmhouse, the urge to kill building with every home he passed. As the sun rose over the prairie, he pulled into the driveway of an unknown residence, and approached the door with his rifle.

THY WILL BE GUN

Dawn came, opened up like a wound, bleeding streams of light across the endless prairie sky. In a white five-room farmhouse west of Shell Lake, Jim and Evelyn Peterson sat on the edge of their bed, readying themselves for their day. As baby Larry suckled gently at Evelyn's breast, the bucolic silence was broken by the sound of tires in the yard, and the slamming of a car door. Jim was likely confused, since he had expected Wildrew to drop by early to help empty the feed bins, but certainly not at sunrise.

"Who is it?" Jim hollered. The door swung open, and a young blond man entered carrying a .22-calibre pump-action rifle. Jim rose to grapple the intruder, but the rifle roared, spitting four bullets into his belly. At once, the quiet country home was shaken by screams. Then, as soon as he had appeared, the gunman left. Terrified, the Peterson children — Mary, Pearl, Jean, William, and Colin — sat trembling in their bedroom, while Evelyn remained in her own chamber, clutching baby Larry to her chest. Seconds later, the maniac re-entered and fired three more times into the dying farmer. He strode over Jim's body to where his daughter Dorothy cowered on the living-room cot. The eleven-year-old could only close her eyes and scream as the barrel of the rifle exploded into her head. Marching into the bedroom off the living room, the gunman spotted the huddled children.

"Don't shoot me, I don't want to die!" one of them screamed. Ignoring their pleas, he began firing into their faces at point blank range. Blood spattered the walls and drenched the sheets, as his targets flopped around like fish in a barrel. In the opposite bedroom, Evelyn Peterson managed to squeeze through the window with Larry in her arms, but the gunman heard them. With almost supernatural speed, he climbed past the bloodied children, slipped out their window, and took aim at Evelyn from the hip. The rifle fired four times, dropping her and baby Larry into the husky grass. Continuing indoors, the gunman finished off the wounded children one by one, before returning outside to execute the baby. With his grim task complete, Victor Ernest Hoffman retrieved seventeen bullet casings, along with two wallets containing $7, then departed, leaving Saskatchewan's worst mass murder in his wake.

QUESTIONS AND CONFESSIONS

On August 21, 1967, Victor Ernest Hoffman was charged with the capital slaying of James Peterson. He was removed to the University Psychiatric Hospital in Saskatoon to be assessed by department head Dr. Donald McKerracher, who was presented with the task of determining if Hoffman was fit to stand trial. During two days of interviews from August 23 to 24, the accused informed Dr. McKerracher that if Mr. Peterson "had talked quiet and told me I was wrong, it would have been all right. He could have helped me and I wouldn't have killed him, but he tried to stop me." In this belief, Victor Ernest Hoffman had never been more deluded. "I was a little scared when I shot him, but I wasn't sorry," he added.

> If I had had someone to talk to, I wouldn't have committed murder. I could talk to Mr. X, a patient at North Battleford. I told him I would commit murder, he told me not to do it. I knew when I left I would commit murder…. I feel guilty. I am scared I will spend the

rest of my life in prison. I will never see the outside world again…. I didn't know what I was doing. I didn't know how I started to do it. My mind was blank, it was kill, kill, kill.[72]

Hoffman concluded that the devil had tricked him into a life of imprisonment, but could offer no rational explanation as to why he had been specifically targeted. Ultimately, Dr. McKerracher diagnosed Hoffman schizophrenic, but deemed him fit to stand trial. Considering the accused expressed his wish to die, the timing was less than fortuitous: as of December 1966, capital punishment in Canada was strictly reserved for convicts who had murdered on-duty police officers or prison guards. Hoffman's capital murder charge was thus changed to two counts of non-capital murder for the deaths of James and Evelyn Peterson. His preliminary hearing was set for October 24. Judge J.M. Policha appointed G.E. Noble, a tall, grey-haired attorney who had been practising law for eighteen years, to act in Hoffman's defence. A meticulous and strategic thinker, Noble privately concluded that the Saskatchewan Hospital in North Battleford had "really boobed" in discharging Hoffman, and would never admit its mistake. If he sent his client back to that institution to be examined by the same psychiatrists who had released him, their findings would undoubtedly be biased. Instead, he had Hoffman transported to Saskatoon where he was examined by private psychiatrist Dr. Abram Hoffer. He spent the first day completing a diagnostic test, and the second being interviewed. Victor told Dr. Hoffer that he did not consider himself guilty of his crimes, because he was following the devil's instructions. Nor did he believe that God was angry with him. Strangely, Hoffman felt more remorse for the burglaries he had committed in his teens, as he believed theft to be thoroughly sinful. Hoffman had expected an important visit from the devil in February 1968. He had not seen his diabolical master in quite some time.

In his final report, Hoffer recorded that, in his experience, he had "not run across any patient who had quite as many different perceptual changes…." Furthermore, he noted that Victor had recently scored ninety-nine on the Hoffman-Osmond Diagnostic test, which measures a schizophrenic patient's perceptual disorders. Comparatively, his score upon leaving the hospital in North Battleford had been a meagre sixty-five, implying that he had still been insane when he had left the institution three weeks before the murders. Like his colleague Dr. McKerracher, Hoffer diagnosed Victor Hoffman as suffering from a "very serious form of paranoid schizophrenia" over a minimum period of ten years. From a legal and psychiatric standpoint, Hoffman had been completely insane at the time of the Shell Lake Massacre.

His trial opened in North Battleford on January 8, 1968, presided over by Justice M.A. Macpherson. The turn-of-the century courthouse was packed from wall to wall, forcing onlookers to stand in the hallway outside during a raging snowstorm. Among the evidence presented by the prosecution were bloodstained boots, lead bullets removed from the victims' corpses, grinding compound, a pull-through gun cleaner found on the Hoffman's property, and fourteen used .22 cartridges recovered from the Peterson farm. Perhaps most incriminating was a tape recording from the RCMP North Battleford subdivision headquarters featuring Victor describing the murders in vivid detail.

There was little doubt that Hoffman had pulled the trigger, so the defence's strategy focused on the issue of the killer's sanity — or lack of it. In the late sixties, psychosis was still widely misunderstood by the general public. Noble realized that if he was going to convince the jury that Victor was not criminally responsible for his actions, he would have to place them temporarily into the headspace of a paranoid schizophrenic. To do so, he called Dr. Hoffer to the witness stand, and over the next hour they described in laymen's terms the severe sensory and cognitive effects associated with the mental illness. After breaking for lunch, Dr. Hoffer returned to the witness stand to explain that Hoffman "was doing what he had to do in terms of these delusions he was suffering at the time. Though Hoffman might have had a legal awareness of his acts, he was working for a higher [divine] injunction which set him above and apart from the ordinary man." Their approach was successful, and following three and a half hours of deliberation, the jury returned a verdict of not guilty by reason of insanity for Hoffman's slaying of James and Evelyn Peterson. Victor Ernest Hoffman was incarcerated at a psychiatric hospital in Penetanguishene, Ontario, where he remained for the duration of his life.

In the end, there were still a number of "what ifs" hanging like storm clouds over Shell Lake. G.E. Noble maintained that if Hoffman had discarded his boots or substituted the hammer marks on his rifle, he might never have been fingered for the crime. Moreover, the murders could have been avoided altogether. On January 10, 1969, Noble received a letter from Hoffman that read, "I am going to tell you something. The North Battleford hospital reduced my resistance for acting out in violence. Before I went to North Battleford hospital, I was always tempted to kill but could always put it out of my mind."[73] A painful indictment of a failed system, or another of Victor Hoffman's deadly delusions? In 1992, Hoffman reported to journalist Peter Tadman that he continued to be haunted by the ominous black devil. On May 21, 2004, Hoffman died of cancer, having never been released from custody.

CONCLUSION

The number of known victims of every Canadian serial murderer chronicled in my previous work, *Cold North Killers*, barely surpasses the 329 deaths attributable to a single Canadian mass slaying: the Air India bombings. Given these statistics, it seems reasonable to proclaim that mass murderers represent a significantly larger threat to the Canadian public than serial killers. Yet as Fox and Levin discuss in *Extreme Killing*, serial slayers usually garner greater media attention, and linger in the public conscious far longer than rampage murderers. For some reason, we tend to think that the Paul Bernardos (three murdered) and Russell Williamses (two murdered) of the world are somehow "worse" than men like **Marc Lépine** (fourteen murdered) and **Alexander Keith Jr.** (eighty-one murdered). This attitude is reflected in forensic psychiatrist Michael Stone's Scale of Evil, popularized on the television program *Most Evil*, where mass murderers indefinitely end up occupying lower levels than serial killers. Perhaps this is because, like Dr. Stone, we tend to focus on the *quality* of the pain inflicted, rather than the *quantity*. Where the 329 Air India bombing victims were likely killed quickly, Paul Bernardo tortured, humiliated, and terrified schoolgirls Leslie Mahaffy and Kristen French for days. This begs the question: as a society, are we more focused on gory details than body count?

Let me be clear where I stand: it is both impossible and tactless to quantify pain on any macrocosmic level. The 329 victims claimed in the Air India bombing may not have suffered anywhere near the prolonged agony of Bernardo's, but we mustn't forget that by murdering 110 times as many people, the terrorists left a much greater legacy of surviving victims. That means thousands upon thousands of friends and family members, forever damaged by the knowledge that their loved ones' lives were stolen. Unlike that of the slain, who no longer suffer, the survivors' agony is ongoing, and may last for generations. What unites serial killers, spree murderers, and mass slayers is that they are all the bringers of unfathomable pain and, barring the profoundly mentally ill, their motivations are always selfish: to experience pleasure or catharsis at the expense of others.

Where anybody with a rudimentary understanding of serial killers knows that violent fantasy plays a crucial role in the build-up to their crimes, I was shocked to discover that it also occurred in many rampage murderers. **Marc Lépine**, **Peter John Peters**, **Swift Runner**, **Robert Poulin**, **David Shearing**, **Valery Fabrikant**, **James Roszko**, **Marcello Palma**, **Dale Nelson**, **Jonathan Yeo**, **Pierre Lebrun**, and **Denis Lortie** all seem to have become immersed in varying degrees of fantasy leading up to their crimes. Maybe Fox and Levin are correct in asserting that the differences between the three types of multiple murderers are ultimately superficial.

It is also interesting to note that, although rampage murders in Canada often spark debates about gun control, our worst massacres have always come by way of explosives and fire. To put it bluntly, if you want to kill as many people as possible, a pack of matches and a can of gasoline are far deadlier (and more accessible) than even the highest-grade firearm. Consider the seven most lethal Canadian mass homicides, four of which (in *italics*) are documented in this book.

Table 10: The Seven Deadliest Massacres Perpetrated by Canadians

Name	Murdered	Weapon Used
Air India Bombings	329	Time bomb
Alexander Keith Jr.	*81*	*Time bomb*
Louis Chiasson	*40*	*Fire*
O'Brien, Boutin, and Eccles	37	Fire
Albert Guay	*23*	*Time bomb*
Marc Lépine	*14*	*Gun*
Gargantua Nightclub Fire	13	Fire

The sum total of all the firearms-related rampage murders in this book does not add up to even half the number killed in the Air India bombing alone. To foray into the controversial waters of gun control is beyond the scope and purpose of this writing; however, I felt it would be irresponsible to overlook this glaring fact. Rampage killers generally seem to have a predilection for fire. All four of our earliest mass murderers (**Thomas Easby, Henry Sovereign, Patrick Slavin,** and **Alexander Keith Jr.**) employed it to different degrees in the commission of their crimes; along with **Pierre Lebrun, Robert Poulin, David Shearing, Albert Guay, Louis Chiasson,** and the **Order of the Solar Temple.** There are other incidents of Canadian mass murder involving arson or explosives that I did not have space to detail in this book, including the devastating Air India bombings, and the Gargantua Nightclub and Bluebird Cafe fires. Perhaps this reveals something about the psychology of a rampage murderer — the subconscious desire to unleash a force of sheer chaotic destruction upon society. Still, of the firebugs listed in this book, only **Poulin, Lebrun,** and the disciples of the **Order of the Solar Temple** committed suicide — metaphorically burning with the rest of the world. Rather, fire seems to be the weapon of choice for the mass killer who seeks to avoid detection, reducing evidence to ash — another reason why it is the deadliest of methods.

While constructing the four categories of spree killer, it occurred to me that some of the mass murderers also fell into these groups. It could be argued that **Robert Raymond Cook** and **Leonard Hogue** had elements of the Utilitarian in them, while **Marc Lépine** and **Denis Lortie** fit perfectly into the Exterminator type. **Victor Hoffman** also correlates to some extent with the Marauder. Maybe, in time, my system may be expanded to include both types of rampage killers. Frankly, I feel that the Holmes and Holmes typology is inconsistent, alternating between motivation (Psychotic, Disciple) and modus operandi (Set and Run, Family Annihilator). Obviously, plenty more research needs to be devoted to this field. I hope this contribution has been an engaging read and of some value.

NOTES

Preface

1. James Fox and Jack Levin, *Extreme Killing: Understanding Serial and Mass Murder* (Thousand Oaks, CA: Sage, 2005), 156.

PART A

2. *Natural Born Killers*, directed by Oliver Stone (Lion's Gate: 1994).

CHAPTER 1

3. This table is reproduced in part from Robert K. Ressler, *Sexual Homicide: Patterns and Motives* (New York: Simon & Schuster, 1992), 138.
4. As serial homicide is not considered a "rampage"-style multiple murder, such cases have been purposefully excluded from this book. I have mentioned the category solely to contrast it with spree killing, with which it is often confused. To learn more about the phenomenon in Canada, please read my 2012 work, *Cold North Killers: Canadian Serial Murder*. Also note that many modern definitions of the term require only two or more victims, incidences, and locations, rather than the three listed here.
5. John E. Douglas, Ann W. Burgess, Allen G. Burgess, and Robert K. Ressler, *Crime Classification Manual* (San Francisco: Jossey-Bass, 1992), 20.

6. *Ibid.*

7. Katherine Ramsland, *Inside the Minds of Mass Murderers: Why They Kill* (Westport, CT: Praeger, 2005), xiii–xiv.

8. Fox and Levin, *Extreme Killing*, 18.

9. John Douglas, *The Anatomy of Motive* (New York: Pocket Books, 1999), 237.

10. Another spooky coincidence for this author (see the Russell Williams case in my earlier work *Cold North Killers*). From 2004 to 2005, I lived in an apartment at 3495 Ridgewood with my girlfriend while I attended Concordia University. It is not a particularly well-known street, and until recently I had no idea that Lépine had ever resided there.

11. Monique Lépine, *Aftermath* (Toronto: Penguin, 2008), 143.

12. "The Montreal Massacre," Canada.com, accessed February 8, 2012, *www.canada.com/ottawacitizen/features/rapidfire/story.html?id= bd7367a7-1f49-4c5d-949d-7e5a85941b40.*

13. *Ibid.*

14. *Ibid.*

15. Lépine, *Aftermath*, 137.

16. "The Montreal Massacre," *Canada.com*.http://www.canada.com/ottawacitizen/features/rapidfire/story.html?id=bd7367a7-1f49-4c5d-949d-7e5a85941b40.

17. *Ibid.*

18. *Ibid.*

19. *Ibid.*

20. *Ibid.*

21. *Ibid.*

22. Richard Ouzounian, "Paying Tribute to Unseen Victims of Montreal Massacre," *Toronto Star* (website), accessed April 25, 2012, *www.thestar.com/entertainment/theatre/article/409267.*

23. Ingrid Peritz, "A Survivor Speaks," *Globe and Mail* (website), accessed April 22, 2012, *www.theglobeandmail.com/news/national/a-survivor-speaks/article1390009/.*

24. This version of Lépine's suicide note is an amalgamation of the translation found at "The Montreal Massacre" (*Canada.com*) and the near-identical replication in Denis Villeneuve's 2009 film *Polytechnique*.

25. Lépine, *Aftermath*, 96–97, 195.

CHAPTER 2

25. American Psychiatric Association, *Diagnostic and Statistical Manual of Mental Disorders: Fourth Edition, Text Revision* (Washington, D.C: Jaypee, 2005), 573.

26. *Ibid.*, 898.

27. A.C. Gaw and R. L. Bernstein, "Classification of Amok in *DSM-IV*," *Hospital and Community Psychiatry* 43(8): 789–793, via National Center for Biotechnology Information (website), accessed June 10, 2012, *www.ncbi.nlm.nih.gov/pubmed/1427677*.

28. Fox and Levin, *Extreme Killing*, 208.

29. Ramsland, *Inside the Minds of Mass Murderers*, 93.

30. Mike Eastham, *The Seventh Shadow: The Wilderness Manhunt for a Brutal Mass Murderer* (Toronto: Warwick, 1999), 77.

CHAPTER 3

31. "McKenzie Murders," University of New Brunswick website, accessed September 9, 2012, *www.unb.ca/saintjohn/arts/projects/crimepunishment/cases/mckenzie.html*.

32. *Ibid.*

33. *Ibid.*

34. Ann Larabee, *The Dynamite Fiend* (Halifax: Nimbus, 2005), 147–148.

PART B

CHAPTER 4

35. Morris Wolfe, "Dr. Fabrikant's Solution," Grubstreet Books (website), accessed July 15, 2012, *www.grubstreetbooks.ca/essays/fabrikant.html*.

36. *Ibid.*

37. *Ibid.*

38. *Ibid.*

39. *Ibid.*

40. *Ibid.*

41. *Ibid.*

42. *Ibid.*

43. H.W. Arthurs, *Integrity in Scholarship: A Report to Concordia* (1994), 69.

44. APA, *Diagnostic and Statistical Manual of Mental Disorders*, 717.

45. Diane Anderson, *Bloodstains* (Calgary: Detselig, 2006), 48.

46. APA, *Diagnostic and Statistical Manual of Mental Disorders*, 706.

47. "A Hail of Bullets: The Shootings — Timeline," *CBC.ca*, accessed October 2, 2012, *www.cbc.ca/fifth/hailofbullets/timeline.html*.

48. Gordon K. Wong, *Report on James Michael Roszko: Prosecution History*, September 23, 2005.

49. R.D. Hare, *Psychopathic Checklist Revised 2nd Edition* (Toronto: MHS, 2003).

PART C

47. Robert J. Morton, ed., *Serial Murder: Multi-Disciplinary Perspectives for Investigators* (U.S. Department of Justice), 9.

CHAPTER 5

48. "Imeson Lived Hard-Knock Life: Lawyer," *Canada.com*, accessed September 28, 2012, *www.canada.com/story_print.html?id=d08c313b-5d49-4455-a976-c6a48490778a&sponsor*.

49. "Avenging Angel: Timeline," *CBC.ca*, accessed March 27, 2012, *www.cbc.ca/fifth/avengingangel/chronology.html*.

CHAPTER 6

50. Steve Marshall, "Guns and Their Relation to Juvenile Crime," via *CBC.ca*, accessed March 27, 2012, *www.cbc.ca/fifth/avengingangel/paper.pdf*.

51. Steve Marshall, email message to Derek McFarland, via *CBC.ca*, accessed March 27, 2012, *www.cbc.ca/fifth/avengingangel/scan.pdf*.

CHAPTER 7

52. Kevin Marron, *Fatal Mistakes* (Toronto: Doubleday, 1993), 139–140.

PART D

53. Material gains seem slightly more prevalent in Canadian "set and run" mass murders. See the cases of Alexander Keith Jr. and Albert Guay.

54. This seems to imply that most Set and Run types are actually serial mass murderers. Curiously, the only Canadian example of this is Alexander Keith Jr.

CHAPTER 8

55. Numbers represent levels in 2010 reported in "Homicide in Canada, 2010," Statistics Canada, October 26, 2011.
56. Months later, the two would post bail, and on June 8, they absconded to Scotland on an Air Canada flight out of Calgary. They were eventually recaptured by Lanarkshire County police.
57. "Vancouver Police Linked With Second Major Crime in B.C.," *Saskatoon Star-Phoenix*, April 23, 1965.

CHAPTER 10

58. Bruce Cheadle, "Man Who Heard Death Plot Dead," *Kingston Whig-Standard*, January 11, 2000.
59. *Ibid.*
60. "Chretien Among Crowd of Hundreds at Memorial Service," *Saskatoon Star-Phoenix*, April 19, 1999.

CHAPTER 11

61. Lortie's erratic behaviour and demeanour can be extensively viewed on several YouTube videos.

CHAPTER 12

62. Another news source reports that Chiasson claimed the time was 6:30 a.m. A journalistic mishap, or inconsistency on the part of the witness?
63. "Survivor Tells a Gruesome Tale of Flames," *Montreal Gazette*, December 3, 1969.
64. Ronald M. Holmes and Stephen Holmes, *Profiling Violent Crimes* (Thousand Oaks, CA: Sage, 2009), 104.
65. Dean Rhodes, "Heart Attack Kills Chiasson in Prison," *Bangor Daily News*, December 20, 1972.

CHAPTER 13

66. APA, *Diagnostic and Statistical Manual of Mental Disorders*, 297.

67. Anderson, *Bloodstains*, 77.

68. F.H. Kahan, "Schizophrenia, Mass Murder, and the Law," *Orthomolecular Psychiatry*, 2, no. 3 (1973): 129.

69. *Ibid.*, 130.

70. *Ibid.*, 131.

71. *Ibid.*, 132.

72. *Ibid.*, 135.

73. *Ibid.*, 146.

BIBLIOGRAPHY

General

American Psychiatric Association. *Diagnostic and Statistical Manual of Mental Disorders: Fourth Edition, Text Revision.* Washington, D.C.: Jaypee, 2005.

Douglas, John E. *Crime Classification Manual.* San Francisco: Jossey-Bass, 1992.

Fox, James, and Jack Levin. *Extreme Killing: Understanding Serial and Mass Murder.* Thousand Oaks, CA: Sage, 2005.

Holmes, Ronald M., and Stephen Holmes. *Mass Murder in the United States.* New Jersey: Prentice Hall, 2001.

Holmes, Ronald M. and Stephen Holmes. *Profiling Violent Crimes.* Thousand Oaks, CA: Sage, 2009.

Leyton, Elliott. *Hunting Humans: The Rise of the Modern Multiple Murderer.* Toronto: McClelland & Stewart, 1995.

Pantziarka, Pan. *Lone Wolf: True Stories of Spree Killers.* London: Virgin, 2000.

Ramsland, Katherine. *Inside the Minds of Mass Murderers: Why They Kill.* Westport, CT: Praeger, 2005.

Ressler, Robert K. *Sexual Homicide: Patterns and Motives.* New York: Simon & Schuster, 1992.

MARC LÉPINE

Lépine, Monique. *Aftermath.* Toronto: Penguin, 2008.

Sourour, Theresa Z. *Report of Coroner's Investigation.* May 10, 1991.

WEB

"The Montreal massacre." *Canada.com. www.canada.com/ottawacitizen/ features/rapidfire/story.html?id=bd7367a7-1f49-4c5d-949d-7e5a85941b40,* accessed February 8, 2012.

Ramsland, Katherine. "Marc Lépine's gendercide, the Montreal massacre." *truTV.com. www.trutv.com/library/crime/notorious_murders/mass/ marc_lepine/index.html,* accessed February 8, 2012.

Peritz, Ingrid. "A survivor speaks." *Globe and Mail* (website). *www.theglobe andmail.com/news/national/a-survivor-speaks/article1390009/,* accessed April 22, 2012.

"Victims of Montreal school massacre remembered 15 years later." *Peace, Earth & Justice News. www.pej.org/html/modules.php?op=modload& name=News&file=article&sid=1126,* accessed April 22, 2012.

FILM

Polytechnique. Directed by Denis Villeneuve. Montreal: Remstar Media Partners, 2009. DVD.

PETER JOHN PETERS

Cheney, Peter. "29 charges for rampage suspect." *Toronto Star.* January 27, 1990.

"Inner demons boiled within seductive killer of women." *Waterloo Region Record.* December 24, 1990.

Cherry, Tamara. "Murderer slips away from prison; inmate who killed two during Ontario crime spree was serving life sentence in B.C." *Toronto Star.* February 14, 2007.

TELEVISION

"The Tattoo Man." *Crime Stories.* History Channel.

SWIFT RUNNER

Thomson, Colin A. *Swift Runner*. Calgary: Detselig, 1984.

ROSAIRE BILODEAU

"Confessed slayer leads constables to three corpses." *Globe and Mail*. October 26, 1934.

"Quebec veteran kills 6 persons wounds 2 others." *Toronto Star*. October 26, 1934.

"Ex-postman to hang for killing official." *Toronto Star*. January 30, 1935.

"Hanged for killing post-office supt." *Toronto Star*. June 14, 1935.

ROBERT POULIN

Haines, Max. "Robert Poulin," in *The Collected Works of Max Haines, Volume 6*. Toronto: Penguin, 2008.

Langman, Peter. "Expanding the sample: Five school shooters." *SchoolShooters.info*. *www.schoolshooters.info/expanding-the-sample.pdf*, accessed September 9, 2012.

DAVID SHEARING

Anderson, Diane. *Bloodstains*. Calgary: Detselig, 2006.

Eastham, Michael. *The Seventh Shadow: The Wilderness Manhunt for a Brutal Mass Murderer*. Toronto: Warwick, 1999.

THOMAS EASBY

Code, Susan. "The Devil and Thomas Easby," in *A Matter of Honour: And Other Tales of Early Perth*. Burnstown, ON: General Store Publishing House, 1996.

Lane, Brian. *The Encyclopedia of Mass Murder: A Chilling Record of the World's Worst Cases*. London: Robinson, 2004.

HENRY SOVEREIGN

Lane. *The Encyclopedia of Mass Murder.*

Schwass, Kate. "Norfold's mass murder 1832." *Simcoe Reformer.* April 13, 2006.

WEB

Brock, Daniel J. Entry for Sovereene, Henry. *Dictionary of Canadian Biography Online. www.biographi.ca/EN/009004-119.01-e.php?&id_nbr=3141*, accessed July 15, 2012.

PATRICK SLAVIN

Lane. *The Encyclopedia of Mass Murder.*

WEB

"McKenzie murders." University of New Brunswick (website). *www.unb.ca/saintjohn/arts/projects/crimepunishment/cases/mckenzie.html*, accessed September 9, 2012.

ALEXANDER KEITH JR.

Larabee, Ann. *The Dynamite Fiend.* Halifax, NS: Nimbus, 2005.

WEB

"Canadian News and British American Intelligencer 1857." The Ships List (website). *www.theshipslist.com/ships/Arrivals/Canada1857b.shtml*, accessed September 21, 2012.

VALERY FABRIKANT

Crude, Wilfred. *The PhD Trap Revisited.* Toronto: Dundurn, 2001.

Fox and Levin. *Extreme Killing.*

Kelleher, Michael. *Profiling the Lethal Employee: Case Studies of Violence in the Workplace.* Westport, CT: Praeger, 1997.

Wolfe, Morris. "Dr. Fabrikant's solution." Grubstreet Books (website). *www.grubstreetbooks.ca/essays/fabrikant.html*, accessed July 15, 2012.

ROBERT RAYMOND COOK

Anderson. *Bloodstains.*

Haines. "Robert Rae Cook," in *The Collected Works of Max Haines, Volume 6.*

JAMES ROSZKO

Butts, Ed. *Line of Fire.* Toronto: Dundurn, 2009.

Hnatiw, Mike. *Bailiff's Report: Addendum.* March 16, 2005.

Wong, Gordon K. *Report on James Michael Roszko: Prosecution History.* September 23, 2005.

WEB

Logan, Matt. "No more bagpipes: The threat of the psychopath." *FBI.gov. www.fbi.gov/stats-services/publications/law-enforcement-bulletin/july-2012/case-study,* accessed October 3, 2012.

"The suspect: Jim Roszko." CBC News Online. *www.cbc.ca/news/background/rcmp/suspects.html,* accessed October 3, 2012.

"Officer who exchanged gunfire with James Roszko testifies at inquiry." CTV Edmonton (website). *http://edmonton.ctvnews.ca/officer-who-exchanged-gunfire-with-james-roszko-testifies-at-inquiry-1.596316,* accessed October 3, 2012.

"What went so wrong with Roszko's head?" *Canada.com. www.canada.com/saskatoonstarphoenix/news/weekend_extra/story.html?id=a6b27f6a-6252-4fc0-93ea-23258593186b&k=75863,* accessed October 3, 2012.

"A hail of bullets." *CBC.ca. www.cbc.ca/fifth/hailofbullets/index.html,* accessed October 3, 2012.

"Portrait of a predator: Part 1." *Canada.com. www.canada.com/story.html?id=0a7c758c-15ad-4ff5-ac39-35dd911fd62b,* accessed October 3, 2012.

"Portrait of a predator: Part 2." *Canada.com www.canada.com/story.html?id=e2acf1fb-afe9-4a31-9064-e9695c17fb3c,* accessed October 3, 2012.

LOUIS CHIASSON

"Fire disaster probe promised." *Montreal Gazette*. December 3, 1969.

"Survivor tells a gruesome tale of flames." *Montreal Gazette*. December 3, 1969.

"Town's centennial turns into tragedy." *Montreal Gazette*. December 3, 1969.

"Chiasson charged in blaze." *Montreal Gazette*. January 16, 1970.

"Chiasson, 65, goes to trial Monday on murder by fire." *Bangor Daily News*. January 11, 1971.

Rhodes, Dean. "Testimony begins on fatal fire." *Bangor Daily News*. January 12, 1971.

"Chaisson said he set fire nine witnesses tell court." *Bangor Daily News*. January 14, 1971.

"Chiasson gets life in 40-death blaze." *Montreal Gazette*. January 16, 1971.

Rhodes. Dean. "Heart attack kills Chiasson in prison." *Bangor Daily News*. December 20, 1972.

GREGORY MCMASTER

WEB

Schmitz, Cristin. "Failure to replace old shoes 'misfeance in public office.'" The Lawyers Weekly (website). *www.lawyersweekly.ca/index.php?section=article&articleid=1007*, accessed September 25, 2012.

Davidson, Terry. "Killer shows no remorse for 1978 murders." *Toronto Sun* (website). *www.torontosun.com/2011/07/02/killer-shows-no-remorse-for-1978-murders*, accessed September 25, 2012.

"Jailed killer wins $6K settlement." CBC News Online. *www.cbc.ca/news/canada/story/2011/06/24/convict-lawsuit-correctional-services-newpaper.html*, accessed September 25, 2012.

Davidson, Terry. "Killer awarded settlement." *Toronto Sun* (website). *www.torontosun.com/2011/06/27/killer-awarded-settlement*, accessed September 25, 2012.

Davidson, Terry. "Families of McMaster's victims forgive but can't forget." *Toronto Sun* (website). *www.torontosun.com/2011/07/02/families-of-mcmasters-victims-forgive-but-cant-forget*, accessed September 25, 2012.

"Ottawa appeals award to shoeless inmate." *Canada.com. www.canada. com/calgaryherald/story.html?id=32b326ad-f588-4ef7-a20f-79b2d1889a65*, accessed September 25, 2012.

Entry for Deputy Richard Magnuson. Minnesota Law Enforcement Memorial Association (website). *www.mnlema.org/fallen_insert. php?officer_id=70*, accessed September 25, 2012.

Clarification re. "Serial killer wants a clean slate." *Toronto Sun* (website) *www.torontosun.com/news/canada/2009/05/20/9508861-sun.html*, accessed September 25, 2012.

JESSE IMESON

WEB

"Imeson wanted to strip at gay bar." *Canada.com. www.canada.com/ nationalpost/news/story.html?id=a4503099-d356-40de-bda7-b9df4f39bb91*, accessed September 29, 2012.

Sims, Jane. "Jesse Imeson: Sentenced to life." *London Free Press* (website). *http://pbdba.lfpress.com/perl-bin/publish.cgi?x=articles&p=248361& s=manhunt*, accessed September 29, 2012.

Kemik, April, Vera Ovanin, and Randy Richmond. "Young woman linked to Imeson." *http://cnews.canoe.ca/CNEWS/Canada/2007/ 07/24/4365117.html*, accessed September 29, 2012.

"Is murdering a gay man less heinous than murdering a straight couple?" Xtra! (website). *www.xtra.ca/public/Vancouver/Is_murdering_a_gay _man_less_heinous_than_murdering_a_straight_couple-5904.aspx*, accessed September 29, 2012.

"Accused's family 'all just in shock.'" *Canada.com. www.canada.com/ topics/news/story.html?id=e34452a0-01e9-4e67-8306-d58b72eeefb8*, accessed September 29, 2012.

Dipierdomenico, Frank. "Wolf in sheep's clothing: The sociopath." Trauma Injury Professional Solutions (website). *www.tipsco.org/?p=231*, accessed September 29, 2012.

"Windsor man gets life for three murders." *Canada.com. www.canada. com/story.html?id=38635fe4-313c-4bf5-80f2-51c5178e877c*, accessed September 29, 2012.

"Suspected triple killer suffers stomach pains after capture." *Canada. com.* *www.canada.com/story.html?id=d4bc370a-7701-4800-a1e8-ea7221d3d97d*, accessed September 29, 2012.

Piercy, Justin. "Police capture murder suspect." *Toronto Star* (website). *www.thestar.com/news/article/241933—police-capture-murder-suspect*, accessed September 29, 2012.

"Triple murder suspect arrested in Quebec." *Canada.com.* *www. canada.com/montrealgazette/news/story.html?id=c7516396-8f98-4dbd-8db4-bc176210f5b2&k=84795*, accessed September 29, 2012.

MARCELLO PALMA

TELEVISION

"The Victoria Day Shooter." *Crime Stories*. History Channel.

STEPHEN MARSHALL

WEB

"Avenging angel." *CBC.ca.* *www.cbc.ca/fifth/avengingangel*, accessed March 27, 2012.

"Suspected killer accessed online sex offender registry, Maine police say." CBC News Online. *www.cbc.ca/news/world/story/2006/04/17/newmaineshooting20060417.html*, accessed March 27, 2012.

Canfield, Clarke. "Suspect in Maine slayings had strong feelings about sex offenders." *Boston.com.* *www.boston.com/news/local/maine/articles/2006/04/20/suspect_in_maine_slayings_had_strong_feelings_about_sex_offenders*, accessed March 27, 2012.

"Sex offender murder suspect kills self." CBS News (website). *www.cbsnews.com/stories/2006/04/17/national/main1501271.shtml*, accessed March 27, 2012.

"No clear reasons for N.S. man's suspected murder-suicide outburst." *Canada.com.* *www.canada.com/topics/news/story.html?id=2302ee1b-2370-4da8-b4c7-f980c16c104f&%3Bp=1*, accessed March 27, 2012.

"Police seek link between Canadian man's suicide, double killing in Maine." CBC News Online. *www.cbc.ca/news/world/story/2006/04/17/maineshooting20060417.html*, accessed March 27, 2012.

DALE MERLE NELSON

Anderson. *Bloodstains*.

Haines. "Dale Merle Nelson," in *The Collected Works of Max Haines, Volume 6*.

JONATHAN YEO

Clark, Doug. *Dark Paths, Cold Trails*. Toronto: Harper Collins, 2002.

Marron, Kevin. *Fatal Mistakes*. Toronto: Doubleday, 1993.

LEONARD HOGUE

"Policeman slays six children." *Ottawa Citizen*. April 22, 1965.

"Bullets fell policeman, 7 of family in midst of robbery investigation." *Saskatoon Star-Phoenix*. April 22, 1965.

"Spring 'snap' turns into family tragedy." *The Deseret News*. April 22, 1965.

"Vancouver police linked with second major crime in B.C." *Saskatoon Star-Phoenix*. April 23, 1965.

Porter, Bob. "Last ride linked to big theft." *Sunday Sun*. April 24, 1965.

"CPR policeman lent slaying gun." *The Leader-Post*. April 29, 1965.

"$1,185,165 in mutilated money." *Saskatoon Star-Phoenix*. June 14, 1965.

JOEL EGGER; JOSEPH DI MAMBRO AND LUC JOURET

Collins, Harvey T. *God: The Perverted Realism, the Universal Fraud — Part Two*. Pittsburgh: Rose Dog, 2010.

Harriss, Joseph. *About France*. iUniverse, 2005.

Lewis, James R. *The Order of the Solar Temple: The Temple of Death*. Hampshire, UK: Ashgate, 2006.

Klein, Shelley. *The World's Most Evil Secret Societies in History*. London: Michael O'Mara, 2005.

WEB

Ramsland, Katherine. "The Order of the Solar Temple." *truTV.com. www. trutv.com/library/crime/notorious_murders/mass/solar_temple/1. html*, accessed May 17, 2012.

"Solar Temple cult: The gory details of Morin Heights." *CBC.ca. www. cbc.ca/archives/categories/society/crime-justice/solar-temple-a-cult-gone-wrong/the-gory-details-of-morin-heights.html*, accessed May 17, 2012.

PIERRE LEBRUN

Cheadle, Bruce. "Man who heard death plot dead." *Kingston Whig-Standard.* January 11, 2000.

Corbett, Ron. "Gunman in bus garage 'had blank eyes': Inquest hears of panic as Lebrun opened fire." *National Post.* January 15, 2000.

WEB

"Ottawa grieves after bus terminal massacre." CBC News Online. *www. cbc.ca/news/story/1999/04/07/bushooting4_7_99.html*, accessed March 12, 2012.

"OC Transpo inquest rocked by revelation." CBC News Online. *www. cbc.ca/news/story/2000/01/10/suicide000110.html*, accessed March 12, 2012.

"Workplace mistrust persists, 20 years after OC Transpo shooting: driver." CBC News Online. *www.cbc.ca/news/canada/ottawa/story/ 2009/04/06/ot-090406-transit-shooting.html*, accessed March 12, 2012.

"Pierre Lebrun profiled at inquest." CBC News Online. *www.cbc.ca/news/ story/2000/01/28/Lebrun000128.html*, accessed March 12, 2012.

"OC gunman's friend latest victim." OHS Canada (website). *www. ohscanada.com/news/oc-gunman-s-friend-latest-victim/1000156887*, accessed March 12, 2012.

"OC Transpo remembers ..." CBC News Online. *www.cbc.ca/news/story/ 2000/04/06/octranspo000406.html*, accessed March 12, 2012.

DENIS LORTIE

"National Assembly gunman kills 3 in a bloody bid to 'destroy the PQ.'" *Montreal Gazette*. May 9, 1984.

Nagle, Patrick. "Lortie had access to weapons." *Calgary Herald*. May 10, 1984.

Drolet, Daniel. "Lortie not insane: psychiatrist." *Montreal Gazette*. February 1, 1985.

"Lortie trial judge withdraws at request of the Crown." *Ottawa Citizen*. February 11, 1987.

TELEVISION

"Gunman kills 3 at Quebec legislature." *The National*. CBC. Broadcast May 8, 1984.

WEB

"Parole conditions eased for Assembly killer." *Canada.com. www.canada. com/montrealgazette/news/story.html?id=885c67db-68e2-4a59-bccc-26cba6d512b6&k=95107*, accessed October 3, 2012.

"Interview: René Jalbert." Canadian Parliamentary Review (website). *www. revparl.ca/english/issue.asp?param=110&art=603*, accessed October 3, 2012.

ALBERT GUAY

Haines. "Albert Guay," in *The Collected Works of Max Haines, Volume 6*.

Jones, Frank. "The Great Pretender," in *Trail of Blood: A Canadian Murder Odyssey*. Toronto: McGraw-Hill, 1981.

WEB

Duffy, Andrew. "'Your crime … has no name': The bombing of Flight 108." *www2.canada.com/pure+grandstanding/1317470/story.html?id=1320228*, accessed August 26, 2012.

VICTOR ERNEST HOFFMAN

Anderson. *Bloodstains*.

Haines. "Victor Hoffman," in *The Collected Works of Max Haines, Volume 6.*

Kahan, F.H. "Schizophrenia, mass murder, and the law." *Orthomolecular Psychiatry.* 2, no. 3 (1973): 127–146.

WEB

"Living in the shadow of tragedy." *Canada.com. www.canada.com/ ch/chcanews/news/story.html?id=fc3d2f3e-aa0b-4f3e-bbb8- 31499a4b71c0*, accessed May 27, 2012.

INDEX

Cold North Killers
Canadian Serial Murder
9781459701243
$26.99

There are more than sixty serial murderers in Canadian history. For too long, awareness of serial murder in Canada has been confined to West Coast butcher Clifford Olson and the "Schoolgirl Murderers" Paul Bernardo and Karla Homolka, along with the horrific acts of pig farmer Robert Pickton. Unlike our American neighbours, Canada has been viewed as a nation untouched by the shadow of multiple murder. Then came Colonel Russell Williams and his bizarre homicides and serial home invasions, which were sensational news worldwide on the Internet and television and in scores of newspapers and magazines. The reason for Canada's serial killer blackout is clear: until now such information has never been compiled and presented in a single concise work. *Cold North Killers* is a wake-up call. This detailed and haunting account of Canada's worst monsters analyzes their crimes, childhoods, and inevitable downfalls. It is an indispensable compendium for any true crime lover, criminologist, or law-enforcement officer.

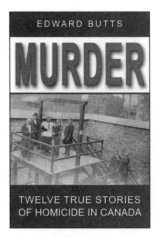

Murder
Twelve True Stories of Homicide in Canada
by Edward Butts
9781554887620
$24.99

Who committed Toronto's Silk Stocking Murder? Why did a quiet accountant in Guelph, Ontario, murder his wife and two daughters? When did police in Alberta hire a self-styled mind reader to solve a mass murder? How did an American confidence man from Arizona find himself facing a murder charge in Cape Breton, Nova Scotia? These questions and more are answered in *Murder: Twelve True Stories of Homicide in Canada*, the latest collection of thrilling true Canadian crime stories by Edward Butts. The keenly researched chapters tell the stories behind some of Canada's most fascinating murder cases, from colonial times to the twentieth century, and from the Atlantic provinces, to the West Coast, and up to the Arctic.

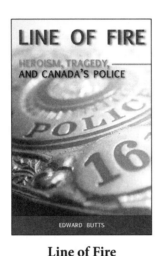

Line of Fire
Heroism, Tragedy, and Canada's Police
by Edward Butts
9781554883912
$24.99

Across Canada, peace officers put their lives on the line every day. Edward Butts takes a hard-hitting, compassionate, probing look at some of the stories involving the hundreds of Canadian law-enforcement officers who have found themselves in harm's way. Some, like the four RCMP officers who perished in the Northwest Territories on the "Lost Patrol" of 1910, died in horrible accidents while performing their duties. Others, such as the Mounties involved in the manhunts for Almighty Voice and the Mad Trapper of Rat River, found themselves in extremely dangerous, violent situations. One thing is certain about all of these peace officers: they displayed amazing courage and never hesitated to make the ultimate sacrifice for their fellow citizens.

DUNDURN
www.dundurn.com

Visit us at
Dundurn.com
Definingcanada.ca
@dundurnpress
Facebook.com/dundurnpress